FRANK CAPRA

Authorship and the Studio System

In the series

CULTURE AND THE MOVING IMAGE

edited by Robert Sklar

FRANK CAPRA

Authorship and the Studio System

edited by
Robert Sklar
and
Vito Zagarrio

TEMPLE UNIVERSITY PRESS
Philadelphia

TEMPLE UNIVERSITY PRESS, PHILADELPHIA 19122
Copyright © 1998 by Temple University.
All rights reserved
Published 1998
Printed in the United States of America

Interior design by Gary Gore

♾ The paper used in this publication meets the requirements of
American National Standard for Information Sciences—Permanence of Paper
for
Printed Library Materials, ANSI Z39.48-1984

Library of Congress Cataloging-in-Publication Data

Frank Capra : authorship and the studio system / edited by Robert Sklar and
Vito Zagarrio.
    p.   cm. — (Culture and the moving image)
Filmography: p.
Includes bibliographical references and index.
ISBN 1-56639-607-7 (cl : alk. paper). — ISBN 1-56639-608-5
(pb : alk. paper)
    1. Frank Capra, 1897–   — Criticism and interpretation.   I. Sklar, Robert.
II. Zagarrio, Vito.   III. Series.
PN1998.3.C36F73   1998
791.43′0233′092—dc21   97-43140
                                                                CIP

In memory of William K. Everson

film historian

teacher, colleague, friend

CONTENTS

CONTENTS

ACKNOWLEDGMENTS

This project began at a retrospective and conference on Frank Capra in Ancona, Italy, sponsored by the Mostra Internazionale del Nuovo Cinema, organizer of the annual Pesaro Film Festival. The editors thank the Mostra's president at that time, Lino Miccichè; Bruno Torri; and its current president and director, Adriano Aprà. Marco Müller, Adriano Levantesi, Ricardo Redi, Angela Prudenzi, Paola Di Michele, Oretta Lo Faso, and Giuliana La Volpe also gave support. James Jeneji and Lynne Larsen of Columbia Pictures, Paolo Ferrari of Columbia Tri-Star Films Italia, and Steven Ricci of the UCLA Film and Television Archive graciously assisted in supplying prints and other materials for the retrospective. Conference participants Tino Balio, Lea Jacobs, Francesco Casetti, Leonardo Gandini, and Claver Salizzato contributed to the development of the concepts debated in these essays.

We are grateful to Frank Capra, Jr., for his encouragement. Jeanine Basinger, curator of the Capra Archives at Wesleyan University, and Bruce Goldstein of Film Forum, New York, also offered assistance. Leith Johnson of the Capra Archives provided research support. Mary Corliss and Terry Geeskin of the Film Stills Archive, Museum of Modern Art, New York, aided in gathering the illustrations. Roy Grundmann, Giorgio Bertellini, Paul Sellors, Alyssa Gallin, Ryan DeRosa, and Daisuke Miyao of New York University and Monica Bottini of IULM, Milan, provided research assistance. Paul Blanchard and Mariella Minna helped in the translation and editing of the Italian essays. Janet Francendese of Temple University Press supported the book to completion; thanks also to Fred Thompson and Linda Forlifer.

Introduction

We found Harry Cohn, president of Columbia, in a bungalow in the garden, sitting in the sun on the flat roof. He was in his sixties, short and bulky, with a bronzed, bald head. This was the man who had made Frank Capra into one of the world's greatest directors. I remembered the spectacular films—*Submarine, Dirigible, Platinum Blonde, The Bitter Tea of General Yen*—the explosive arrival, out of what appeared to be nowhere, of *It Happened One Night*, starring Clark Gable and Claudette Colbert in what is still one of the most human, most civilized, and most American of comedies.

Michael Powell, *Million Dollar Movie* (1992)

Why would one film director—Britain's Michael Powell, who held independence and artistic freedom among his highest values—praise another by giving credit to the filmmaker's producer and boss? "This was the man who had made Frank Capra"; Powell's remark, meant no doubt to be complimentary all around, strikes at the heart of the Frank Capra paradox. Acclaimed as one of the world's great directors, he is still not secure in reputation as an auteur, or author, in his own right.

Frank Capra occupies a unique place in American culture. His name has become an instantly recognizable signifier, loosely defined but clearly understood, standing for a particular strain of national self-conception. An idealistic nobody runs for office against the political machine and wins. A community rallies around a good but burdened citizen. Little people triumph over arrogant

1

plutocrats. Events that seem simultaneously sentimental, improbable, and uplifting invariably are described as Capraesque.

Capra's films (or a specific viewpoint toward them) have created Capra the adjective, but along the way Capra the filmmaker has become obscured. Like Michael Powell, he, too, valued independence and artistic freedom, yet commentators are loath to acknowledge that he gained them. Credit for Capra's films remains contested. Powell grants producer Cohn substantial measure. Capra biographer Joseph McBride, in the most tortured formulation, castigates the director for his films' concepts and values while seeking to credit their authorship to scriptwriter Robert Riskin.[1]

Capra remains one of the most significant test cases for the theory and historiography of film authorship. The influential evaluations of directors by 1950s French critics, who promulgated a *politique des auteurs*, gave him short shrift.[2] While some Hollywood directors of his age cohort, particularly Alfred Hitchcock and Howard Hawks, were highly praised, Capra was almost entirely ignored. It was not that he was dismissed as a stylist. "Capra is a genuine auteur," wrote Andrew Sarris, the leading American proponent of the auteur theory, in his 1968 book *The American Cinema*.[3] The auteurists were indifferent if not hostile to Capra because they disliked the ideology they found in his films—what Sarris called his conformism, his sentimentality, his "populist demagoguery." The most that was said for him among the French critics was Jean-Louis Comolli's remark that he was among those American directors for whom "the battle has still to be fought."[4]

A battle of sorts has been fought over Capra during the intervening years—in part around style, in part around ideology, but most of all about the terms of his authorship. Meanwhile, the ground of the wider debate on authorship has altered. Under the influence of structuralism and the work of French philosopher Michel Foucault, film theory shifted attention from questions of an individual author's subjectivity to concern with the social function of the authorship concept.[5] Concluding his concise survey of the range of author theory in a 1983 article, "Authorship and Hollywood," Stephen Crofts emphasized "the possibility of thinking of Authorship in historical and cultural terms."[6]

Above all, the development of film historiography has shaped the most recent discourses on authorship in the medium. Robert L.

Carringer's *The Making of Citizen Kane*, on the 1941 Orson Welles classic, was among the first works using studio archives to analyze specific details of collaboration between a director and other creative contributors, giving support to the *politique des auteurs* notion of a director-auteur providing the dominant aesthetic conception of a film to co-workers.[7] Thomas Schatz's *The Genius of the System* studied MGM, Warner Bros., Universal, and the independent Selznick company, developing a perspective on authorship as a function of even broader collaborations and conflicts within the creative operations of the studio system.[8] It became possible to acknowledge that Hollywood directors such as Capra were neither solitary geniuses nor sly transgressors slipping personal touches into factory products—as some earlier versions of authorship might have put it—but auteurs, indeed, working out their ideas and visual styles in an industrial mode of production.

This viewpoint did not answer the question of authorship, of course, but merely focused it on the specific circumstances of individual auteurs. In Capra's case, authorship issues had been framed by the biographical legend the director had offered in his 1971 autobiography, *The Name above the Title*, and by scholarly concentration on a few of his most ideologically pointed films: *Mr. Deeds Goes to Town* (1936), *Mr. Smith Goes to Washington* (1939), *Meet John Doe* (1941), and *It's a Wonderful Life* (1946).[9] This situation changed in the late 1980s, however, when Columbia Pictures, the studio at which Capra had worked for more than a decade, made available restored prints of nearly all the films he had directed there from 1928 through 1934. Some of these works—*Platinum Blonde* (1931), *American Madness* (1932), *The Bitter Tea of General Yen* (1933), and, of course, the Academy Award-winning *It Happened One Night* (1934)—had been in general circulation, but others were unfamiliar even to specialists.

A new view of Capra emerged from this cinematic effusion. It became clear, as never before, that these early years at Columbia were quantitatively the most productive of his career: nineteen films from 1928 through 1933, considerably more than the number of features he directed over the following three decades. It became possible to observe the auteur's emergence in precisely the industrial context that the new film historiography required. One could understand why Michael Powell, a few years younger than

4

Capra, would begin his list of Capra's "spectacular films" with *Submarine* (1928) and *Dirigible* (1931), films that he surely first saw when he was himself a beginning filmmaker in London. (Powell reports that his quota-quickie, *The Star Reporter* [1932], played in Britain as the bottom half of a double bill with *Platinum Blonde*.)[10]

Capra's pre-1934 Columbia films were screened in retrospectives in the United States and overseas. In Italy, the Mostra Internazionale del Nuovo Cinema organized an event that interrogated both Capra and the development of Columbia Pictures, curated by this volume's co-editor Vito Zagarrio, with screenings and a conference with contributions from American and European scholars.[11] This book is an outgrowth of the investigations begun there. It extends the dual focus on both the director and the studio for which he worked, and it retains the multiple approaches offered by American and European viewpoints. Although it emphasizes Capra's work at Columbia between 1928 and 1934, it also treats later works at that studio throughout the 1930s.

On the relationship between authorship and the studio system, this book offers a dossier of perspectives. Was Harry Cohn the man who made Frank Capra into one of the world's greatest directors, as Powell states? Was Capra his own self-creation, in implacable struggle with Cohn, as a reader might glean from the director's autobiography? Or did Frank Capra emerge as an auteur in conflict but also in collaboration with the studio head and with Columbia's creative personnel? With their differing approaches to Frank Capra and his movies, the following essays suggest the breadth and complexity of current historiography on cinema authorship. Capra's claims to authorship, as with all filmmakers, emerge in a setting of multiple relationships—with an industry's and a studio's modes of production, with the talents of other film workers, with the culture and ideologies of his times, and with the evolving discourses of film theory and history, as cinema historians seek to deepen their understanding of how lives, institutions, and ideas are inscribed in works of art and entertainment.

Thomas Schatz opens the book with a detailed analysis both of Capra's career at Columbia Pictures and of the studio's development during Capra's years there, from 1928 to 1939. Columbia in the late 1920s was a "Poverty Row" company lacking its own theaters. However, when the Great Depression hit, this circumstance left Columbia in a stronger position than the fully integrated companies, which were burdened by real estate debt. Guided by the autocratic Harry Cohn, the studio devised a distinctive house style of romantic comedies, which enabled its films to play in major first-run theaters. Capra's contribution to Columbia's rise was significant, but so too, Schatz argues, was the studio important to Capra, as evidenced by the director's later failure to match his Columbia success. Schatz suggests that Capra and Cohn were alike in their ambitions and that the situation at Columbia in the early 1930s gave Capra a unique opportunity to thrive as a "studio director."

Noting how strongly Capra's historical reputation is bound up with the decade of the 1930s, Robert Sklar's essay (chapter 2) utilizes the recent availability of the director's pre-1934 films to shift focus and examine Capra's relation to 1920s American society and culture. The earlier decade, belying its Jazz Age reputation, has reengaged scholarly interest because of the era's conflicts over race, gender, and ethnicity, in contrast to the 1930s quest for a unitary culture in which Capra played such an important part. Sklar's essay explores four themes: the links between *It Happened One Night* and an earlier literary genre of genteel romantic comedy, Capra's ethnic identity in an era hostile to immigrants and the way ethnicity is represented in several of his films, issues of spectacle and realism in Capra's visual style, and the emergence of a new ideological role in American culture for Capra, Columbia, and Hollywood with *American Madness*.

From a European, more specifically Italian, perspective, Vito Zagarrio offers a counter-reading of a director whose reputation has suffered, the author says, because many critics find his works too sentimental, even reactionary. Drawing on the writings of Italian historian Carlo Ginzburg, Zagarrio proposes looking for signs, clues, and "slips" in the director's films that go against the grain of their optimistic surfaces. His search for such traces in the pre-1934 films reveals a darker Capra, one who, in spite of himself, made films with unhappy endings, was obsessed with the theme of suicide, dealt with family and social conflicts, and shaped more an American Nightmare than an American Dream. Capra-corn, he suggests, can be bitter, even tragic. Zagarrio's essay (chapter 3) also encompasses an extensive critique of Joseph McBride's biography of the director, *Frank Capra: The Catastrophe of Success*.

Charles J. Maland addresses themes related to Zagarrio's through a detailed analysis of three Capra films: *American Madness* from the pre-1934 period and *Mr. Deeds Goes to Town* and *Mr. Smith Goes to Washington* from the period of Capra's highest reputation. Maland focuses on the narrative and stylistic aspects of these works that drive their male protagonists into moments of despair. He argues that these moments are tied to tensions in the wider culture between private interest and pursuit of the common good, a conflict between the ideologies of capitalism and democracy that was particularly exacerbated by the crisis of the Great Depression. Maland seeks to show a Capra different from the fantasist of goodwill postulated by earlier critics. By demonstrating how deeply the theme of despair is embedded in the filmmaker's visual style, he also makes a strong case for Capra as an auteur.

It Happened One Night is the subject of Richard Maltby's comprehensive cultural and cinematic analysis (chapter 5). Maltby positions the film in the framework of the motion picture industry's internal code of censorship, which was in itself, he argues, linked to a cultural crisis for men brought about by the Great Depression. Capra's multiple Academy Award-winning comedy emerged as a response to this crisis. Both the male and female protagonists, news reporter Peter Warne and socialite heiress Ellie Andrews, were reconceptualized from the original short story to the characters portrayed by Clark Gable and Claudette Colbert. (Gable's screen persona also went through a significant transformation in the process.) Drawing on comedic archetypes elucidated by literary theorist Northrup Frye, Maltby views the film as a marker of the restoration of patriarchal order in American culture after the advent of the New Deal.

Giuliana Muscio's essay expands the discussion of Capra's relation to the New Deal to a more general level of ideological critique. In chapter 6 she explores the differences between federalism and populism as conceptions of politics and power and notes how these two opposites paradoxically mingled in the rhetoric of the Roosevelt administration, particularly in the writings of New Deal ideologist Thurman Arnold. Capra's ideological tendencies in his 1930s films of social commitment were not immune to this contradiction, she argues, although the director's dominant perspective was neopopulist, with his heroes small-town folk and his villains from big business and big cities. However, of greatest importance, according to Muscio, was Roosevelt's and Capra's shared desire to address society's emotional needs through media. During the New Deal era, she writes, politics turned its public into spectators while cinema turned its spectators into a public.

Capra's direct representation of national politics is examined in Charles Wolfe's historical critique of *Mr. Smith Goes to Washington*. Wolfe grounds his approach in a setting not so much of shared ideologies as of competing discourses of power—not only between government and media, but also among the press, movies, and the newest medium, radio, growing in importance for its immediate dissemination of news bulletins during the impending world crisis. Chapter 7 stresses the role in politics of performance and the media's function as spectators and transmitters of that performance to the public. *Mr. Smith* dramatizes how the Washington press corps and an actual, high-profile radio correspondent, inserted into the fiction, carry out this function. At the same time, it enacts a performance of cinema, using film techniques to assert the primacy of its own modes of discourse for communication to the public on issues of culture and politics.

The last two essays in this book return to the history of Columbia Pictures. Brian Taves's detailed account of the studio's mode of production in the 1930s cautions against placing too much emphasis on Capra's role. In fact, Capra's rising budgets through the 1930s made it more difficult for his films to turn a profit, whatever their prestige. Taves argues that Columbia's development as a major studio rested on its capacity to turn out a steady supply of effective, low-cost B pictures for the double-feature programs common in Depression-era exhibition. In chapter 8 he highlights the range of genres, directors, and performers significant in the studio's 1930s output. The studio's strategy, in his view, was unique in the Hollywood industry, enabling it to survive and ultimately to thrive.

Columbia, Taves remarks, has not yet received the extensive study accorded to most other studios by cinema historians. One of the earliest explorations of the studio's history continues to rank among the most significant—Edward Buscombe's "Notes on

Columbia Pictures Corporation 1926–1941," first published in 1975 and reprinted here with a new afterword by its author. Under the circumstances of its writing, Buscombe's essay by necessity demonstrated a hunt for clues and traces similar to the historical method proposed by Vito Zagarrio. Looking back, Buscombe observes that we have not come much closer to the answers that he sought, but perhaps we have learned to phrase the questions more clearly.

"The project of film history," Edward Buscombe writes, "is still substantially what it was: how to account for films as both the result of individual human actions and the product of impersonal forces." In this book we have undertaken this project in the case of Frank Capra's relationship to Columbia Pictures, over the question of authorship and the studio system, and have demonstrated more fully how both the individual and the system contributed to some of the most interesting and important works in American cinema.

Notes

1. Joseph McBride, *Frank Capra: The Catastrophe of Success* (New York: Simon & Schuster, 1992), 290 ff. In his definition of authorship, McBride emphasizes a concern with "the thematic content of a film" (290), whereas the founding terms of the authorship debate centered on mise-en-scène, or visual style.

2. The authorship debate stems from a polemic begun during the 1950s in the French film journal *Cahiers du cinéma*, in which future filmmaker François Truffaut and other writers criticized what they regarded as an overly literary, dialogue-dominated tendency in French cinema. They wanted film technique and visual style to be dominant, and they ranked as auteurs those directors whom they admired as stylists. An auteur, they argued, was a director who embraced the contributions of collaborators such as screenwriter, art director, and cinematographer within an overall conception that shaped a film's technique. This viewpoint became known as the *politique des auteurs*, rendered in English, slightly askew, as "auteur theory." François Truffaut, "A Certain Tendency of the French Cinema," in *Movies and Methods: An Anthology*, ed. Bill Nichols (Berkeley and Los Angeles: Univ. of California Press, 1976), 224–37, originally published as "Un Certain tendance du cinéma français," in *Cahiers du cinéma* 31 (January 1954). See also *Cahiers du cinéma, the 1950s: Neo-realism, Hollywood, New Wave*, ed. Jim Hillier (Cambridge: Harvard Univ. Press, 1985).

3. Andrew Sarris, *The American Cinema: Directors and Directions 1929–1968* (New York: Dutton, 1968), 87.

4. Jean-Louis Comolli, Jean-André Fieschi, Gérard Guégan, Michel Mardone, Claude Ollier, and André Téchiné, "Twenty Years On: A Discussion about American Cinema and the *politique des auteurs*," in *Cahiers du cinéma, the 1960s: New Wave, New Cinema, Reevaluating Hollywood,* ed. Jim Hillier (Cambridge: Harvard Univ. Press, 1986), 196–209, quotation on 205; originally published as "Vingt ans après: le cinéma américain et la politique des auteurs," *Cahiers du cinéma* 172 (November 1965).

5. See Michel Foucault, "What Is an Author?" in *The Foucault Reader,* ed. Paul Rabinow (New York: Pantheon, 1984), 101–20, and *Theories of Authorship: A Reader,* ed. John Caughie (London: Routledge & Kegan Paul, 1981).

6. Stephen Crofts, "Authorship and Hollywood," *Wide Angle* 5, no. 3 (1983): 17–22, quotation on 20. Croft's categories of authorship discourse are as follows: (1) Author as expressive individual. (2) Author as constructed from the film or films: (2.1) as thematic and stylistic properties impressionistically and unproblematically read off from the film or films. (2.2) as a set of structures identifiable within a body of films by the same author. (2.3) as a subject position within the film. (3) Author as social and sexual subject. (4) Author as author-name, as function of the circulation of the film or films.

7. Robert L. Carringer, *The Making of Citizen Kane* (Berkeley and Los Angeles: Univ. of California Press, 1985). Carringer was in part defending the director from the claim that screenwriter Herman Mankiewicz deserved the credit as "author" of *Citizen Kane,* made by Pauline Kael in "Raising Kane," her introduction to *The "Citizen Kane" Book* (Boston: Little, Brown, 1971), 1–84. Ironically, Joseph McBride, who has played the Kael role in claiming credit for screenwriter Robert Riskin as "author" of the Capra films on which they collaborated, defended Welles against Kael in "Rough Sledding with Pauline Kael," *Film Heritage* 7, no. 1 (1971): 13–16, 32.

8. Thomas Schatz, *The Genius of the System: Hollywood Filmmaking in the Studio Era* (New York: Pantheon, 1988).

9. Frank Capra, *The Name above the Title: An Autobiography* (New York: Macmillan, 1971).

10. Michael Powell, *A Life in Movies: An Autobiography* (New York: Knopf, 1987), 223.

11. See *Accadde una Notte: Frank Capra (1928–1934) e la Columbia (1934–1945),* ed. Vito Zagarrio (Rome: Di Giacomo, 1988).

1

Anatomy of a House Director: Capra, Cohn, and Columbia in the 1930s

Thomas Schatz

Whether filmmaking success is measured in terms of box-office revenues, critical and popular acclaim, or Academy statuettes, Frank Capra was without question the most successful American movie director during the 1930s. In a meteoric rise that coincided with Hollywood's so-called Golden Age, Capra directed a remarkable string of hits: *Lady for a Day* (1933), *It Happened One Night* (1934), *Mr. Deeds Goes to Town* (1936), *Lost Horizon* (1937), *You Can't Take It with You* (1938), and *Mr. Smith Goes to Washington* (1939). All were huge moneymakers for Columbia Pictures, which shed its Poverty Row stigma during the 1930s to compete with the top studios. All six films received Oscar nominations for best picture, and five brought Capra nominations for best director. *It Happened One Night* and *You Can't Take It with You* went on to win Academy Awards for best picture, and Capra himself won three Oscars for best director in a five-year span (1934–38), a feat unmatched in industry history.

Not surprisingly, Capra's success also won him considerable clout in Hollywood. He served as president of the Motion Picture Academy from 1935 to 1939 and then became president of the newly formed Screen Directors Guild, mounting an outspoken campaign for directorial authority and creative freedom. Capra had been battling studio boss Harry Cohn for those same rights and privileges, and in 1939 he finally won them—though not at Columbia. After a decade as Cohn's top contract director and principal combatant, Capra bolted Columbia and signed a deal as an "in-house independent" producer-director at Warner Bros., allowing him more creative, administrative, and financial freedom than virtually any other filmmaker in Hollywood.

Capra's defection was not unexpected, given his success and his well-publicized clashes with Cohn. What was unexpected was his steady, inexorable decline after leaving Columbia. Capra had a somewhat tentative start at Warners with *Meet John Doe* (1941) and *Arsenic and Old Lace* (produced in 1941, released in 1944) and then left Hollywood when the war broke out to produce a series of Why We Fight documentaries for the government. Capra's postwar tour de force, *It's a Wonderful Life* (1946), produced through his independent company, Liberty Films, suggested a return to his 1930s form. Remarkably, however, Capra managed only five more features during the remainder of his career, and none of them, not even the remakes of two earlier Columbia hits, had anywhere near the commercial, popular, or critical success of his 1930s output.

Capra's postwar decline scarcely affected his critical reputation. On the contrary, Andrew Sarris anointed him "a genuine auteur" in 1968, and Capra came to be regarded as an exemplary Hollywood individualist, a director who overcame the avaricious, dehumanizing machinery of the industry to express his distinctive "vision" and personal style.[1] And though auteurism has declined in the face of more sophisticated approaches to Hollywood's industrial and institutional history, film critics and historians still celebrate Capra as the visionary artist who put Columbia on the industry map. Neal Gabler, for example, in his 1988 study of the Hollywood moguls and the studios they built, *An Empire of Their Own*, posited that "it is safe to say that no other studio was as dependent on a single artist as Columbia would be on Capra, and no other studio was built through a single talent the way Columbia was built through Capra's."[2] Ethan Mordden, in another 1988 study of the industry, *The Hollywood Studios*, wrote that "the reason for Columbia's graduation from quickie to major status was a director who worked for peanuts in order to command his films autonomously. This was Frank Capra, destined to be one of Hollywood's greatest self-defining talents."[3]

There is a certain irony in this latter statement, since the Capra mythos was most emphatically self-defined in the filmmaker's autobiography, *The Name above the Title*. Published in 1971 as auteurism was just taking hold and with its guiding "one man, one film" epithet planted every two or three pages, Capra's memoir contributed mightily to the romanticized conception of the movie director as lone artist battling the system. "Regardless of the origin of a film idea—I made it mine," asserted Capra. "Regardless of differences with studio heads, screenwriters, or actors—the thought, heart, and substance of a film were mine."[4] After his mid-1930s triumphs, *It Happened One Night* and *Mr. Deeds Goes to Town*, Capra claimed that he could feel "the 'one man, one film' concept nearing fruition; at a time when the power-structure of executive control was at its zenith, I was the maverick demanding total control. That meant total responsibility."[5]

The antagonist in this scenario, of course, was Harry Cohn, the embodiment of executive control at Columbia. Capra portrayed Cohn as more of an impediment than an advocate in his climb to greatness, someone who hitched his studio to Capra's rising star. "I had to hit a home run every time I came to bat to keep [Columbia] out of the cellar," recalled Capra. "Atlas carried only the world—I was carrying Harry Cohn on my back."[6]

In retrospect, it's quite remarkable that Capra's account sold so well—and that it continues to sell, as Gabler's and Mordden's accounts well indicate. The fact is that neither Capra nor his work can really be understood or appreciated in terms of personal style and individual authorship. Nor can Columbia's emergence as an industry power during the 1930s be attributed to its Capra-directed releases. This is by no means a dismissal of the notion of directorial authorship—a notion that was even more important to top movie directors in the 1930s and 1940s than to auteurists in the 1960s and 1970s. As we will see in Capra's negotiations with David O. Selznick, United Artists, Warner Bros., and others when he decided to go independent in the late 1930s, individual authority and creative control were crucial bargaining chips during Hollywood's classical era. It is significant that other studio contract directors like William Wellman, John Ford, and William Wyler made the successful transition to independent producer-director status at about the same time. But Capra's steady decline after leaving Columbia suggests that he was a filmmaker whose talents, personality, and working methods were best suited to a studio-based production process. His "one man, one film" bombast aside, Capra may have been essentially a house director, a collaborative artist whose vision and artistry were inextricably wed to Columbia's 1930s house style.

The Rise of Columbia Pictures

As with the other Hollywood studios, Columbia's house style coalesced during the early 1930s, mainly because of the effects of the Depression. The Capra films were key markers in Columbia's output, of course, but they represented only one facet of the company's overall production and marketing strategy, which actually took shape during the company's decade-long rise to power during the 1920s. Columbia began its corporate life in 1920 as the CBC Film Sales Company, a modest operation created by Joe Brandt, Jack Cohn, and Harry Cohn.[7] Brandt and Jack Cohn had worked together in advertising years earlier, before Jack decided in 1908 to join Carl Laemmle's IMP, the forerunner of Universal Pictures. Cohn learned the business end of the industry operating out of the New York office of Laemmle's bicoastal operation. In 1918 Jack's younger brother Harry, a former vaudevillian and song peddler in New York, joined Universal and was sent to the West Coast, where he was schooled in motion picture production. In 1920, Jack convinced Harry and Joe Brandt to join him in creating CBC (Cohn-Brandt-Cohn) to produce the kind of short subjects that Universal and other companies included on their programs. Seed money of $100,000 for CBC came from the Bank of Italy, a California-based concern run by A. H. and A. P. Giannini, two second-generation Italian-Americans vital to Columbia's development. Brandt and Jack Cohn ran CBC and handled sales out of New York, while Harry set up production on Hollywood's legendary Poverty Row, a block-long stretch of low-rent offices and studios on Beechwood Drive between Sunset Boulevard and Fountain Avenue.

CBC was successful enough that, in January 1924, the company went public and was incorporated as Columbia Pictures Corporation. Company headquarters remained in New York, with Brandt as president and Jack Cohn as his vice president in charge of sales. Harry Cohn remained in Hollywood as vice president in charge of production, with sole authority over the studio. Columbia expanded both its distribution and production operations in the next few years, developing a national merchandising setup and moving tentatively into feature film production. Columbia also began absorbing its Poverty Row environs until it encompassed most of the city block bordered by Sunset, Beechwood, Fountain, and Gower—thus the appellation "Gower Gulch." By the late 1920s Columbia Pictures, despite its low-rent facility and generally low-grade output, was beginning to look very much like a major Hollywood power, standing alongside the studios that would dominate the movie industry for decades to come.

Of those studio powers, Columbia most resembled Warner Bros. In fact, the similarities and differences between Columbia and Warners are quite illuminating. Both companies started virtually from scratch in Hollywood just after World War I, when powerhouses like Paramount and First National were already fully integrated companies with nationwide theater chains, global distribution networks, and factories on the West Coast turning out fifty to sixty feature films annually. Columbia and Warner Bros., conversely, began as small companies distributing via states-rights exchanges, gradually developing both the production and distribution systems to attain major studio status.[8]

Another obvious similarity between Columbia and Warners was the "family run" aspect. Both the Cohns and the Warners came from families of East European Jewish immigrants with four sons, and in each case only two of the sons (named Harry and Jack in both companies, coincidentally) remained heavily involved in the movie business, with the elder sibling running the New York office while his younger brother ran the studio. Thus, fraternal seniority reflected the hierarchy of authority in the industry, with the corporate headquarters in New York directing the "factory" in L.A. The older brother in each case—Jack Cohn and Harry Warner—was fiscally conservative, which meant limited operating budgets and cautious market strategies. Rather than the costly and highly differentiated prestige pictures that companies like Paramount, Fox, and MGM were turning out, Columbia and Warners relied on standardized story formulas even among their top features. What's more, both stressed contemporary genres—urban crime films and melodramas at Warners, romantic comedies at Columbia—which were more economical and efficient to produce.

Studio bosses Harry Cohn and Jack Warner also had a good deal in common. Both were ruthless autocrats who converted fiscal restraint into oppressive filmmaking policies; they did constant battle with their top talent, especially their directors, writers, and stars. Both Harry Cohn and Jack Warner overworked and ruthlessly typecast their contract players, and both routinely put their contract talent on suspension for failing to cooperate. Interestingly, however, both studio bosses had a tendency to hire left-leaning writers, in part because of the renegade status of each company and also because of the topical, socially conscious nature of their output. In fact, Warners and Columbia were home to far more blacklisted writers (and members of the infamous Hollywood Ten) than was any other studio.

Both Harry Cohn and Jack Warner also did constant battle with the New York office, which was a function of sibling rivalry as well as of their efforts to secure larger operating budgets and more authority over sales and marketing. But here the Columbia-Warners comparison breaks down. Unlike Columbia, Warner Bros. was among the industry's elite "integrated majors." Along with Paramount, Fox, MGM, and RKO, Warners not only produced and distributed its own motion pictures, but also owned a theater chain and thus had a guaranteed outlet for its products. Columbia, along with Universal and United Artists, was considered a "major minor" (or "nonintegrated major") because, even though the company owned no theater chain, it did develop a distribution system to complement its production operation. This rendered Columbia a legitimate Hollywood power, since distribution was widely considered the most crucial element of the industry's production-distribution-exhibition process. Indeed, the five integrated majors and the three major minors were referred to as the "Big Eight" because of their complete domination of movie distribution.

Columbia's nonintegrated status put added pressure on its West

Coast operations, of course. Without a theater chain, Columbia had to rely more on the commercial strength and quality of its products for survival in the movie marketplace. The lack of theaters also meant that Columbia's only significant real estate holding was its studio, which, because of its Poverty Row location, was scarcely among the more attractive properties in and around Hollywood. This lack of valuable real estate helps explain the general indifference toward Columbia on the part of Wall Street financiers, who were becoming increasingly involved in the financing and corporate control of other Hollywood studio powers. Columbia maintained its ties to the Gianninis' (renamed) Bank of America, which, as Edward Buscombe has pointed out, was itself something of a renegade outfit in relation to its East Coast counterparts.[9]

So, despite its Big Eight status, Columbia was still very much a minor-league studio at the dawn of Hollywood's classical era. In 1930, one year after Columbia's first issue on the New York Stock Exchange, the company showed assets of only $5.8 million, a tiny fraction of the value of the integrated majors like Paramount ($306 million), Warner Bros. ($230 million), and MGM ($128 million).[10] Even the nonintegrated Universal was valued at $17 million, over three times Columbia's worth, largely because of the value of Universal City, the massive production facility on a 350-acre site outside Los Angeles. Moreover, Columbia's features were scarcely on a par with even the routine first-run output of the majors. Paramount, for example, released sixty pictures for its 1929–30 program on a total budget of just under $20 million; its top dozen releases ("New Show World Specials") were budgeted at over $500,000 apiece.[11] Even Universal, with its relatively meager assets, was turning out ambitious and costly prestige pictures in 1929–30, like *All Quiet on the Western Front* and *Broadway*, budgeted at well over $1 million each. Columbia, meanwhile, cranked out two dozen features per annum in 1929 and 1930, each budgeted from $50,000 to $150,000, with an occasional project in the $200,000 range.

Though Harry Cohn well realized his studio's limitations, still he was intent on upgrading Columbia's output and industry status. He had taken two major steps in that direction in 1929, both of which were acknowledged in a trade press ad in which Cohn announced: "Capra will make nothing but 'specials' for Columbia from now on. Our stock is on the Big Board now—and going up fast."[12] The references here were to Columbia's successful stock issue in 1929 and also to the success of contract director Frank Capra, whose recent films were scoring well in the first-run market, those deluxe downtown theaters that played only top features and generated the lion's share of the revenues in the movie business.

Capra, Cohn, and the Columbia House Style

Capra had arrived at Columbia in 1928, recruited by studio manager Sam Briskin to write and direct a typically modest feature, *That Certain Thing*, and he had quickly established himself as the company's top director. In his early thirties when he joined Columbia, Capra already had done stints with comedy producer Hal Roach and then with Mack Sennett, for whom he had co-written and directed several Harry Langdon silent comedies. Capra parlayed his experience into feature assignments at Columbia, notably a cycle of "service pictures" with Jack Holt and Ralph Graves (*Submarine* in 1928, *Flight* in 1929, and *Dirigible* in 1931) that helped carry Columbia into the first-run market. *Submarine* was Columbia's biggest moneymaker to date and also its first sound picture, although without synchronous dialogue. (Capra did direct Columbia's first talkie, *The Donovan Affair*, in 1929.) *Dirigible*, Capra's thirteenth feature for the studio during a three-year span, was the first Columbia feature to play in L.A.'s most prestigious movie palace, Grauman's Chinese Theater.[13]

Clearly, the Capra-directed pictures were bringing Columbia the income and credibility that were so essential to compete with the established powers. The studio's competitive position improved even more, paradoxically, when the Great Depression caught up with the movie industry in 1931–32. Although the stock market crash in October 1929 had had little immediate effect on Hollywood because of the tremendous talkie boom, the Depression hit the industry with a vengeance in 1931. As the other studios struggled, Columbia found itself in a relatively stable position for three basic reasons. First, because Columbia owned no theaters, it was not saddled with the debilitating mortgage payments that drove all the integrated majors except MGM to the

1.1. One of the earliest publicity portraits of Frank Capra after he joined Columbia Pictures in 1927. (Museum of Modern Art/Film Stills Archive)

brink during the early 1930s. Second, Harry Cohn's cost-efficient factory system was well suited to the depressed economic climate and limited resources of that era. And third, a regulated output of shorts, modestly priced features, and B-grade "programmers" jibed perfectly with the changing marketplace, as double features and evening-long programs created a huge demand for Columbia's product.

In a sense, the Depression forced the other Hollywood powers to operate with much the same efficiency and economy as Columbia, and in the process all of the studios developed more distinctive house styles.[14] As audiences dwindled, money grew tighter, and resources became increasingly scarce during the early 1930s, the studios were forced to operate within their means, maximizing available resources and developing clear-cut market strategies. And, since Roosevelt's 1933 National Recovery Act sanctioned block booking, whereby companies foisted up to an entire year's output on exhibitors, each studio became keenly aware of the need for the "collective differentiation" of its products. Consequently, each company developed a regulated output of readily identifiable story cycles, star-genre formulations, and specialized programs, which might include cartoons, shorts, newsreels, and serials, as well as feature films.

Columbia cranked out shorts in assembly-line fashion throughout the 1930s, while Cohn steadily upgraded feature production from fewer than thirty pictures per year to roughly one feature per week at decade's end.[15] Most of these features were still low-budget programmers and B-grade Westerns; indeed, Douglas Gomery notes that the average length of Columbia's features as late as 1938 was a mere sixty-six minutes, indicating all too clearly that most of its features were destined to fill out the bottom half of double bills.[16] While these low-grade products kept the Gower factory running at full capacity and ensured an income base, even more crucial to Columbia's Depression-era fortunes were its occasional top features, those calculated star vehicles of sufficient quality and box-office appeal to compete in the lucrative first-run market. Not only was there greater profit potential for first-run features, but, in an era of intensive block booking, these top pictures quite literally carried the freight, enticing exhibitors to take a release schedule laden with second- and third-rate features.

The Capra-directed "specials" were among Columbia's most profitable and readily identifiable products, of course, but they were simply one facet of the production operations and overall market strategy that Harry Cohn refined during the 1930s. In a feat matched only by MGM, Columbia actually turned a profit every year during the Depression and saw its assets increase (from $5.8 million in 1930 to $15.9 million in 1940).[17] Significantly enough, Metro had a team of executives overseeing operations, from president Nick Schenck in New York to studio boss Louis B. Mayer and production chief Irving Thalberg in Hollywood. Columbia, meanwhile, had Harry Cohn. In fact, none of the Big Eight had anything like Columbia's one-man management operation, particularly after its severe executive shakeup in 1932. Joe Brandt, after a decade of running the company and mediating the endless sibling squabbles between the Cohns, had decided to sell his stake in Columbia. Jack Cohn was in line to succeed Brandt as chief executive but, in an unexpected turn of events, A. H. Giannini of the Bank of America backed Harry Cohn. Buying out Brandt for a reported $500,000, younger brother Harry assumed the presidency of Columbia, while Jack emerged from the internecine power struggle as vice president and treasurer. Even after taking over Columbia, Harry Cohn stayed in Hollywood to oversee studio operations, which put him in a class by himself as the only movie mogul to run the company out of L.A. while overseeing studio operations.

Harry Cohn's ascension only intensified his autocratic methods. In fact, after assuming the company presidency, Cohn began to act on his growing fascination with Italian dictator Benito Mussolini. Columbia produced a generally flattering (and commercially successful) 1933 documentary, *Mussolini Speaks*, and a trip to Italy inspired Cohn to remodel his studio offices to replicate those of *Il Duce*. One entered Cohn's office through two outer offices and, finally, a massive, sound-proofed door with no knob or keyhole on the outside, which was opened via a buzzer operated only by Cohn or his secretary. Cohn's office was spacious and elongated, with his huge semicircular desk at the far end of the room, dimly lit on a slightly raised platform. Cohn himself became more authoritarian and belligerent after assuming the company presidency, which observers also related to his naive infatuation with Mussolini—though few went so far as to dub Cohn a fascist. Biographer Bob Thomas, for instance, held that Cohn "had no comprehension of the Mussolini ideology, but he could understand and appreciate the Mussolini style." [18]

Although Cohn was perhaps an extreme case of the studio despot, he was not all that different from the other 1930s studio bosses, the men (and they were always men) who, year after year, were responsible for the companies' output. These privileged few transformed an annual budget into a program of specific pictures, coordinated operations of the entire plant, conducted contract negotiations, developed stories and scripts, screened "dailies" as pictures were being shot, and supervised editing until a picture was ready for release. These were the men Capra himself railed against in a 1939 open letter to the *New York Times*, complaining that "about six producers today pass on about 90 percent of the scripts and edit 90 percent of the pictures."[19] These were the men referred to by F. Scott Fitzgerald in 1940, when he wrote: "Not half a dozen men have been able to keep the whole equation of pictures in their heads."[20] And these were the men who shaped each company's house style. As sociologist Leo Rosten put it in his 1941 study, *Hollywood: The Movie Colony, The Movie Makers*: "Each studio has a personality; each studio's products show special emphases and values. And, in the final analysis, the sum total of a studio's personality, the aggregate pattern of its choices and tastes, may be traced to its producers . . . who establish the preferences, the prejudices, and the predispositions of the organization and, therefore, of the movies which it turns out."[21]

Of Hollywood's top studio executives, Cohn was among the least creative and yet the most heavily involved in day-to-day operations. One reason Cohn preferred to stay in the Gower facility, even though Columbia could afford to move or to build elsewhere, was that it kept him in close proximity to all phases of production. In terms of his own tastes, perhaps the closest Cohn ever came to articulating a film aesthetic was in a rare interview given in March 1928, in which he stated: "If your story has novelty, human appeal, humor, and pathos without being too morbid, your chances are very good."[22] Cohn gave that interview at about the same time he hired Frank Capra, who would effectively translate Cohn's vaguely defined aesthetic into actual filmmaking practice. This style did not really begin to coalesce, however, until 1932, the year of Cohn's ascendence and of the veritable birth of the "Capra unit" at Columbia.

Like the other Hollywood studios during the early 1930s, Columbia was turning to a unit production approach to first-run features, whereby particular star-genre formulas were sustained by specific producers, writers, directors, and others who collaborated on a succession of predictable star vehicles.[23] These star-genre formulas were crucial during the early years of the Depression, providing a means of stabilizing marketing and sales, of bringing efficiency and economy to the production of top features while ensuring consistent production values, and of distinguishing one company's output from another's. The integrated majors, with their superior resources and legions of top contract talent, were able to cultivate a number of star-genre formulas and distinct production units. But the major minors, given their limited resources and contract personnel, had difficulty sustaining unit production at the top feature level. Universal's only consistent unit-produced star-genre formula in the early 1930s, for instance, was its horror cycle starring Boris Karloff and Bela Lugosi. Columbia, too, had only one collaborative team working on successive first-run feature productions—its Capra unit.

Although Capra and others often mention his relative autonomy at Columbia, they rarely point out how heavily Capra relied on certain top studio personnel from one production to another. Capra did work without direct supervision by Harry Cohn, which was a clear exception to the studio boss's usual practice of personally overseeing the preparation and editing of other top features and of prowling the set during shooting. Cohn's interests were well served by Sam Briskin, Columbia's vice president and studio manager, whom Capra himself termed "my unit manager," the studio functionary who took "all the production details—money, sets, locations—off my hands."[24] Briskin assumed that role from the time Capra arrived, acting as what would have been termed at Metro or Paramount an *associate producer*, a middle-management position that Cohn could scarcely tolerate (or afford) on other Columbia productions.

The key creative collaborators in the Capra unit were writer Robert Riskin and cinematographer Joseph Walker. Riskin's role was particularly important, and indeed the unit as such did not really exist until Riskin became involved. Riskin signed with Columbia in 1931 and immediately began working with Capra, providing input on both *The Miracle Woman* and *Platinum Blonde*. The first full-blown Capra-Riskin collaboration came in 1932 with *American Madness*, and over the next six years—clearly the most successful in Capra's entire career—Riskin scripted seven of eight Capra-directed pictures.[25] With each project, it became more obvious that Riskin's glib, rapid-fire dialogue, Runyonesque characters, and tightly constructed plots were ideally suited to Capra's deft pacing, his feel for visual and physical humor, and his skill in working with actors. Together, Capra and Riskin forged a world view that was given shape by Joe Walker, who served as director of cinematography on all of Capra's 1930s pictures—and on most of Columbia's other important features, as well. In supervising the lighting and camera work on Capra's pictures, Walker ensured consistent production values and on-set efficiency despite Columbia's limited financial, material, and technical resources.

Cohn oversaw the production of Capra's pictures, of course, albeit in this case from the distance of his executive offices. Cohn determined Capra's budgets and decided what story properties were worth pursuing (and at what price), and he also handled casting—which, for Capra's productions, invariably meant bringing in freelance stars or loan-outs from other studios. From the mid-1930s onward, Capra worked most frequently with either Gary Cooper or James Stewart, two "outside" stars, who played the male lead opposite either Jean Arthur or Barbara Stanwyck, two nonexclusive Columbia contract players. In whatever pairing, these co-stars represented what became the essential Capra screen types: the aggressive, fast-talking, quick-witted career woman, more comfortable in a tweed suit than a designer gown, and the deliberate, low-key, tongue-tied man, out of his element among city slickers but ultimately capable of timely, heroic action. Capra's comedies usually centered on the man, whose common sense and homespun values put him at odds with the hustling heroine and with some political or industrial power as well. The hero triumphs, of course, and both the heroine and the larger institutional forces are won over, thus projecting a world in which sexual antagonism and deep-seated ideological conflicts might be resolved.

With Capra's increasing success, Cohn repaid his star director not only with salary increases but also with greater creative and administrative freedom. After the enormous success of *It Happened One Night* in 1934, Cohn offered Capra producer-director status and a six-picture deal, at $100,000 per picture plus 25 percent of the net profits.[26] This was unprecedented at Columbia but was hardly a risk or a sacrifice for Cohn. By 1934 Frank Capra, whatever his "one man, one film" precept and his perception of himself as maverick, was a known quantity at Columbia and in the industry generally, just as a Capra film was a known commodity in the movie marketplace.

Although the Capra-directed features were the most consistent and well publicized of Columbia's top features in the 1930s, they scarcely provided an adequate supply of first-run product for Cohn's run at the majors, particularly with Capra's output falling to only one picture per year. So Cohn developed other projects—and other production strategies—to supplement Columbia's first-run output and carry the overall schedule. Two key strategies were initiated in 1934, the year of Columbia's breakthrough success with *It Happened One Night*. One was a cycle of operatic romances starring the vivacious and somewhat portly blonde soprano Grace Moore. Success on Broadway and at the Metropolitan Opera had won Moore a contract at MGM in the early 1930s and, when weight problems cost her the Metro contract, Cohn signed Moore for *One Night of Love*. The film, which cast Moore as a rebellious opera star in comic conflict with her oppressive mentor, was a surprise runaway hit of 1934, especially in urban markets. While *It Happened One Night* was breaking box-office records in the hinterlands, *One Night of Love* had record-setting engagements in first-run theaters in both the United States and Europe. In fact, the Moore operetta was the first Columbia release to be booked in the prestigious and profitable Loew's Incorporated theater chain.[27] After the success of *One Night of Love*, which brought Moore an Oscar nomination for best actress, Columbia turned out similar vehicles during three successive years: *Love Me Forever* in 1935, *The King Steps Out* in 1936, and *When You're in Love* in 1937.

The other and more significant trend for Columbia was its A-class romantic comedies with top talent recruited from outside the studio. This trend also took shape in 1934, with two releases: *Twentieth Century*, a screwball comedy directed by Howard Hawks, co-scripted by Ben Hecht and Charles MacArthur, and starring John Barrymore and Carole Lombard, and *The Captain Hates the Sea*, directed by Lewis Milestone and starring John Gilbert, the fallen MGM silent star in what was to be his last feature. Although the Gilbert picture proved disappointing, *Twentieth Century* gave Columbia another sizable hit and an emergent star in Carole Lombard. What's more, it featured the same breakneck pacing, witty repartee, and sexual jousting as *It Happened One Night*. Cohn decided to continue the trend with two 1935 releases, *The Whole Town's Talking* and *She Married Her Boss*.

These two pictures solidified Columbia's commitment to "packaged" comedies, though with modifications. Cohn went outside the studio for the directors and top-billed stars—John Ford and Edward G. Robinson in *The Whole Town's Talking* and Gregory La Cava and Claudette Colbert in *She Married Her Boss*—but the co-stars in each were rising Columbia ingenues: Robinson teamed with Jean Arthur, Colbert with Melvyn Douglas. These and other emerging studio stars, like Cary Grant, were under nonexclusive contract, and Cohn displayed remarkable savvy not only in casting them in his own productions but in maneuvering their careers elsewhere.

Another important modification involved the scriptwriters on these 1935 hits. Both were written by staff scribes—*The Whole Town's Talking* by Jo Swerling and Robert Riskin and *She Married Her Boss* by Sidney Buchman. These were Columbia's three top contract writers, who not only scripted but also acted as informal supervisors as Cohn's penchant for packaged comedies grew with such notable releases as *Theodora Goes Wild* in 1936, *The Awful Truth* in 1937, *Holiday* in 1938, and *Only Angels Have Wings* in 1939, all of which were crucial to Columbia's Depression-era fortunes. *She Married Her Boss* and *Holiday*, for instance, were among the top box-office hits in their respective release years, and in 1937 *The Awful Truth* actually scored more major Oscar nominations—five, including best picture, best director (Leo McCarey), and best actress (Irene Dunne)—than did *Lost Horizon*, Capra's 1937 epic and Columbia's most ambitious production to date.[28]

The success of Columbia's packaged projects along with Capra's output established the contemporary romantic comedy as Columbia's trademark A-class commodity. Technically, they were fast-paced and elliptical, with an ideal balance of visual and verbal humor and of sophisticated comedy and broad farce. The stories invariably centered on a couple whose comic antagonism was related to differences in class or background, with the dominant situation usually turning on some case of mistaken or altered identity. The lovers' differences generally involved larger cultural oppositions and social conflicts of special significance to 1930s audiences—between the leisure and working classes, for example, or between the values and attitudes of city slickers and shysters and those of small-town or rural-agrarian types. These films all displayed solid production values although, with budgets of under a half-million dollars, they were inexpensive by Hollywood's standards for first-run features. Even with top talent, Cohn well appreciated the essential economy of these topical comedies, which required relatively little investment in the way of sets, costumes, score, and effects.

Capra versus Cohn

As important as the battling co-stars were to Columbia's screwball formula, the studio's crucial antagonists were Frank Capra and Harry Cohn. Indeed, the primary impetus for Columbia's 1930s rise was the Cohn-Capra symbiosis. The two had similar backgrounds, coming from immigrant stock and impoverished childhoods. Each also developed a proclivity for hustling, risk taking, and performing that eventually led to the movie business. Whatever their similarities, the two were bitter adversaries from the moment Capra arrived in 1928. This resulted, to an extent, from the division of labor and hierarchy of power in the studio system. Equally important, however, were the ambitions and personalities of the two. Capra and Cohn each harbored a paradoxical desire for success on his own terms and for acceptance within the Hollywood elite. Each also realized that only an outfit like Columbia could accommodate those desires, precisely because of its second-rate status and meager resources. As Capra said of the long-term contracts signed with Columbia in the 1930s, "I was trading away money for power I couldn't get at any other studio." He also realized that his desire for power was directly related to Cohn's. "He used me as a battering ram," Capra said of Cohn. "I used his ambition to get control of my films."[29]

Cohn, for his part, accepted Columbia's relative financial weakness as a fair trade-off for the degree of power it gave him within the company and also for the independence from the Wall Street financiers and Eastern power brokers who wielded so much control over the other studios. As Neal Gabler suggested, Cohn had a personal stake in the mythology that the Capra-directed films espoused. "For all the balm this myth provided to a country divided by class and riddled with anxiety, it also had a particular resonance at Columbia. . . . Capra's 'little men' fighting against and often overcoming entrenched powers had direct application to [Cohn]. It was, after all, a description of his life in Hollywood."[30]

That mythology extends beyond Capra's and Cohn's personalities, of course, particularly in 1930s America. In fact, 1932 was a key year in the Cohn/Capra/Columbia accord, not only because it marked Cohn's ascent to Columbia's presidency and the coalescence of Capra's production unit with *American Madness*. The year 1932 also saw the election of FDR and the emergence of the New Deal as a consummate populist scenario—and one that jibed remarkably well with the general outlook at Columbia, from the filmmakers on the set to the front-office personnel and even the Gianninis at the Bank of America. As Edward Buscombe has suggested, once we recognize what was virtually a corporate mind-set at Columbia during the early to mid-1930s, we necessarily move beyond the facile notion that Capra's Depression-era success was a function of his singular empathy with the American public.[31]

It is also significant that, when Cohn yielded to Capra's continual pleas to tackle more ambitious projects, the results were disastrous. This occurred on two occasions, with *The Bitter Tea of General Yen* in 1933 and *Lost Horizon* in 1937, two lavish, costly, and high-minded costume dramas designed to compete more aggressively in the high-stakes prestige market. Such projects were inevitable, perhaps, given Capra's and Cohn's ambitions. But both pictures fared poorly commercially and critically, and on each occasion the Capra unit reverted to the screwball comedies that it knew best, with *It Happened One Night* in 1934 and *You Can't Take It with You* in 1938, two of Columbia's biggest hits of the decade. Although these hits confirmed how well Capra's talents and sensibilities jibed with Cohn's and with the studio generally, Capra grew ever more determined to parlay his success into commercial and artistic independence.

Not surprisingly, Capra's strongest motivation to leave Columbia was his relationship with Harry Cohn, which reached a flash point in 1937 when Capra discovered that a low-grade Jean Arthur comedy, *If You Could Only Cook*, had been released in Britain as "A Frank Capra Production," cashing in on his increasing marquee value. Capra promptly sued Cohn, initiating a legal battle that went on for over a year and kept Capra out of active filmmaking—though he kept busy negotiating with other studios and independent producers.

Those negotiations clearly indicated Capra's market value at the time, as well as the premium placed on creative autonomy and administrative control by Capra and others. Capra's most ardent suitor in 1937 was David O. Selznick, who a few years earlier had bolted an executive position at MGM to create Selznick International Pictures (SIP). In August 1937 Selznick wrote to SIP board chairman Cornelius Vanderbilt "Jock" Whitney and treasurer John Wharton that "it looks almost certain that we can make a deal with Frank Capra . . . if he is successful in breaking his Columbia contract, which confidentially he is suing to do." Capra, who had never used an agent before, now was being represented by David's brother Myron Selznick, an aggressive and successful

1.2. Harry Cohn (left) with Frank Capra at the 1939 Academy of Motion Picture Arts and Sciences awards ceremony. Capra holds his Oscar for best director for *You Can't Take It with You* (1938). (Museum of Modern Art/Film Stills Archive)

"ten percenter." Myron was demanding a flat fee of $200,000 for Capra's services, which David considered excessive, although he recognized (as had Cohn) that "Capra's name alone on a picture is worth a fortune" both at home and abroad, especially in England, where SIP did roughly one third of its business. Selznick closed the letter with this assertion: "I do not need to tell either of you that Capra is unquestionably the ranking producing director in the business and I think we should move fast on this."[32] Wharton wired Selznick that he and Whitney "approve two hundred thousand figure provided you can specify type of story and control budget."[33] Those terms were not acceptable to Capra, and indeed they were plaguing Selznick's efforts to sign several of Hollywood's "producing directors," notably Gregory La Cava, Mervyn LeRoy, and Leo McCarey.

By November 1937 Cohn and Capra had settled their differences, temporarily at least, and had began another project that clearly indicated how desperately Cohn wanted to keep Capra at Columbia. Cohn agreed to purchase the screen rights to George S. Kaufman and Moss Hart's Pulitzer Prize-winning stage hit "You Can't Take It with You" for the unprecedented price of $200,000.[34] He also secured the services of James Stewart to co-star opposite Jean Arthur, with a supporting cast that included such top character actors as Lionel Barrymore, Edward Arnold, Spring Byington, and Harry Davenport. *You Can't Take It with You* reconvened the Capra unit for the first time since *Lost Horizon* over a year before—and for their first romantic comedy since *Mr. Deeds Goes to Town* in 1936.

The outcome was not only another huge hit and Oscar winner (for best picture and best director), but also a canny portrait of Cohn's Columbia. *You Can't Take It with You* centers on the efforts of a young couple (James Stewart and Jean Arthur) to reconcile the worlds of their two very different patriarchs. Stewart's father (Edward Arnold) is a scion of big business, while Arthur's father (Lionel Barrymore) is an inspired eccentric whose rickety mansion in New York City houses his own unconventional family along with a collection of inventors, poets, actors, and other assorted misfits who have taken refuge there against the corrupt and decadent world outside. Arnold and Barrymore seem a dual extension of Cohn's own split personality—on the one hand, the vulgar, bullying industrialist and, on the other, the determined idealist, out to live life on his own terms. Barrymore's addled, ramshackle household was itself reminiscent of Gower Gulch. "Decorwise, Columbia was a junkyard," Capra once said, "but brainwise it was a gold mine."[35] The same was true of the Barrymore household in *You Can't Take It with You*, although in that utopian fantasy everyone comes to love the place. In the picture's finale, Arnold learns to play the harmonica, approves the marriage of the young lovers, and relents in his plan to replace Barrymore's house with a skyscraper.

Capra scarcely expected that kind of rehabilitation on Cohn's part, nor was he willing to persevere at Gower Gulch. The success of *You Can't Take It with You* bolstered Capra's status and further enhanced his resolve to go his own way. In fact, his key collaborator, Bob Riskin, had already left the fold; after adapting *You Can't Take It with You*, Riskin signed as a writer-producer with

1.3. On the set of *Mr. Smith Goes to Washington* (1939). From the left: James Stewart, Jean Arthur, Frank Capra, and cinematographer Joseph Walker. (Museum of Modern Art/Film Stills Archive)

Sam Goldwyn. Capra was committed to one more Columbia picture, and for that project he collaborated with the studio's top comedy writer, Sidney Buchman. The picture was *Mr. Smith Goes to Washington*, a Jimmy Stewart-Jean Arthur comedy in the vein of *Mr. Deeds*, to which Cohn gave maximum studio support. *Mr. Smith Goes to Washington* was another commercial and critical success, but it was scarcely enough to keep Capra at Columbia. Even before he had finished shooting the picture, Capra had determined to set out on his own.

Mr. Capra Goes Independent

Selznick continued to dominate Capra's outside negotiations, in spite of the concerns voiced by board chairman Jock Whitney, an Eastern aristocrat who told Selznick during negotiations with Capra that he considered *You Can't Take It with You* "the most vicious piece of anticapitalist propaganda since Capra made *Mr. Deeds*."[36] But Selznick persisted, even working Riskin into the deal with an offer for him to write and produce two pictures per year for SIP, at $50,000 plus 10 percent of the net profits.[37] That was only a fraction of his offer to Capra, which escalated as a virtual bidding war broke out for his services. Capra continued to favor SIP, and in August 1939 he and Riskin set up a partnership, Frank Capra Productions, with headquarters on the RKO lot in a bungalow leased from Selznick.[38] (At the time SIP had taken over much of the RKO facility in Culver City for the production of *Gone with the Wind* and *Rebecca*.)

This was a heady period for Capra, who not only was a free agent and valued artist in Hollywood but also was heavily involved in industry politics. He had been president of the Motion Picture Academy since 1935, helping to guide the industry through a difficult period as actors, writers, and directors organized viable "guilds" to challenge the power of the studios. Capra left that post in 1939 to preside over the newly created Screen Directors Guild, mounting an outspoken campaign for directorial authority and artistic freedom. He staked out that position publicly in the open letter to the *New York Times* quoted earlier, in which he lamented that in Hollywood there were "only half a dozen or so directors who are allowed to shoot as they please and who have any supervision over their editing."[39] At issue was the refusal by Hollywood's top producers and studio bosses to recognize the guild as the bargaining agent in labor-management negotiations for directors and assistant directors. The issue eventually was resolved in favor of the Screen Directors Guild, adding to Capra's clout and prestige.

Actually, Capra had come to think of himself as a producer and was being actively recruited to join a group Selznick termed "the more important independent film producers" in Hollywood, who wanted to create a trade association of their own.[40] That effort came to naught, and Capra eventually decided that, to maximize his own individual power and status, he was better off committing to a major studio as an "in-house independent" than to SIP. Many of the majors were willing to sign one- and two-picture deals with independent producer-directors, and they would provide both a base of production operations and a solid distribution-exhibition setup. In February 1940, Capra signed a one-picture deal with Warner Bros. for *Meet John Doe*, and he immediately went to work with Bob Riskin on the project.

Warners secured Gary Cooper and Barbara Stanwyck for the Capra picture; along with Riskin they resembled the old Columbia unit. But the remaining personnel were provided by Warners, and although the film was an obvious reformulation of two Columbia projects (*Mr. Deeds* and *Mr. Smith*), the outcome was scarcely up to Capra's earlier standards. Indeed, *Meet John Doe* indicated that, although he finally had the creative freedom, authority, and resources that he had so sorely coveted during the years with Columbia, Capra was not altogether able to handle them. But Capra sought even more autonomy with his next production, dissolving Frank Capra Productions after *Meet John Doe*, which marked the end of his decade-long collaboration with Bob Riskin. There followed yet another round of offers from Selznick, United Artists, and Fox, but again Warner Bros. came up with the most attractive deal. In August 1941 Capra signed another one-picture deal with Warners to produce and direct an adaptation of a then-current stage hit, "Arsenic and Old Lace," and his contract with Warners well evidenced Capra's market value.

Capra was to be paid $100,000 plus 10 percent of the gross receipts of *Arsenic and Old Lace* in excess of $1.25 million; his name was to appear above the title and in type size at least 50 percent that of the title. The contract further stipulated that "the duties of the Director shall include those customarily rendered by a producer and/or a director, and shall include the cutting, titling, and editing of such photoplay."[41] A Warners "deal memo" further stipulated that "Capra as producer will, of course, collaborate and assist in the writing and development of the screenplay, and we agree to furnish Capra with competent scenario writers at our cost."[42] That clause underscored the degree of control Capra wielded over the production, and it also signaled Robert Riskin's absence—and thus the ultimate dissociation of the Capra unit.

Arsenic and Old Lace did quite well when Warners sent it into general release in 1944 (after holding it up because of an agreement with the play's producers), but it provided further evidence that the famed Capra touch had not survived his defection from Columbia and his split with Riskin. The film was little more than a serving of canned theater, an entertaining and straightforward recreation of the stage play with virtually none of the style or substance of the earlier Capra-directed pictures. And, over the following decade in a sequence of increasingly disappointing efforts, Capra proved to be utterly out of his filmmaking element. Nor was there any going back, as he learned with two failed remakes of previous Columbia hits. Though still a relatively young man and seemingly at the height of his powers when he went independent, Capra saw his career—even as a director for hire, let alone as a leading independent filmmaker—completely unravel within a decade.

Columbia, meanwhile, which had sagged briefly after Capra's departure, surged through the ensuing war years and into the uncertain postwar era under Harry Cohn's autocratic command, turning a profit every year until Cohn's death in 1958.[43] Columbia's success came via new stars and genres and a new crop of filmmaking talent, of course, though Cohn relied ever more heavily on the kind of packaged projects he had developed in the 1930s. But, just as Capra never duplicated his Columbia success as an independent, Columbia itself never found another Frank Capra. His was a singular talent, and one perfectly suited to the studio's particular fusion of resources and personnel, management style, and market strategy. What Columbia had provided Capra was not only a viable working environment and a top collaborative team, but also an ideal balance of creative freedom and institutional constraint. Capra proved that he was not simply another house director but a consummate studio auteur, in the same mold as such inimitable studio-based talents as Josef von Sternberg at Paramount, Michael Curtiz at Warners, and Vincente Minnelli at MGM. In the final analysis, Frank Capra's distinctive artistry was impracticable—and remains inconceivable—in any milieu other than that provided by Harry Cohn and Columbia Pictures.

Notes

1. Andrew Sarris, *The American Cinema: Directors and Directions, 1929–1968* (New York: Dutton, 1968), 87.

2. Neal Gabler, *An Empire of Their Own: How the Jews Invented Hollywood* (New York: Crown, 1988), 165.

3. Ethan Mordden, *The Hollywood Studios: House Style in the Golden Age of the Movies* (New York: Knopf, 1988), 174.

4. Frank Capra, *The Name above the Title: An Autobiography* (New York: Macmillan, 1971), 185.

5. Ibid., 185–86.

6. Ibid., 172.

7. There are various accounts of Columbia Pictures' history, most notably Rochelle Larkin, *Hail Columbia* (New Rochelle, N.Y.: Arlington House, 1975); Bob Thomas, *King Cohn: The Life and Times of Harry Cohn* (New York: Putnam's, 1967); Douglas Gomery, "Columbia," in *The Hollywood Studio System* (New York: St. Martin's, 1986), 161–172, along with the Gabler, Mordden, and Capra books cited above.

8. Gomery, "Columbia," 161.

9. Edward Buscombe, "Notes on Columbia Pictures Corporation 1926–1941," *Screen* 16, no. 3 (1975): 65–82, reprinted as chapter 9 of this book.

10. Figures are culled from various chapters in Gomery, *Hollywood Studio System*.

11. Paramount figures are taken from an interoffice memo dated 20 June 1929, outlining the budget and release schedule for each of Paramount's 1929–30 productions; David O. Selznick Collection, Humanities Research Center, University of Texas at Austin (hereafter HRC/UT).

12. Quoted in Capra, *Name above the Title*, 103.

13. Thomas, *King Cohn*, 89.

14. For a more detailed and extensive treatment of the emergence of the studios' distinctive house styles during the early Depression, see Thomas Schatz, *The Genius of the System: Hollywood Filmmaking in the Studio Era* (New York: Pantheon, 1988), 69–155.

15. Figures are cited in Christopher R. Sterling and Timothy R. Haight, *The Mass Media: Aspen Institute Guide to Communication Industry Trends* (New York: Praeger, 1978), 31.

16. Gomery, "Columbia," 167.

17. Sterling and Haight, *Mass Media*, 184.

18. Thomas, *King Cohn*, 102.

19. Quoted in Leo Rosten, *Hollywood: The Movie Colony, the Movie Makers* (New York: Harcourt, Brace, 1941), 302.

20. This oft-quoted passage appears on the opening page of F. Scott Fitzgerald, *The Last Tycoon: An Unfinished Novel* (New York: Scribner's, 1941), which he was writing in Hollywood at the time of his death.

21. Rosten, *Hollywood*, 242–43.

22. Quoted in Thomas, *King Cohn*, 46.

23. For more detailed treatment of unit production, see Schatz, *Genius of the System*, 159–270, and Janet Staiger, "The Producer-unit System: Management by Specialization after 1931," in David Bordwell, Janet Staiger, and Kristin Thompson, *The Classical Hollywood Cinema: Film Style and Mode of Production to 1960* (New York: Columbia Univ. Press, 1985), 320–29.

24. Capra, *Name above the Title*, 97.

25. For more on the 1930s screen comedy and the Capra-Riskin collaborations, see "The Screwball Comedy," in Thomas Schatz, *Hollywood Genres: Formulas, Filmmaking, and the Studio System* (New York: Random House, 1981), 150–85.

26. Capra, *Name above the Title*, 177.

27. Thomas, *King Cohn*, 99.

28. Cobbett Steinberg, *Film Facts* (New York: Facts on File, 1980), 18, 202–3.

29. Capra, *Name above the Title*, 105.

30. Gabler, *Empire of Their Own*, 173.

31. See chapter 9.

32. Selznick to C. V. Whitney, 12 August 1937, David O. Selznick Collection, HRC/UT.

33. John Wharton to Selznick, 13 August 1937, David O. Selznick Collection, HRC/UT.

34. Capra, *Name above the Title*, 234.

35. Ibid., 82.

36. C. V. Whitney to Selznick, 27 December 1938, David O. Selznick Collection, HRC/UT.

37. Selznick to Henry Ginsberg, 11 July 1938, David O. Selznick Collection, HRC/UT.

38. The deal is outlined in a letter from E. L. Scanlon to Selznick, 12 February 1940, David O. Selznick Collection, HRC/UT; also described in Capra, *Name above the Title*, 294–95.

39. Quoted in Rosten, *Hollywood*, 302.

40. Selznick to Lloyd Wright, 17 February 1940, David O. Selznick Collection, HRC/UT.

41. Capra-Warner Bros. contract dated 1 August 1941, Warner Bros. Legal Files, United Artists Collection, Wisconsin Center for Film and Theater Research, State Historical Society, Madison, Wis. (hereafter WB-UA/Madison).

42. Roy Obringer to Ralph Lewis (both were Warners attorneys), 23 July 1941, WB-UA/Madison.

43. Sterling and Haight, *Mass Media*, 184.

2

A Leap into the Void: Frank Capra's Apprenticeship to Ideology

Robert Sklar

As with few other American filmmakers, Frank Capra's historical reputation seems inextricably bound up within a specific
social and political conjuncture: the years of Franklin D. Roosevelt's presidency, 1933–45. *It Happened One Night* (1934),
the *Mr. Deeds*, *Mr. Smith*, and *John Doe* trilogy (1936–41), the
World War II Why We Fight series, and, slipping just over the
chronological terminus, the postwar *It's a Wonderful Life* (1946)
form a primary canon for debate over the director's cultural significance. These works, along with a few others, such as *American
Madness* (1932) and *You Can't Take It with You* (1938), represent
Capra's ideological contribution to capitalism's crisis in the Great
Depression, to national myths of popular power and individual
leadership.

This dominant temporal framework has tended to eclipse the
fact that, in quantitative terms, Capra's most prolific period occurred during the years before *It Happened One Night*. The films
he directed at Columbia Pictures from 1928 through 1934, along
with a handful of titles he made for other companies in 1926–27,
make up well more than half of his total feature film output. During the 1970s revival of interest in the director's work, following
the 1971 publication of his autobiography *The Name above the
Title*, Capra himself may have discouraged close attention to these

early films when he famously fostered a legend of an epistemolog-
ical break between his 1930s period of self-consciously important
work and all that came before it, or perhaps he was simply inter-
nalizing the existing critical emphasis.[1] The unavailability during
the 1970s of many of his early films provided no opportunity to
test the prevailing viewpoint.

Since the late 1980s, however, most of Capra's pre-1934 work
has been returned to circulation.[2] We now have a foundation in
available texts for the first time to approach these early years in
broader and more comprehensive terms, as a distinctive temporal
unit of their own. Given the dominant critical focus on Capra's
social and cultural significance in the 1930s, the question necessarily arises: What kinds of social and cultural discourses appear in
the pre-1934 films? From this particular perspective, are there
grounds to revise our understandings of Capra's canonical works
or of his directing career as a whole?

This essay seeks to shift the concern with Capra's representation of American society and culture into that earlier temporality:
the 1920s and the period between the 1929 stock market crash
and Roosevelt's inauguration in 1933. Such a move, however,
confronts a historiographical problem: other than popular legends
of the Roaring Twenties and the Jazz Age, to what historical referents about this era can Capra's films be related? The 1920s period has for some time lacked focus and attention in contemporary historiography—and this has been the case as much for the
history of American cinema in that era as for American society at
large. In contrast, recent scholarship in both fields concentrates on
the 1930s as a fundamental period of struggle and transformation,
during which the principal events and issues are clearly demar-
cated even as their meaning and interpretation may be in dispute.

Nevertheless, there are signs that the emerging concerns of the
1990s are making analysis of 1920s American society and culture
relevant once again. New, broadly interpretative studies of the era
have emphasized continuities with later times rather than an epis-
temological break between the 1920s and 1930s, which has been
a common concept in writings about the period that was echoed
by Capra's personal recollection.[3] The era's freshly conceived relationship of continuity with later times rests on two related argu-

ments: that the 1920s generated an ethos of "modernity" in the arts and popular media that remains central to the contemporary cultural landscape and that this ethos was strongly animated by conflicts over race, gender, and ethnicity not unlike those in late twentieth-century America. The 1930s, so one may summarize and extend this viewpoint, was a period in which government, media, and the arts alike were striving to construct a unitary American culture, an effort in which Frank Capra played a prominent role. The 1920s, on the other hand, was an era in which the dominant forces of state, society, and culture all struggled over the desire, or the necessity, to shape a multicultural nation.

In this essay I explore four aspects of cultural and social representation in Capra's early career and films: the generic and cultural background of *It Happened One Night*, issues of ethnicity and social mobility, the stylistics of spectacle and realism, and the emergence of an ideological project. Each topic is introduced through a contemporary quotation.

The Background of *It Happened One Night*

At any given moment he might be running a pirate fleet or landing on the throne of the Kingdom of Boopadoopia.

Let us for the moment allow the source of this quotation to remain unknown. If you were to pursue its identity through some form of keyword cross-check, you might come across "The Offshore Pirate," a short story by F. Scott Fitzgerald published in the *Saturday Evening Post* of 29 May 1920. I take the liberty of quoting myself in describing how this fiction begins:

> A beautiful, willful, temperamental young girl, Ardita Farnam, is cruising with her uncle on a yacht off the Florida coast. She is fed up with stuffy, boring, moralizing, conventional suitors. She has taken up with a bad man, because he seems the only one who can give her life the romance and power she desires. "He's the only one I know, good or bad," she says, "who has an imagination and the courage of his convictions."[4]

With a few nips and tucks, this scene setting bears an uncanny resemblance to the opening sequence of *It Happened One Night*. And, indeed, the sentence quoted anonymously above turns out to be from the popular magazine short story from which Capra's film was adapted, "Night Bus," by Samuel Hopkins Adams, published August 1933 in *Cosmopolitan*.[5] "Night Bus" opens not on a yacht but in a Miami, Florida, bus station where a beautiful, willful, temperamental young woman, Elspeth Andrews, has run away from her father, the yachting millionaire, to take up with a bad man who is the only one she knows with imagination and the courage of his convictions.

The male pronoun in the Samuel Hopkins Adams sentence refers to the story's hero, Peter Warne. With his links to pirate fleets and exotic kingdoms, Peter sounds not unlike Toby Moreland of "The Offshore Pirate," who indeed poses as a pirate to commandeer Ardita Farnam's yacht (her uncle having conveniently gone ashore) and sail it to a palm-fringed island. Eventually he is revealed as one of her previously rejected conventional suitors, but his capacity for fantasy performance wins her over entirely. " 'What an imagination!' she said softly and almost enviously. 'I want you to lie to me just as sweetly as you know how for the rest of my life.' "[6]

As many commentators have noted, the fictional Peter Warne went through a substantial transformation to become Clark Gable's character in *It Happened One Night*. He was "a sort of high-class gadabout in the story," write the editors of *Stories into Film*, but "this characterization was rightly rejected as too outré to evoke the audience's sympathy."[7] "Rightly rejected," of course, from the viewpoint of the film's extraordinary success and classic status. But Adams's Peter Warne was not too outré for readers of popular magazine fiction in 1933, any more than Fitzgerald's Toby Moreland was in 1920. To understand not only *It Happened One Night* but also much of Capra's earlier work in the framework of 1920s culture, we need to know something more of the genre in which characters such as Peter and Toby, not to speak of Ardita and Elspeth, flourished.

In my study on F. Scott Fitzgerald, quoted above, I sought to define a branch of 1920s commercial fiction to which Fitzgerald was a frequent contributor—and which, in his serious fiction, he critiqued and overcame. What made these popular narratives significant was their manner of constructing a romantic couple on the basis of particular kinds of middle-class and male ideological fantasies. The hero was a solid middle-class figure with a capacity for masquerade, who could perform feats of imaginative fancy sufficient to entertain and divert and win the heart of—and here is the key point—a woman of a social class higher than his own. The man, whom I called the genteel romantic hero, was a somewhat conventional figure of popular literature. The woman, whom I called the genteel romantic heroine, was, I argued, a new literary type, "a young woman who dares to use her independent will for what she wants, and is not punished for it."[8] But she is, to repeat, a daughter of the yacht-owning, plutocratic upper classes.

The terminology, arising from earlier discourses concerning what was called the genteel tradition in American literature, may seem at best quaint. More recent cultural studies would almost surely want to ground analysis of these texts in terms such as *patriarchy* and *bourgeois culture*, but these, we also know, are blunderbuss terms, cutting a wide swath, leveling all before them. There are many forms of patriarchal and bourgeois discourse, and the genteel romantic hero and heroine form but one strand. For readers of the *Saturday Evening Post* and *Cosmopolitan* and their many kindred periodicals, stories like these provided reassurance that women's new freedoms—and particularly the possibility of sexual license that great wealth conferred on young women— could be safely controlled within the bounds of middle-class male imagination.

If "The Offshore Pirate" in 1920 is a relatively early and innovative work, "Night Bus" some thirteen years later reads as a fully mature and conventionalized example of the genre. Adams, perhaps confident of his readers' familiarity with the tropes, provides only sketchy narrative background. We meet Elspeth at a bus terminal and through subtle behavioral codes intuit her leisure-class status; a third of the story passes before we learn of her flight from her father, the millionaire yachtsman. Information about Peter is in like manner dribbled out tantalizingly throughout the tale. A premise of the genre is that evidence of character is more significant than outward signs of social position, especially when enough signals are present to assure that social status will ultimately be adequate. Peter, it turns out, knew Elspeth's cousin at college, but perhaps while he was in a serving position, such as valet or butler, which might account for his poise and resourcefulness. Such enigmatic clues are all part of the story's gamesmanship. When Elspeth surreptitiously telegraphs the cousin to inquire about Peter, she receives in reply the mention of a pirate fleet and the Kingdom of Boopadoopia—the proverbial smoking gun for readers of the genre.[9]

By story's end the genteel hero's imagination and courage have quite overshadowed those reputed qualities in the bad man, aviator King Westley, whom Elspeth had escaped her father to join. What is perhaps most significant about "Night Bus," however, is not the hero's behavior, but the heroine's. The link between Elspeth's independent will and the possibility of sexual license is more vivid in the Adams story than the standard for the genre and certainly than in Claudette Colbert's performance as Ellie Andrews in *It Happened One Night*. Elspeth is the one who comes to chafe at the propriety of "the walls of Jericho"—the blanket Peter rigs to separate their tourist camp bunks—and at the end is the sexually forward partner who suggests marriage and gives Peter the trumpet to blow down the "walls." Although considerable attention has been given to the changes of Peter Warne's character from story to film, as noted above, the question of Elspeth's transformation to Ellie may be of equal importance and has hardly been remarked upon at all.

Beyond the popular narratives of genteel romance, a further source for understanding the Elspeth/Ellie characterizations lies with the representation of women in Capra's pre-1934 films. I have in mind specifically three works, none of which shares any of the comedic elements of either the fiction genre or *It Happened One Night*, yet all of which feature prominently a woman of independent will. In each film this figure is portrayed by Barbara Stanwyck. The films are *Ladies of Leisure* (1930), *The Miracle Woman* (1931), and *Forbidden* (1932). Stanwyck's performances—she also appeared in *The Bitter Tea of General Yen* (1933) during this pre-1934 period—are central aspects of Capra's representation of 1920s-era American culture and society.

All three films open with gestures of defiance by the beautiful, willful, and temperamental women whom Stanwyck plays. In

Ladies of Leisure, based on a 1924 stage play, Kay Arnold is introduced as a disheveled "party girl" rowing away from a party on board a yacht, where what she regards as an untoward incident has occurred. In *The Miracle Woman*, based on a 1927 stage play, Florence Fallon opens the film by delivering an impassioned attack on the parishioners of her deceased father's church, whom she regards as hypocrites. In *Forbidden*, credited as an original story by Capra but acknowledged by him to be drawn from Fannie Hurst's *Back Street* (1931), the work opens with a vehement revolt by small-town librarian Lulu Smith against her constricted life; she takes all her money out of the bank and sails off on a cruise ship to Cuba.

These three films, as noted, are not comedies; they are melodramas. Their female protagonists are not genteel heroines (i.e., wealthy daughters of the yacht-owning class), they are figures on the social margin, even if they may be described, as in the case of the librarian and the minister's daughter, as respectably lower-middle class. In their genre, they are not entertained and beguiled by the imagination of genteel heroes. If they are not chastised or rendered odious by their authors, as was often the case with women of independent will in the American literary tradition, the outcome of their impetuous acts is loss and suffering. Lulu Smith of *Forbidden* meets the love of her life in Havana, but he is a married man and politically ambitious; she lives a shadowy, unacknowledged, and renunciatory life as the "other woman," even committing murder to protect their secret. Florence Fallon of *The Miracle Woman* becomes a sensational evangelist dominated by a charlatan promoter and ends in a similarly anonymous way, in the Salvation Army. Of the three films, only *Ladies of Leisure* hints at a "happy ending," but even there it follows Kay Arnold's suicidal leap into the sea from a cruise ship, and the reunion of thwarted lovers appears as a false, double ending to a work already tragically concluded.

The ideological implications of these narratives are plain. All three Stanwyck characters are "new women" of the 1920s, women who work outside the home and who desire to change their social status as well as their prospects for happiness.[10] Yet the boundaries posed by class, by institutions, or by conventional morality are almost entirely insurmountable.

2.1. Wealthy yachtsman Alexander Andrews (Walter Connolly) pleads with daughter Ellie (Claudette Colbert) not to jump ship, in a publicity still from *It Happened One Night* (1934). (Museum of Modern Art/Film Stills Archive)

It Happened One Night also opens (as the short story "Night Bus" decidedly does not) with a gesture of defiance by a beautiful, willful, temperamental woman—Ellie Andrews's leap into the sea from her father's yacht. That impetuous act of independent will deserves comparison with those of Stanwyck's characters. In breaking out of their socially sanctioned cages, the latter set in train possibilities of change across the full spectrum of social and emotional outcomes, from desire's fulfillment to suicidal despair. In contrast, Ellie's leap is always provisional; it can be retracted by a word. In her flight Ellie is exposed—on the bus, at the tourist courts—to the experiences of women outside her own class, as she would not otherwise have been; yet her social position erects a wall of glass between her activities and their possible consequences. This is not to say that there are no dangers or risks in exerting her independent will, but hers is not the challenge to fate thrown out by the party girl Kay Arnold, the orphaned daughter Florence Fallon, or the librarian, soon to be kept woman, Lulu Smith.

In light of this comparison, whatever else may be said about the ideological implications or the historical importance of *It Happened One Night*, it marks for Capra a significant class shift. He had made comedies before, he had represented upper-class women before (e.g., the Jean Harlow character in *Platinum Blonde* [1931]). *It Happened One Night* is his first genteel romantic comedy, a work featuring a rich woman of independent will who is not punished because she accepts the yoke of the genteel hero's imagination.

It has been argued, of course, that *It Happened One Night*'s hero Peter Warne is decidedly no longer genteel.[11] Clark Gable's Peter is indeed a figure whose potential for danger and sexual allure is considerably greater than anything Peter of "Night Bus" had to offer. Yet danger and sexual allure are not alien to the genteel romantic hero in his performer's role, as with Fitzgerald's Toby Moreland masquerading as an outlaw to win Ardita's heart in "The Offshore Pirate." We need to interrogate the Capra-Gable version of Peter—who is, as a newspaper reporter, likely to be no less a middle-class "college man" than earlier genteel heroes— to see whether his renegade persona may also be something of a masquerade.

We need to pay attention not only to transformations in the hero but also in the structure of the couple, the economy of emotion and will shared by male and female. Elspeth, as noted, also becomes different in Claudette Colbert's Ellie. The film's heroine loses some of the brash edge of the story's, while the hero takes on some of the impetuosity and potential self-destructiveness previously seen in the willful, temperamental woman.

It Happened One Night has been claimed as the founding text for important 1930s comedy genres. Thomas Schatz, in his book on *Hollywood Genres*, regards the film as the prototype for screwball comedy; William Rothman, speaking with reference to "the comedy of remarriage," remarks that "the world never before knew the genre of comedy that Capra's film inaugurates."[12] These assertions work most persuasively if the basis for comparison is 1930s sound film comedy in relation to the genres of 1920s silent film comedy. But here we are casting a wider cultural net and postulating close links between a 1920s literary genre of romantic comedy and Capra's film.

It Happened One Night does make what could be regarded as substantial revisions to that genre's codes by creating an impression of a wider class and cultural gulf that hero and heroine have to traverse in forming the romantic couple. However, later screwball comedies as a rule restore the romantic couple to a narrower upper-class range, reestablishing the conventions of 1920s popular fiction. Placing Capra's work more fully in the framework of 1920s culture and society tends to disperse accepted notions of generic origins and of *It Happened One Night* as a popular narrative the likes of which the world had never before seen.

Ethnicity and Social Mobility

> Many people in Hollywood will tell you that the three top directors are Italian: Borzage, La Cava, and Capra. But when anyone in Hollywood says "The Little Wop," anyone in Hollywood knows that that means Frank Capra. And nobody's offended, even the Italians. Certainly Capra isn't. He'd probably be uncomfortable if anyone tried to link him up with the kind of imperial, orotund Latinity in which Mussolini and his more fiery followers specialize. For he was, and still largely is, just that—a little wop.
>
> John Stuart, "Fine Italian Hand" (1935)

Film director Frank Borzage (1893–1962) was born in Salt Lake City to parents of Swedish descent; director Gregory La Cava (1892–1952) was born in Pennsylvania. So much for what people in Hollywood will tell you. Frank Capra (1897–1991) was born, of course, in the Sicilian village of Bisacquino and left it in 1903, a few days before his sixth birthday, to travel by ship to the United States. Standard American dictionaries of the late twentieth century define *wop* as a disparaging and offensive term pertaining to Italians or persons of Italian descent. Was the journalist who wrote, in 1935, the *Collier's* article quoted above aware that he was describing Capra—whatever Hollywood or even Capra himself may have told him—in a disparaging and offensive way? We'll never know, but at least Stuart has made us aware of racist discourses in the American popular press pertaining to Italians and of the director's ethnic and immigrant status during an era when such markers mattered a very great deal.

"I have no identity because I cancelled my identity," Capra told an Italian film historian during an interview in the 1980s. "I have no fatherland."[13] Spoken by a frail old man some eight decades removed from his birthplace, this declaration is both deeply poignant and highly conventionalized—an American myth and a familiar trope of the Western genre, the man who has wiped out every vestige of his past, even to his name. No matter what one may feel in mind and heart, however, identity is dialogic and performative, involving display of self to others who may see what one wishes to cancel, discard, or hide. As the *Collier's* article makes clear, in the world's eyes during the 1930s Frank Capra possessed a very clear identity.[14]

Nevertheless, to say that a person was Italian or even Sicilian in an American context might miss the transformations in identity impelled by the variables of the immigration experience. For Capra, the primary variable was his destination in the United States; one of his older brothers, who had preceded and paved the way for the Capra family exodus, had settled in Los Angeles, so the 1903 journey ended there. This was in marked contrast to most other Italian immigrants. In the decade 1900–1910, when more than two million Italians came to the United States, the great majority settled in the large industrial cities of the East and Midwest.[15] Fully one fourth of the nation's Italian-born population in 1930 lived in New York City, according to the United States census of that year, with smaller concentrations in Chicago, Philadelphia, Boston, and Detroit. Four hundred thousand New Yorkers had immigrated from Italy, and an additional six hundred thousand New Yorkers were of "Italian stock"—the immigrants' children and grandchildren. Thus, a million ethnic Italians comprised one fifth of the city's population in 1930.

By contrast, the Italian-born population of Los Angeles in 1930 numbered 12,685. "In California," historian Alexander DeConde has written, "little Italies were less crowded . . . , less provincial, and more prosperous."[16] Lured by the discovery of gold in 1849, a small number of Italians had begun migrating to California in the mid-nineteenth century. Many became wealthy in commerce and agriculture. By the time the Capra family arrived, Italians in California—particularly in San Francisco—were among the state's economic and social elite.

Thus, from the beginning Capra's experience of being "Italian," as well as of living in the United States, would have been different from that of other Sicilian boys whose families settled in the Italian ghettoes of eastern cities. The critic and historian Jerre Mangione, who chronicled Sicilian life in the United States, wrote in an essay, "On Being a Sicilian American," "Instinctively, most Sicilians kept away from the 'Americans,' if it was at all possible. They shopped in Italian stores, and frequented Italian dentists, doctors, lawyers, shoemakers, and barbers. Nearly all of their business and social life was conducted in their native tongue."[17] In Los Angeles, Capra did not have the opportunity to grow up within such an isolated, self-enclosed Sicilian community. Unlike the Sicilians whom Mangione described, by necessity or by desire Capra actively sought to become "American." In his autobiography Capra wrote with some bitterness about being excluded from a college preparatory public high school, Los Angeles High, and shipped with the "culls, rejects, and 'bad guys'" to the technical-vocational high school, Manual Arts, among "the riff-raff of Dagos, Shines, Cholos, and Japs."[18] This was yet another variation on the immigrant experience—neither the unitary culture of a Sicilian enclave nor the Anglo-American elite of L.A. High, Capra's high school experience was a multicultural encounter in which the degrees of ethnic separateness and hybrid-American assimilation were matters to be negotiated.

Capra had moved past his high school years when the advent of World War I, and the subsequent U.S. intervention, changed the terms and structures of power in which immigrants conducted these negotiations. Conceiving the war, in the framework of British propaganda, as a struggle between civilization and barbarism, the dominant Anglo-American culture took a strongly nativist turn. Up to this point, the traditional culture had been able to maintain the belief that it had been transforming immigrants into Americans through the famous myth of the melting pot. Now the adherents of the old American culture began to acknowledge— and to reject—the way immigrants had been transforming the character of American life. The solution was stark: put an end to immigration.

A series of laws placing increasing restrictions on immigration culminated in the Immigration Act passed in May 1924. This law set quotas for immigration based on the national origins of the American population recorded in the census of 1890—a date picked because it preceded the mass immigration of Italians and other southern and eastern Europeans. David Rieff, a writer on ethnic issues, described it thus:

> The 1924 law (also known as the National Origins Act) was one of the last gasps of Protestant, white picket-fence America. Its supporters were motivated not only by anti-Catholicism, and, to a lesser extent, anti-semitism, but by small-town America's distrust of the big cities in which such people lived and the big capitalism that gave them jobs. Indeed, the act is probably best viewed as part of a triptych of enthusiasms (the other two being Prohibition and Creationism) that inflamed the American heartland between the 1890s and the Great Depression . . . At the time, of course, most of the immigration was from Sicily, the Jewish Pale, or from Poland, and since people from these areas still constituted a relatively small part of the American population taken as a whole, the new rules had the (intended) effect of barring any more from coming.[19]

Italy's quota under the law was 3,800 immigrants per year, a tiny fraction of the numbers that had been arriving annually.[20]

The ending of European mass migration to the United States had as profound an effect on American society and culture as did its flourishing. For the immigrants—and particularly for their American-born children—the question of their status in American culture became perplexing. The melting pot had been declared

2.2. Frank Capra and his wife Lucille at the 1935 dinner of the Academy of Motion Picture Arts and Sciences. (Museum of Modern Art/Film Stills Archive)

a failure. A linguistically and socially separate life, such as that of Mangione's Sicilians, could only wane with the passing of generations and the absence of new immigrants. In this framework, the old cultures of Europe and traditional U.S. culture were equally inaccessible. Among immigrant groups, notions of cultural pluralism and hyphenated Americanism (i.e., Italian-American, Polish-American, etc.) found favor. But to American-born children of immigrants, who lacked ties of memory and often of language to the old country, a more appealing allegiance was to the emerging American cultures of mass communication and consumption.[21]

Frank Capra was a paradigmatic figure who emerged from an immigrant background to become, not a spectator and consumer of this new culture nor one of its economic entrepreneurs, but one of its leading creative artists. Did he seek to represent the struggles and transformations of immigrant life in his pre-1934 film work? The text that most intrigues is one that is unavailable—*For the Love of Mike*, the comedy-drama he directed in 1927 after several years as a writer for Mack Sennett comedies and after directing two Harry Langdon comedy features, *The Strong Man* (1926) and *Long Pants* (1927). No prints of this low-budget, independent East Coast production, distributed by First National, are known to have survived. Charles Wolfe's description of the story suggests this work's mediation in the conflicts of immigrant life and American culture.[22]

For the Love of Mike is based on an apparently unpublished story, "Hell's Kitchen," by John Moroso, with a scenario credited to J. Clarkson Miller and/or Leland Hayward. As recounted by Wolfe, the narrative concerns an abandoned baby boy who found in a New York Hell's Kitchen tenement and raised by three men: a German delicatessen proprietor, a Jewish tailor, and an Irish street cleaner. Grown up to college age, the boy, Mike, resists the idea of furthering his education because he doesn't want to continue as a financial burden on the men. However, he is persuaded to go to college by a pretty Italian girl who works in the German's deli. Mike enrolls—at an Ivy League bastion of Anglo-American culture, Yale University. Social origins prove irrelevant as Mike gains success as a sports star, yet his upward mobility and personal transformation inevitably estrange him from his roots. He insults his "fathers" and begins to associate with gamblers; he owes them money, and they demand that he deliberately lose the big rowing race with Harvard. But the fathers and the Italian girl come to support him, and they inspire him to defy the gamblers and win the race for Yale. At the end he is reconciled with the men who raised him and in love with the Italian girl.

Interpreting a text solely from a plot summary is not to be recommended, but *For the Love of Mike* offers much to consider should a print ever be found. From the available information, Mike's ethnic origins are unknown. How does the film represent his formation by multiethnic "fathers"—is this a version of the obsolescent melting pot that prepares him for easy assimilation into the traditional American elite? Apparently his college triumphs do not inure him from the psychic crisis involved in constructing a new self in a previously alien class environment, which seems to require a form of self-destruction in order to slough off the outgrown past. It seems that the solution this particular work offers enables the youth rising from humble ethnic origins both to gain entry into the upper classes and to retain his earlier allegiances—but only after those who love him also cross the social barriers and assist him on the new territory he has penetrated.[23]

Returning to Hollywood and beginning to work steadily as a director for Columbia, Capra dealt centrally with ethnic issues in only one other film over the next few years—*The Younger Generation* (1929), his eighth film at the studio during a period of sixteen months. Sonya Levien wrote the scenario, from a 1927 play, *It Is to Laugh*, by Fannie Hurst. The change of title calls attention, in the context of its ethnic story, to the challenge for children of immigrants (like Capra himself), negotiating loyalty to the past with desire for a different future. The narrative circumstances are sharply different from *For the Love of Mike*. Morris, a Jewish boy growing up with his family in a Lower East Side tenement, has a clear ethnic identity that Mike lacked; more significantly, Morris has what the earlier film completely effaced, a mother who dotes on him and channels her ambitions into him (while his ineffectual old-worldly father sells pots from a pushcart). Morris becomes a successful Fifth Avenue antiques dealer, hobnobs with the elite, and shortens his name from Goldfish to Fish. He attempts to bring his family with him, but this effort is doomed to embarrassment and failure on both sides. The narrative provides no psychic crisis for Morris in his upward mobility and personal transformation, nor is there a love interest or even a friend who could come to his support. For Morris, rising out of the immigrant ghetto brings estrangement, loneliness, and family tragedy.

Morris, however, has a sister, Birdie, who suffers many vicissitudes but ends up back on the Lower East Side, running a music store on Delancey Street with her husband, a songwriter who has sold some numbers to Tin Pan Alley. The culture of mass communication and consumption provides an avenue to fulfillment without ever having to leave home.

The Stylistics of Spectacle and Realism

BELASCO'S SKILL PUT INTO A TAWDRY PLAY
Some Fine Acting in "Ladies of the Evening," a Meretricious
Drama Handsomely Mounted.

New York Times, 24 December 1924

Frank Capra's eleventh film for Columbia Pictures, *Ladies of Leisure* (1930), was based on the play *Ladies of the Evening*, which received, as this headline indicates, decidedly mixed reviews when it opened at the Belasco Theatre the night before Christmas Eve, 1924. "It would be idle for this reviewer to pretend that he was not entertained by large parts of it," the *Times* critic wrote of the play, "but tinged with his reluctant enjoyment was always a feeling of shame." [24]

No such shame attended the *Times* movie critic's appraisal of *Ladies of Leisure*. Under the headline, "Miss Stanwyck Triumphs," the review began, "Whether or not 'Ladies of Leisure,' at the Capitol, differs from the play, 'Ladies of the Evening,' from which it was adapted . . . matters little. The fact remains that the photoplay . . . stands quite alone for its amusing dialogue, the restrained performances of nearly all the players and a general lightness of handling that commends the direction of Frank Capra." [25] This is particularly significant praise because movie reviewers at that time often ignored the director entirely. *Variety*'s review, which found the film inferior to the original play—"the Belasco original has been sadly mistreated"—failed to mention Capra at all in its text and listed him as A. Frank Capra in the credits. [26]

What is of interest for our purposes is not the difference of opinion over the adaptation from stage to screen. (Jo Swerling wrote the screenplay for Capra's film.) It is the conjunction of the names Capra and Belasco. Though by now largely forgotten, David Belasco by any measure is a major figure in the history of American popular entertainment. His power and aura in his own time are attested by the fact that both the *Times*'s theater reviewer in 1924 and *Variety*'s movie reviewer in 1930 credit him as the auteur of *Ladies of the Evening* ("the Belasco original") when he functioned solely as the play's producer and director. One Milton Herbert Gropper was the playwright.

Are there fresh perspectives on Capra's pre-1934 work to be gleaned by exploring the implications of linking his name with Belasco? The theatrical impresario, who was winding down a long career and was in his early seventies at the time of *Ladies of the Evening*, was famously associated with stage naturalism.[27] He also played a role in the early discourse concerning cinematic realism, an aspect of his work that has been even more thoroughly neglected. In Belasco's heyday, however, the poet Vachel Lindsay discussed some terms of this debate in his pioneering 1915 book on film aesthetics, *The Art of the Moving Picture*:

> Belasco's attitude toward the stage has been denounced by the purists because he makes settings too large a part of his story-telling, and transforms his theatre into the paradise of the property-man. But this very quality of the well spaced setting, if you please, has made his chance for the motion picture anthology. As reproduced by Jesse K. Lasky the Belasco production is the only type of the old-line drama that seems really made to be the basis of a moving picture play. Not always, but as a general rule, Belasco suffers less detriment in the films than other men.[28]

In his 1949 book *Stage to Screen: Theatrical Method from Garrick to Griffith*, A. Nicholas Vardac elaborated this viewpoint in arguing that early cinema arose out of nineteenth-century realist theater. Since then, nearly half a century of scholarship has passed with scant interest in the relationships between theater and early cinema, until in recent years the debate has resumed on the ground of lighting technology.[29]

Realism becomes an element in the discourse on Capra's pre-1934 films in connection with his work on *Submarine* (1928), generally regarded as an early turning point in the director's career. He was still in his first calendar year at the Columbia Pictures job when studio head Harry Cohn ordered him to take over directing the film, which had already been in production for three weeks with another director. Previously, Capra had directed five (or perhaps six) low-budget films at breakneck speed over a period of some eight or nine months.[30] *Submarine* was Capra's first opportunity to work on a major production; indeed, the film was one of the studio's earliest attempts to compete with the established movie companies at the same level of production values, with a budget estimated at $250,000.

In his account of this episode in his autobiography, *The Light on Her Face*, cinematographer Joseph Walker suggests that Cohn's principal dissatisfaction with the original director, Irving Willat, concerned the performances he was getting from the leading actors, Jack Holt and Ralph Graves. Yet, as Walker describes it, Capra's response to this complaint dealt not with acting styles but with external appearances. When he took over as director, he told Holt and Graves that they had been wearing too much makeup, and he ordered them not to wear any at all.

The terms with which Walker summarizes this incident are significant. "The story needed strong realism," Walker explains. "Hollywood shied away from unflattering realism—but in this case, the story, the actors, even the photography would gain . . . The natural look of [*Submarine*'s] characters set a precedent that would influence motion pictures from then on; and it firmly established Frank Capra's innovative talent." Strong realism, unflattering realism, natural look—these are phrases that recall the debates over theatrical realism and the cinema to which Lindsay alluded in 1915 and more specifically suggest the concept of "Belasco atmosphere" that was a way of describing naturalistic effects.[31]

Walker's remarks call attention to the frequency with which large-scale action and frightening disasters—hallmarks of Belasco's naturalism[32]—became central to Capra's mise-en-scène after *Submarine*. Two more films pairing Holt and Graves, *Flight* (1929) and *Dirigible* (1931), follow a similar story line and add even more elaborate realist visual effects. Both involved aerial photography, in *Dirigible* with lighter-than-air craft. The collapse and crash of a dirigible in the 1931 film was the most spectacular of many scenes giving spectators a heightened sense of the experience of flight. During this same period two other films provide another kind of naturalistic action by staging raging fires as a climax: a circus tent burns down in a roaring blaze at the end of *Rain or Shine* (1930), and flames consume the evangelist's temple in a concluding sequence of *The Miracle Woman* (1931).

What connections can be found between Capra and Belasco in

the work that most directly brings them together, *Ladies of Leisure*? Here we might turn to another version of Belasco that surfaces in the discourse of theater history, espoused perhaps by those "purists" who, according to Lindsay, deplored the idea of theater as a "paradise of the property-man." One exemplar of the viewpoint was drama historian Arthur Hobson Quinn. Speaking of a quintessential moment of Belasco naturalism, when the impresario put a replica of an actual restaurant on stage, Quinn wrote in his *History of American Drama*, "In his desire to provide reality of stage setting, Belasco placed an utterly absurd last Act in a restaurant which was scrupulously photographic to the last spoon and fork."[33] If Belasco naturalism could be an absurdity in Quinn's view, the historian nevertheless admired Belasco as a playwright and regarded his best work (such as the play *Madame Butterfly*) as belonging to a tradition of romantic tragedy.

2.3. Ralph Graves as Jerry Strong and Barbara Stanwyck as Kay Arnold in *Ladies of Leisure* (1930). (Museum of Modern Art/Film Stills Archive)

This perspective enables us to return to the question of the film *Ladies of Leisure* as an adaptation of the play *Ladies of the Evening*. Both works concern the chance meeting of a socialite artist and a "party girl," his desire to use her as a model for his painting, the love that grows between them, his parents' opposition to their union, their separation. In the stage version, according to the reviews, their final reconciliation seems to be a relatively straightforward dramatic denouement. In the film, something quite different occurs; the party girl, Kay Arnold, portrayed by Barbara Stanwyck, leaps from the deck of a cruise ship into the ocean.

This suicidal act combines both aspects of Belasco's legacy: romantic tragedy and a strong sense of naturalistic disaster. But the scene is followed by another, of Kay in a hospital bed with her lover by her side. She has survived and they are reunited, just as in the play. It is ironic that, of the four films Capra made with Stanwyck before 1934 (*The Miracle Woman*, *Forbidden*, and *The Bitter Tea of General Yen* were the others), only the work drawn from a Belasco production should have swerved from the path of romantic tragedy with which Arthur Hobson Quinn associated Belasco the playwright. Linking Capra with Belasco is not merely an arbitrary exercise based on the fortuity of their shared connection to a text. It provides a historical and intertextual framework both for Capra's naturalism and for the romantic tragedies among his works. It points to a defining moment in Capra's work—Kay's leap and its annulment—when his heroine attained, but was rescued from, the tragic vision of Puccini's Butterfly.[34]

The Emergence of an Ideological Project

The bank stories I think are all right from a policy standpoint and will even do good by helping renew confidence in banking institutions. In fact one of them, a Columbia story tentatively called *Faith* ought to be seen by all the bankers themselves for, in script-form at least, it is a strong preachment of principles I know you thoroughly believe in, namely enough confidence by bankers in human nature to allow them to take leadership and help even these screwy times.

Jason S. Joy to Will H. Hays, 25 March 1932

This internal communication within the Motion Picture Producers Association—from the West Coast head of the Studio Relations Office to the "czar" of the movie industry, based in New York—is a caution against imposing too strict a separation between Capra's post-1934 films and those that came before.[35] *It Happened One Night* is a convenient breakpoint in assessing Capra's career because of its popularity and (with five Academy Awards) the extraordinary recognition bestowed upon it by the film industry, but many of the major issues of the Depression decade were thoroughly debated before 1934, and Capra was well aware of them. Among his pre-1934 films, one deals directly with a crisis of the Great Depression, the "bank story" Jason S. Joy referred to, released in 1932 as *American Madness*.

American Madness bears many similarities to Capra's later 1930s "social message" films—particularly the narrative pattern of the hero's humbling and then his subsequent rescue by the "little people" who confirm him as their leader. The hero of *American Madness*, however, is not a homespun figure called to greatness from the depths of America's heartland, like Deeds, Smith, or Doe, but a powerful urban sophisticate, a bank president. As Edward Buscombe has argued, banker Tom Dickson inevitably calls to mind the banking family that participated in the financing and control of Columbia Pictures, and particularly its most prominent member, Amadeo Peter Giannini.[36]

A generation older than Capra, A. P. Giannini was born in the United States to a family of Italian immigrants who prospered as grape growers in northern California. In 1904 Giannini founded the Bank of Italy in San Francisco—the beginning of what would expand during the course of the twentieth century into one of the world's major banks, Bank of America. Giannini's career and philosophy read almost as a treatment for the script of *American Madness*; his physical stature called for an actor with just the height and bearing of Walter Huston, who played the banker hero in the film—except that neither Huston nor his fictional character Dickson give any sign of ethnic background other than the old American Anglo-Saxon elite.

"Giannini stood six feet two inches tall, weighed more than 240 pounds, had a booming voice, and a near-photographic memory for names and faces," writes Gary Hector, a chronicler of the Bank of America's fortunes.

> He coveted customers that other bankers wouldn't touch, the small businessmen and the working stiffs, many of them immigrants who could barely speak English. In 1930, Giannini told Congress, "The little fellow is the best customer that a bank can have, because he is with you. He starts in with you and stays to the end. Whereas the big fellow is only with you so long as he can get something out of you; and when he cannot, he is not for you anymore." [37]

To top matters off, in the wake of the 1929 stock market crash, an aging and ill Giannini was involved, much like Tom Dickson in *American Madness*, in an effort to prevent a takeover of his financial empire by hostile Wall Street investment bankers. He did indeed lose control of his holdings—not, of course, a local bank, as in the film, but a giant bank holding company, Transamerica. Depositors thereupon lost confidence in his successors, withdrawing their funds from the firm's banks in a manner uncannily like the run on Dickson's bank in *American Madness*. The Bank of America was in danger of failing.

When the Wall Street usurpers began to sell off other banks that were part of the Giannini empire, Giannini organized an effort to regain control. "Restoration of public confidence is a condition prerequisite to success and future prosperity of institutions," he proclaimed. At a shareholders' meeting on 15 February 1932, Giannini won the battle and returned as chairman of the holding company and president of Bank of America. Less than two weeks later, Columbia Pictures informed the Motion Picture Producers Association of its plans to produce a "Bank Story." [38]

When *American Madness* was completed, A.P.'s brother, Attilio (A.H.), the Giannini who had pioneered in bank financing of motion picture production, obligingly wrote a letter to Harry Cohn stating that he believed "that this photoplay . . . will do more than any other single agency to stop runs on banks which are started by false or malicious rumors." [39] Here was a banker's imprimatur on a film that, by its depiction of mob behavior by bank depositors, might be regarded in the historical moment as inflammatory and dangerous. A.H.'s endorsement echoed A.P.'s declaration about restoring public confidence.

Jason S. Joy's letter to Will H. Hays, however, did not address the goal of regaining *public* confidence; it spoke about boosting *bankers'* confidence. It did not say that the general public should go to *American Madness*, but that bankers ought to see it. The purpose of Joy's remarks can only be surmised; certainly the tone of an employee flattering his boss is unmistakable. Nevertheless, the words bespeak an expectation that can clearly be understood as a significant transformation for the motion picture industry. As the traditional elites of American society seemed to lose their hold on power in the 1930s crisis, a film spokesman could anticipate the possibility that the movies might now address more than the masses; they could speak to (and for) the powerful. Having developed his craft in genre works that transmuted into popular entertainment the class and cultural struggles of the 1920s, Frank Capra was prepared—when, as with *Submarine*, he replaced another director on *American Madness*—to intervene in the ideological discourses of his time, respecting no secular power as beyond the reach of his mythologizing grasp.

Notes

1. Frank Capra, *The Name above the Title: An Autobiography* (New York: Macmillan, 1971), 175–76, tells the story of being transformed by a visit from a "little man . . . completely bald, wearing thick glasses," who mysteriously appeared when Capra became ill after the Academy Award triumphs of *It Happened One Night* and called the director a coward for not using his God-given talents for higher purposes.

2. In the late 1980s Columbia Pictures Corp. completed restoration of many of Capra's works for that studio made from 1928 to 1934. Retrospectives of these titles were screened in 1988 at the Museum of Modern Art, New York, and the seventh Rassegna Internazionale Retrospettiva at Ancona, Italy, sponsored by the Mostra Internazionale del Nuovo Cinema. Since that time several additional Capra films from that period, previously believed lost, have been found in archives.

3. New works on the 1920s include historian Lynn Dumenil's *The Modern Temper: American Culture and Society in the 1920s* (New York: Hill & Wang, 1995) and literary critic Ann Douglas's *Terrible Honesty: Mongrel Manhattan in the 1920s* (New York: Farrar, Straus & Giroux, 1995). Douglas's book, as its sub-

title indicates, concerns New York City as a primary site of cultural confluence and influence. The emphasis in these studies on continuity contrasts with a view first articulated as early as 1931 in a best-selling popular history by journalist Frederick Lewis Allen. "The United States of 1931 was a different place from the United States of the post-World War I era," Allen wrote. "An old order was giving place to new." *Only Yesterday: An Informal History of the Nineteen-twenties* (New York: Harper & Brothers, 1931), 351–52. Another important new work is Walter Benn Michaels, *Our America: Nativism, Modernism, and Pluralism* (Durham, N.C.: Duke Univ. Press, 1995), a book-length essay reconsidering the discourses of race and culture in 1920s literature and social thought. It has particular relevance to my discussion of Capra and ethnicity.

4. Robert Sklar, *F. Scott Fitzgerald: The Last Laocoön* (New York: Oxford Univ. Press, 1967), 68–69. Quotation from "The Offshore Pirate," in F. Scott Fitzgerald, *Flappers and Philosophers* (New York: Scribner's, 1920), 20.

5. Samuel Hopkins Adams, "Night Bus," reprinted in *Stories into Film*, ed. William Kittredge and Steven M. Krauzer (New York: Harper & Row, 1979), 32–91; the quoted sentence is on 70.

6. Fitzgerald, "The Offshore Pirate," 46.

7. Adams, "Night Bus," 34.

8. Sklar, *F. Scott Fitzgerald*, 21.

9. In her exchange of telegrams, Elspeth uses the pseudonym Bessie Smith—the name, of course, of a famous African-American blues singer. Fitzgerald's "The Offshore Pirate," in which the hero Toby takes over Ardita's yacht in the guise of a leader of a gang of black thieves, gives even more evidence for the endemic racism of the genre.

10. See the chapter on "The New Woman" in Dumenil, *The Modern Temper*, 98–144, and the bibliography, 321–25.

11. The most historically detailed and compelling instance of this viewpoint is in Richard Maltby's essay "*It Happened One Night*: The Recreation of the Patriarch," chapter 5 of this volume.

12. Thomas Schatz, *Hollywood Genres: Formulas, Filmmaking, and the Studio System* (New York: Random House, 1981), 152. Schatz discusses Capra's relation to screwball comedy throughout his chapter, "The Screwball Comedy," 150–85. William Rothman's reference to *It Happened One Night* occurs in a comparison with Hitchcock's *The 39 Steps* in *Hitchcock: The Murderous Gaze* (Cambridge: Harvard Univ. Press, 1981), 134; his remarks about "the comedy of remarriage" pay homage to Stanley Cavell's *Pursuits of Happiness: The Hollywood Comedy of Remarriage* (Cambridge: Harvard Univ. Press, 1981).

13. Capra quoted by Gian Piero Brunetta, from an interview with the director for a film documentary, *Arriva Frank Capra* (1986), directed by Gianfranco Mingozzi. See *Gianfranco Mingozzi: I Documentari*, ed. Cesare Landricina (Rome: Collana, 1988), 112–19.

14. John Stuart, "Fine Italian Hand," *Collier's*, 17 August 1935, 13, 48–49, quotation from 13.

15. Alexander DeConde, *Half Bitter, Half Sweet: An Excursion into Italian-American History* (New York: Scribner's, 1971), 77.

16. DeConde, *Half Bitter, Half Sweet*, 84; census data drawn from *Studies in*

Italian American Social History: Essays in Honor of Leonard Covello, ed. Francesco Cordasco (Totowa, N.J.: Rowman & Littlefield, 1975), 166–67.

17. Jerre Mangione, "On Being a Sicilian American," in *Italian American Social History*, 40–49, quoted passage, 47. Mangione, who was a professor of English at the University of Pennsylvania, wrote several works on his personal, familial, and community life as a Sicilian American, including *Mount Allegro: A Memoir of Italian American Life* (Boston: Houghton Mifflin, 1943) and *An Ethnic at Large: A Memoir of America in the Thirties and Forties* (New York: Putnam's, 1978).

18. Capra, *Name above the Title*, 6.

19. David Rieff, "The Transformation of America," *Times Literary Supplement*, 25–31 May 1990), 543.

20. DeConde, *Half Bitter, Half Sweet*, 162–81, deals in detail with the restriction issue in the framework of Italian-American relations.

21. My own earlier work on 1920s culture develops this perspective on the era; see the introduction to *The Plastic Age (1917–1930)*, ed. Robert Sklar (New York: Braziller, 1970), 1–24, esp. 14 ff.

22. Charles Wolfe, *Frank Capra: A Guide to References and Resources* (Boston: G.K. Hall, 1987), 44–46. Another description of the film may be found in *Meet Frank Capra: A Catalog of His Work* (Palo Alto: Stanford Theatre Foundation, 1990), 11–12, produced by the staff of the American Film Institute Catalog.

23. In her first film role, Claudette Colbert played the Italian girl, Mary. It would be especially interesting to be able to see this performance in relation to her portrayal of Ellie Andrews.

24. *New York Times*, 24 December 1924, 11. The *New York World* reviewer called it a "bed and butter" play and described it: "Brass bed, street-walker smart, vile joke, stale joke, catchpenny situation, everything to bring them scampering to the box office." *New York World*, 24 December 1924, clipping in the New York Public Library, Performing Arts Collection, Lincoln Center.

25. *New York Times*, 24 May 1930, 21.

26. *Variety*, 28 May 1930, 35, review signed "Rush."

27. Belasco (1853–1931), who was also an actor and playwright, was said to have directed or produced over three hundred plays in New York. He was known as the "Bishop of Broadway" because of his penchant for wearing clerical clothing. He is perhaps most clearly remembered by opera fans as co-author of the play *Madame Butterfly* (1900) that Giacomo Puccini adapted for his famous opera, *Madama Butterfly*, first staged in 1904. Puccini drew on Belasco again for the source text for the opera *La Fanciulla del West* (1910), based on Belasco's 1905 play *The Girl of the Golden West*. Puccini's adaptations of Belasco are discussed in William Ashbrook, *The Operas of Puccini* (New York: Oxford Univ. Press, 1968), 97 ff. John Barrymore's comic portrayal of a megalomaniac impresario in Howard Hawks's film, *Twentieth Century*, produced by Columbia in 1934, was a parody of Belasco. A brief overview of Belasco's career may be found in Garff B. Wilson, *Three Hundred Years of American Drama and Theatre: From "Ye Bear and Ye Cub" to "Hair"* (Englewood Cliffs, N.J.: Prentice-Hall, 1973), 251–56.

28. Vachel Lindsay, *The Art of the Moving Picture* (New York: Macmillan, 1915); passage quoted from 1922 edition (reprinted 1970), 136. At least fifteen American films were produced from plays written or co-authored by Belasco, in-

cluding *The Girl of the Golden West* three times, the last by MGM in 1938; see Larry Langman, *Writers on the American Screen: A Guide to Film Adaptations of American and Foreign Literary Works* (New York: Garland, 1986), 19–20.

29. A. Nicholas Vardac, *Stage to Screen: Theatrical Method from Garrick to Griffith* (Cambridge: Harvard Univ. Press, 1949), 108–35. See Lea Jacobs, "Belasco, DeMille and the Development of Lasky Lighting," *Film History* 5 (1993): 405–16, and Peter DeCherney, "Colonizing Light," unpublished research essay, New York University, 1995.

30. *The Power of the Press* was released after *Submarine*, but Charles Wolfe persuasively argues that it was produced earlier; see Wolfe, *Frank Capra*, 61–62.

31. Joseph B. Walker and Juanita Walker, *The Light on Her Face* (Hollywood: ASC Press, 1984), 169; DeCherney, "Colonizing Light," 11 ff.

32. Vardac recounts a blizzard scene in the stage production of *The Girl of the Golden West* that he describes as "equaling, if not exceeding the reproductional thrill of the cinema." *Stage to Screen*, 128.

33. Arthur Hobson Quinn, *A History of the American Drama: From the Civil War to the Present Day* (New York: Harper & Brothers, 1927, rev. 1936), 1:196. Child's Restaurant was the name of the actual eatery Belasco replicated, and the set appeared in *The Governor's Lady* (1912).

34. Catherine Clement, *Opera, or the Undoing of Women*, trans. Betsy Wing (Minneapolis: Univ. of Minnesota Press, 1988), offers an indispensable perspective on Capra's heroines through her treatment of "The Girls Who Leap into Space" (chapter 4, 78–95); my title, "A Leap into the Void," is drawn from her text. Her viewpoint suggests that further studies on Capra's films in relation to opera could be fruitful.

35. Jason S. Joy to Will H. Hays, 25 March 1932, *American Madness* file, MPAA Collection, Academy of Motion Picture Arts and Sciences, Beverly Hills, Calif.

36. Edward Buscombe, "Notes on Columbia Pictures Corporation 1926–1941," *Screen* 16, no. 3 (1975), 65–82, reprinted as chapter 9 of this volume.

37. Gary Hector, *Breaking the Bank: The Decline of BankAmerica* (Boston: Little, Brown, 1988), 17–18.

38. Hector, *Breaking the Bank*, 41–56, gives an account of Giannini's financial struggles in the 1927–32 period; reference to Columbia Picture's "Bank Story" appears in a letter from Jason S. Joy to Sam Briskin of Columbia, 25 February 1932, *American Madness* file, MPAA Collection.

39. A. H. Giannini to Harry Cohn, 28 May 1932, *American Madness* file, MPAA Collection.

3

It Is (Not) a Wonderful Life: For a Counter-reading of Frank Capra

Vito Zagarrio

Capra's Corpse

Hollywood cinema of the 1990s seemed suddenly to develop a strange longing. In *The American President* (1995), directed by Rob Reiner, a journalist, played by Annette Bening, invited to the White House, says, "Here we are, in Frank Capra's kingdom!" In a moment, she will meet the president, portrayed by Michael Douglas, and she will fall in love with him, as in a Capra fairy tale. Andrew Bergman, who was a scholar before he became a filmmaker, wrote an important book on American cinema during the Depression years that dealt extensively with Capra and, two decades later, directed a kind of Capra remake, *It Could Happen to You* (1994).[1] Stephen Frears's *Hero* (1992), Peter Weir's *Fearless* (1993), Ivan Reitman's *Dave* (1993), the Coen brothers' *The Hudsucker Proxy* (1994), and Robert Zemeckis's *Forrest Gump* (1994), a multiple winner at the 1995 Academy Awards, all somehow evoke a body in the closet: the body of the beloved and detested master of comedy, Frank Capra.

This abundance of references to Frank Capra began during the 1980s. Zemeckis's *Back to the Future* (1985) contains the classic theme of Capra's *It's a Wonderful Life* (1946), namely, the nightmare of never having been born (or, in the case of *Back to the Future*, the fear of not being born, of not being able to return to the future). In *Gremlins* (1984), directed by Joe Dante, Capra's best-known films (from *It's a Wonderful Life* to *You Can't Take It with You* [1938]) are also clearly quoted.

The 1990s have witnessed a genuine wave of Caprian reminiscences. In *Hero* a vagrant, played by Andy Garcia, becomes a media star like Gary Cooper in *Meet John Doe*; in *Fearless*, the character portrayed by Jeff Bridges narrowly eludes death, thanks to his love for his family, and learns to love even his allergy to strawberries, much as James Stewart's George Bailey learns to love the petals of his little daughter's flower in *It's a Wonderful Life*. In *The Hudsucker Proxy* a "black angel" keeps the protagonist, played by Tim Robbins, from killing himself on Christmas eve, as in *It's a Wonderful Life*; Kevin Kline's character in *Dave* resembles similar figures in *State of the Union* and, once again, *Meet John Doe*. *It Could Happen to You* recalls the happy-ending situations of the thirties, and *Forrest Gump* refers back to the naive accidental heroes of the New Deal.

What's behind this Caprian revival? Why is Capra used whenever the need arises? Perhaps this revival has something to do with a return to fashion of populism—an ambiguous notion that can be grasped from the Right or from the Left, scorned or respected for its historical context. (The ideology of Populism, as reconstructed by Jeffrey Richards, can be traced to Jefferson, James Fenimore Cooper, and Horatio Alger. A 1995 issue of *Business Week* was titled "America's New Populism.")[2] The phenomenon of a generalized populism, in fact, seems to be making headway throughout the world. Didn't the tumultuous appearance of Silvio Berlusconi's Forza Italia Clubs on the Italian political scene in the early 1990s, fueling the media baron's successful campaign for the premiership, recall quite clearly the rise of John Doe Clubs in Capra's film?

Certainly, Capra now represents a cumbersome presence for American culture, critics, ideology, and imagination, partly because the body in the closet is real. Capra passed away on 3 September 1991 (he was born at Bisacquino, near Palermo, in 1897), and his death was followed immediately by the publication of a biography written by specialist Joseph McBride, a ruthless recon-struction of the life and career of the director, who is attacked on the personal as well as the artistic level.[3] In the United States, it would appear, a vulture-like attitude predominates in the field of biography: one throws oneself on the still-warm cadaver to scorn it. (It must be admitted, however, that McBride waited, in agree-ment with the family, for the director to die before publishing the book, which had been written while Capra was still alive).

Capra arouses contrasting feelings: there are the cinephiles, who adore his characteristic devices and his somewhat kitsch atmospheres, and his detractors, who accuse him of populism, sticky-sweet optimism, and paternalistic demagogy, a superficial democracy that fades, on close examination, into a substantially reactionary attitude. One understands why the *Cahiers du cinéma* (and the critics most interested in the concept of authorship, in general) have always snubbed him and have never included him in the pantheon of greats.[4]

The recovery and rereading of Capra began in the 1980s. In Italy a conference, a retrospective, and a catalogue/book, *Ac-cadde una notte: Frank Capra (1928–1934) e la Columbia (1934–1945)*, signaled a change in attitude toward the director. The de-bate went a step further in 1989 with the necessary, though belated, translation into Italian of *The Name above the Title*. In 1995 a complete one-man show of the Italian-American director's films was presented, *Frank Capra: Un italiano alla corte di Holly-wood* (an event in which the director's son, Frank Capra, Jr., took part). Capra's birthplace, Bisacquino, Sicily, honored him with a retrospective in 1997, his centenary year.[5]

In the United States, a 1982 issue of *American Film* magazine was dedicated to the director (the cover, showing Capra smiling and holding the Stars and Stripes, bore the title, "America's Love Affair with Frank Capra"). The American Film Institute honored Capra with its Lifetime Achievement award and later published a complete catalog of his films. A Capra archive was opened at Wes-leyan University, and the Cinémateque Française and the Library of Congress in Washington found and restored films believed to have been irredeemably lost (*The Matinee Idol* and *The Power of the Press*). American and European scholars have published new stud-ies (e.g., Raymond Carney's controversial book *American Vision:*

The Films of Frank Capra, Charles Wolfe's handy repertory, and Michel Cieutat's European-style monograph).[6]

Research framing Capra's cinema in theoretical debates on the studio system, on authorship, on the relationship between history and cinema, and, in general, on the so-called modes of production of filmmakers appears continually in new studies.[7] In the framework of these debates, let us try to "revive" Capra's material and symbolic "body" so we can propose a counter-reading.

Another Frank Capra

Frank Capra has gone down in history as the master of the tearjerker, the director who could coolly and professionally tug at the heartstrings. That tug is repeated every Christmas when one sees *It's a Wonderful Life* on television: James Stewart, in a long nightmare, experiences what life would have been like if he had never been born. When he finds the petals of his little girl's flower in his pocket, he realizes that he has returned to the real world. At that moment the audience's deepest emotions are touched in some mysterious way, whereas the critic's perspective produces a negative reaction, an unquestionable rejection of the paternalistic, demagogic components in Capra's work.

The current, conventional image thus portrays Capra as a great craftsman who lacked style, that special touch with which Ernst Lubitsch and Josef von Sternberg were gifted; Capra, in the last analysis, is seen as a teller of conservative fairy tales, a reassuring and conciliatory man on the street.[8] Frank Capra can be interpreted in a new way, however, not only in relation to film history and, more generally, to the history of American society, but also as a case study of historiographic methodology. The central idea of this essay is that the director of *It's a Wonderful Life*, the greatest constructor of happy endings, in fact represented enormous social contradictions and conflicts that clash with the surface message of his films, even if, perhaps, he was unaware of this fact. By reading his films again (between the lines, as it were) and analyzing some key sequences, one can find Freudian slips that reveal very uncomfortable social situations.[9] The director ends up pointing out some of America's social problems in spite of himself. Certain apparently insignificant narrative segments show a sample of the pathologies, problems, and follies of a country whose state of health was always apparent to Capra. Following the leads provided by these sequences, which I believe are fundamental, one is justified in considering Capra a discomforting author. A textual analysis of his films brings to light a pessimistic vision of life based on emigration, poverty, class struggle, and social violence—in a word, many of the contradictions of the American myth.

Carney, by placing Capra within a vast, deterministic line of American modernism and the great tradition of American transcendental expression, accepts completely the positive implication of the American myth. Cieutat, while acknowledging the obvious presence of that myth, also points to its contradictions: the pessimism as well as the optimism; the attempted suicides as well as the strength of character; the duality as well as the simplicity of being; the sense of a society in danger, of a family charged with tensions, of individuals brimming with fear, as well as the pursuit of happiness.

Despite their differences, these two authors study Capra with the affection that is typical of those who pass years of their lives in the reconstruction of the life and work of a historical figure, an artist, an actor, or a director. But there are also those who feel no affection toward the object of their inquiry, such as Capra's biographer, Joseph McBride. Any counter-reading of Capra must come to grips with McBride's volume because of the depth of the work, the fact that it was the first biography published after Capra's death, and the necessity to distinguish one's own position from that of the author. It is not my habit to defend one research project by attacking another. I respect subjective points of view. But McBride's book requires that a stand be taken; indeed, it calls for firm opposition.

First of all, McBride's work is a biography, not a work of filmic analysis, and its arguments reflect the limits of this basic choice. Second, it is a contradictory book that denies Capra authorial specificity, on one hand, but accepts the myth of authorial cinema, on the other. Above all, McBride's biography seems to be a systematic personal attack on the director. Emblematic in this sense is "The Catastrophe of Success," a chapter that gives its title to the entire book (a fine title, which accords with my own contention that Capra is a skillful recorder of great and small, micro- or macrocosmic catastrophes, a sort of seismograph). Unfortunately, the catastrophe of which McBride speaks is of quite another nature: it is borrowed from Tennessee Williams and is directly tied to Capra's personal history. Capra, according to McBride, suffered a manic-depressive crisis typical of the postsuccess phase: "Capra had schemed and sweated since childhood for the fame that was now his . . . but when it came, it left him feeling strangely unworthy."[10]

What, according to McBride, was the source of this malaise? Certain psychologists (McBride cites Joan Harvey) speak of an imposter phenomenon connected with unresolved Oedipal tensions ("which certainly could apply to Capra, who attributed much of his drive for success to a need to impress his defiantly unimpressed mother"). This is part of the genre of biography. Charles Maland, another biographer of the director, links his private insecurities as well as his poetics to his attendance of the Ecumenical Church. McBride substitutes psychoanalysis for religion, but he does so with a vengeance, with an unusual anger that brings to mind his own psychological condition: "Becoming famous gave Capra little real satisfaction but only brought out the bitterness and *rage* that was festering below the surface of his combative personality. His first impulse was not to feel grateful toward those who had helped him succeed, but to feel *revengeful*."[11]

According to McBride, Capra believed that the success of *It Happened One Night* (1934) was an accident; above all, he was unconsciously convinced that he was unworthy of his success, which was due to others: "In Capra's case, the need to appropriate credit belonging to his writers stemmed from his insecurity about the nature of his own abilities and achievements: like his mother, he was never sure that he deserved all of that money and all of that acclaim just for sitting in a director's chair."[12]

The main thrust of McBride's thesis is that Capra was an "impostor," an "angry, vindictive" paranoiac who "appropriated" the work of others. And who were these others? They were the screenwriters—above all, Capra's own favorite, Robert Riskin, the true author, according to McBride, of Capra's cinema. As an example, McBride states that Capra's autobiography contains a revealing error concerning *Lady for a Day* (1934): "He seemed to think that his four-month stay at MGM working on *Soviet* came after the making of *Lady for a Day*, not before it. Such a significant mis-placing of time is hard to accept as a simple memory lapse, and indeed other evidence suggests it may have been a deliberate attempt to obscure the extent of Riskin's contribution to *Lady for a Day*." [13]

If I interpret this correctly, McBride's assertion is that Capra's error in reconstructing the date of a film conceals a background intention, an obsession: to show that he is good, at the cost of stealing credit from Riskin. At least one thing is certain: the autobiography is not credible (like most autobiographies); it must be taken as a text, not as a reliable source for reconstructing a career, especially that of an old elephant of Hollywood at the end of his career. Clearly, an aging protagonist reconstructs events as he likes, even events that span the history of the twentieth century—the Depression and the New Deal, McCarthyism and Fascism, the Hays Code and the studio system, Hollywood stars and, naturally, his co-workers.

It is also clear that an aging protagonist tends to arrogate all the merits of his work to himself, even when, in the case of cinema, the work is a group effort. One need not even trouble with psychoanalysis. I happened to meet the Italian director Alessandro Blasetti before he died, and he claimed to have invented all the techniques of Italian cinema. His daughter, Mara, is still engaged today (and this is normal) with the task of reassessment and re-appropriation. What is distressing, however, is to mistake the memories of an old veteran for a historical source in order to give credit to a revisionist thesis, to attack the veteran pitilessly by focusing on his psychological disorders. This is like interpreting the cinema of Pier Paolo Pasolini only through his homosexuality or interpreting Federico Fellini's films only through his patronizing of the brothels of Rimini. It is akin to a biographer of Vittorio De Sica accusing the neorealist director of stealing from his collaborator and scriptwriter, Cesare Zavattini. Who is the true author, De Sica or Zavattini? In Italy mention has been made, for years now, of joint authorship. [14] But if, following McBride's example, one were to opt only for Zavattini (a credible choice: he is the true author, as well as the theoretician, of neorealism), would this mean that De Sica is a thief?

McBride makes matters even worse. "Capra's sense of ethics

was flexible"; the refusal to cite Riskin is the sign of a "cultivated amnesia"; "he embarked on his crusade to deny Riskin his due credit . . . in attempting to prove his case for authorship." This is a tone more worthy of a lawyer engaged by Riskin's heirs than of a historian. McBride's quotation of David Rintels, president of the Writers Guild of America, is amusing in this connection: "It is indecent of Capra to call Riskin one of his dearest friends while doing everything possible to undermine his reputation." McBride shows no qualms in accepting the position of Rintels, who not only dutifully defends the role of screenwriters, but also marries Riskin's daughter! "Rintels," McBride observes in parentheses, "later married Riskin's daughter Victoria, whom he had known only slightly at the time of the debate." [15] McBride is saying, in effect, that Rintels's judgment is entirely objective, given that he barely knew Riskin.

On the other hand, the Riskin-Capra dispute is old; it certainly was not discovered by McBride. It falls within a broader debate on the relations between the director and his troupe, on the filmic text itself as a *texte entrouvable*. The same argument could be applied to Orson Welles and the cinematographer Gregg Toland, or it could be brought to bear on the relationship between Capra and his trustworthy director of photography, Joseph Walker. The screenwriters are usually angrier, with the director and perhaps even with the actors (a dispute over the authorship of *Mediterraneo* [1991], winner of an Academy Award as best foreign film, has become famous in Italy), but in the division of labor of the studio system it is wrong to call even the contract director the author. Recourse must be made to a vast debate on the policy of authorship. But let us see what McBride has to say about this serious problem:

> It was a battle that went beyond simple questions of fairness into complex philosophical issues about the "authorship" of a film, issues that would be lumped together into an acrimonious debate over the auteur theory. The debate began in 1954 with the proposal in the French film magazine *Cahiers du cinéma* by critic (and later director) François Truffaut of "*un cinema des auteurs*," which included among its tenets the primary role of the director in determining the thematic

content of a film. Truffaut designed *Cahiers*' "*politique des auteurs*" partially to account for a situation like that of *Lady for a Day*, in which the director is not the screenwriter but still exerts his personality over the material. However, in the translation of the *politique* to American criticism, and even more so in its bastardization by its Hollywood detractors, the distinction between writer-director auteurs and nonwriter auteur directors largely became lost, and the debate degenerated into hopeless and irresolvable battles between the defenders of the director and the defenders of the writer.[16]

McBride utilizes his biography of the director to demolish his authorship, and more conventional criticism utilizes Capra's autobiography to produce the usual, commonplace portrait of a reactionary populist in love with the Statue of Liberty. In analyzing Capra *malgré lui* (in spite of himself), I shall take his films, their internal structures, and their language as my primary sources. The biographical and autobiographical facts will help place the case study in a personal and historical context, but what count are the director's texts, which I shall try to analyze in a new way.

Method of Analysis

For historiographic analysis one must adopt a method of investigation that stresses the less significant details, that reconstructs byways, necessarily abandoning the main line of inquiry. The historian must possess intuition and be willing to run risks, arriving at a final judgment that is not based on conventional sources.

The Italian historian Carlo Ginzburg writes that "to narrate means to speak here and now with an authority that derives from having been (literally or metaphorically) there and then . . . What we have tried to analyze here is not one narrative among many, but the matrix of all possible narratives." These are the closing words of Ginzburg's book, *Ecstasies: Deciphering the Witches' Sabbath*, in which the "deciphering of an event such as the witches' sabbath becomes an investigation of an original narrative magma, a synthesis of high and low cultures, of literature and popular fantasy, that underlies all stories. This type of approach brings historical analysis ever closer to fiction, shifting it to a terrain where the reconstruction of facts becomes a reflection on the limits of the historian's work." [17]

Ginzburg has become a standard reference for "new historians." In the wake of the French *Annales* school and of Thomas Kuhn's analysis of the structure of scientific knowledge, Ginzburg launched the Italian historical new wave with his essay, "Clues: Roots of an Evidential Paradigm." The central idea of this work is that the new historian (and every scientist in general) must be like a hunter in search of traces, footprints, and clues, a modern hunter such as Arthur Conan Doyle's Sherlock Holmes, basing his or her work on evidence and on the power of intuition. Systematic analysis is impossible, given the complex social structure of advanced capitalist society. The only solution is to decipher the signs and, hence, the semiotics. Following Ginzburg, a historian is an augur, a diviner, a priest-king like Bloch's "Roi Thaumaturges," an instinctive hunter of clues, a detective. [18]

To bring up "Clues" in order to study a Hollywood director and the witches' sabbath to view *It's a Wonderful Life* may seem somewhat rash, perhaps even irreverent. However, bearing in mind the polemics that have divided historians in recent years, the method hypothesized by Ginzburg can help to provide a new type of historical and scientific approach to an intangible, fleeting medium such as cinema, which is called into existence only when a picture lights up on the screen. Obviously, the historian who pursues this method (regardless of the object of his investigation) must slip into the metaphorical shoes of Sherlock Holmes, as Ginzburg says. He or she must be sensitive to the tiniest traces, the smallest details; must risk an analysis that overturns what is currently accepted; must force himself or herself to reason in probabilities. On this basis one can attempt an investigation of Capra with the aim of conjugating text and context, historical analysis of the social background, evolution of production and ideology, and analysis of the films.

Freudian Slips

I shall start with a flash-forward to a late film by Capra (who was on the threshold of decline at the time), the famous *It's a Wonderful Life*. Here one finds the classical scenario that made the director's films so successful: the humble, solitary hero (this time a young, self-made man running a small family business); the small, anonymous town (called Bedford Falls, potentially any town in the Midwest) as the setting for a fable that is valid for humanity as a whole; the ritual adversary or bad guy (this time a heartless, unprincipled moneylender whose sole ideal is pecuniary); the community of good neighbors, all the ordinary people who hover between refusal and acceptance, their private lives and interpersonal relationships invariably conditioned by their membership in the community. After more than twenty years of Capra's filmmaking, this scenario had been elevated to a style, a repetitive scheme of simple philosophical ideas raised to the status of an existential ethic. A conflict between the planned message and the involuntary message comes to a head here, perhaps at a conscious level. In fact, the film, which met with production difficulties and was made independently by the director without assistance from the Hollywood studios, provides the most obvious example of Capra *malgré lui*, the Capra who was subject to extremely significant slips.

To highlight his message, usually linked to an optimistic, happy ending, Capra uses a contrasting second theme, a theme that also contains contradictions and contrary solutions. In spite of himself, the director transmits a series of negative messages that infringe on the more general message, particularly in certain segments of the narrative. These sequences have a role to play in the final outcome of the story; generally they are the crucial point in the negative situation, the dramatic climax that precedes and prepares the way for the happy ending; but they deserve to be read as independent minifilms. It seems to me that the director loses his ideological control in these fragments and that the images of society and sediments of civil malaise emerge here as from the collective unconscious, contradicting and negating the sweetened Christian and class-struggle-free utopias of Capra's films.

These are the unconscious clues to which attention must be addressed because they can lead to a reversal of current opinion or at least to a new proposal for an overall interpretation. The "slip" in *It's a Wonderful Life* (and I use this term improperly) is in one special portion of the film: the daydream of George Bailey (James Stewart). In this famous sequence an angel, Clarence, stops the hero of the film, George, from committing suicide by jumping off a bridge, convincing him that life is always worth living by allowing him to experience never having been born. This is a classic device of science fiction and of counterhistory: what would have happened if the Germans had won the First World War or the South had won the American Civil War? In this didactic nightmare one finds that George's brother would have died, his wife would have been a spinster, Gower the pharmacist would have ended up in prison, but, most importantly, the town would have been in the power of the wicked Potter (Lionel Barrymore) without the actions of the ordinary citizen, George Bailey.

Bedford Falls, the utopian American town, begins to look like a real contemporary city with all its defects and moral degradation: the violent, vulgar bars; the gambling dens; the roads lit up by too many neon lights; the haunts for men only, lured in by flashy promises of girls. The town is now called Pottersville because the evil moneylender has imposed his values on the community in this other dimension.[19] Pottersville is dominated by violence (the bad cop who shoots to kill, the customers in the bar who beat up George Bailey), by sadness (Gower, the desperate pharmacist who appears as a relic of the Depression), and by solitude (the situations of the wife, Mary, and the prostitute, Violet). This community is more similar to the worst real models of postwar American society than to the village of metaphor and fable. A diabolic, rather than an angelic, trick has transformed the wholesome Bedford Falls of the Golden Age, of good-neighborliness, of loving one's fellow as oneself, into New York, Los Angeles, or Washington. The dream reveals actual society. To provide a distorted picture of Bedford Falls, Capra introduces the realism of the society in which he lives, unconsciously judging that society and destroying the American myth. And the appalled eye of James Stewart, dilated by a wide-angle shot, suddenly catapulted into a horror film, legitimizes this translation into a parallel dimension.

Even in this fable par excellence, this masterpiece of petit-bourgeois agitation and reassurance, one can glimpse a different image of social history. The film is a kind of summation of Capra's dichotomous attitude to history. One part of him presents and reflects the contemporary environment, often intuitively forecasting future developments, while the other part holds up comfortable, optimistic ideological icons. On one hand the director sweetens and doctors the truth in the name of Christian and lay mercy, but on the other he documents and photographs society in a way that is often merciless. To explore this dichotomy more thoroughly, let us now make a long flashback (as Capra does at the beginning of *It's a Wonderful Life*, when God shows the viewer George's life), working backward from this later film to the period from 1928 to 1934.

Frank Capra *Malgré Lui*, 1928–1934

Why the years from 1928 to 1934? First, this is Capra's least-known period, coming as it does before the "catastrophe of success," before *It Happened One Night*. Second, the individual and collective contradictions of American society emerge more clearly during these years; characterized by the beginning of the Depression and the Hays Code, the early thirties are decisive years (think of the events of 1932–33 at Warner Bros.).[20] And, finally, the passage from silence to sound gives this juncture the flavor of a change of epoch.

Generally, those who value Capra place him in one of three traditions: the American vision (as in Raymond Carney's *American Vision*), an ancestral ritual of comedy (*The Cinema of Frank Capra* by Leland Poague),[21] or religious moralism (*Frank Capra* by Charles Maland). I hope to demonstrate that Capra can be read in terms of his relationship to social history, that his work can be analyzed in accordance with historical method, and that he can actually be considered a case study for a new kind of historical analysis.

An incentive and an occasion for a new analysis of Capra's early works was provided in Italy by the 1989 translation of the director's autobiography.[22] The Italian edition appeared at an appropriate moment and invited ordinary readers as well as cinema scholars to reflect on the figure of Frank Capra. The moment was appropriate because a process of rereading the films of this Hollywood master, of reconsidering his work and his artistic and ideological role, had been going on for some time in Europe.

Until recently, Frank Capra has been associated with populism, with the conservative, reactionary demagogy apparent in a cursory reading of his films. The love for the good neighbor and the message that happiness does not come from money, but from small things and correct feelings, reassuring the public that conflicts can be resolved, have contributed to limiting the Italian-American director to the role of the faithful adaptor or even the brilliant forerunner of the optimism that was typical of one aspect of the New Deal.

The sudden return of interest and desire to review entrenched critical judgments are intriguing, but also disconcerting, and raise several questions. Mainly, who is Capra? A knowing and perhaps cynical creator of happy endings, or an often merciless chronicler of the contradictions of American society? A story-teller, a re-counter of fairy tales for grown-ups, or a more tragic ballad singer, brimming with pathos, like those who travel around Sicily, where his family originated. A craftsman without intellectual ambition, or a poet of the imaginary average American, a minimalist ready to claw at the powerful? Which should be considered correct: the many referents that show Capra to be an inconvenient person for the American system, or his declarations, his convictions? Should one believe in the new readings of the last few years, which stress the conflicting elements in Capra, or in his autobiography, which emphasizes the optimism of will power and Christian values?

The most striking element that emerges from Capra's autobi-ography is the gap between reality and his perception of that real-ity. In other words, the ingenuousness of *The Name above the Title*, its rhetorical outbursts, its harking back to old values, its faith in goodness and in a better future authorize the old, con-ventional reading of Capra's work in a way that the films do not, if they are carefully read. In addition, his autobiography came out after he had retired, in the early seventies, and it tends to give a compact, homogeneous reconstruction of his career in accordance with the consolidated view that had by that time immortalized him. Thus, it is a book of memories, like all autobiographies, to be treated with due caution, as it is full of those adjustments and distortions that are natural in a letter to posterity. It can be con-sidered as a source, but not as a reliable guide to an aesthetic or ideological judgment. The judgment must be made *malgré lui*, in spite of the director's conscious self-interpretation.

Capra's early works, the films made from the time he joined Columbia Pictures until he won the Academy Award (from *That*

Certain Thing to *It Happened One Night*) cast doubts on the customary evaluation of the director and throw new light on his subsequent works, from *It Happened One Night* to *It's a Wonderful Life*. The critical judgment of Capra must be revised radically. If one scratches the surface of his films, particularly those made from 1928 to 1934, between the end of silent films and the enforcement of the Motion Picture Production Code by the Production Code Administration, one finds traces of an American history that has not been sweetened, of a dramatic reality that cannot be resolved in a happy ending. Capra's medicine cannot cure the deep-seated ills of the America of those years; on the contrary, it can be a lethal poison, like the "bitter tea" of General Yen (in the 1933 film of that title) or the mistaken prescription of the pharmacist, Gower, in *It's a Wonderful Life*. One must read between the lines and analyze the apparently unimportant clues indicative of personal and social conflicts that are often insoluble—or that can be solved only by a miracle or a fairy tale. If one reads more carefully, one finds elements of individual and collective folly that conflict with the apparently reassuring populist ideology.

A history of conflict emerges *malgré* Capra, in spite of his autobiography and his official statements. One discovers a Capra in whom the American Dream borders on an American nightmare. All one has to do is cut the ending, which is almost always possible in Capra's films, to obtain a different reading. It is sufficient to concentrate attention on a sequence that is not famous, on a revealing passage or sign, or to analyze the sequences constructed by Capra to obtain a dramatic climax, the catastrophic penultimate situations necessary to the solution, to the final deux ex machina, whether it be the angel Clarence or the pilot Lefty (in *Flight* [1929]). These segments can reveal more about society, history, and the author's dynamics than all the rest of the film.

This is where the "Capra-corn," the facile and rather annoying optimism, fails and a pessimistic view of life emerges in its place, rooted in the contradictions of the immigrant's American Dream. If one wishes to reread the Capra of this period, one must analyze certain indicative themes: the unhappy ending, the obsession with suicide, the coming catastrophe, family conflicts, the American nightmares (social conflicts), models and crises of the system, and off-key frames.

Capra's Indicative Themes

The Unhappy Ending

Let us start with *The Way of the Strong*, made in 1928. This is an interesting pastiche of categories—comedy, psychological drama, gangster film, and romance with melodramatic overtones on the theme of Beauty and the Beast. A gangster, ironically known as Handsome because of his monstrous face, covered with scars and marked by cruelty, falls in love with a blind musician, and this romance inevitably changes the atmosphere of violence and harshness that permeates his milieu.[23] One of his friends, a young man who plays the piano in a saloon, also falls in love with the young woman, and his character likewise improves. A classic, tragic case of mistaken identity is a play on the theme of misunderstanding and doubles: Handsome is ashamed to allow his hideous

3.1. From the left: Handsome Williams (Mitchell Lewis) with Nora (Alice Day) and Dan (Theodore von Eltz) in *The Way of the Strong* (1928). (Museum of Modern Art/Film Stills Archive)

face to be touched by the blind girl, so he borrows the face of the young pianist. This gives rise to the tragic comedy of Handsome who, in the end, sacrifices himself for the sake of love in favor of the more physically attractive and younger pianist.

This is a many-faceted film, full of psychological conflict, but the important thing from our point of view is that it has an unhappy ending. To save the girl and the young man who loves her, the gangster allows the police to follow him and, when he realizes that all is lost, turns his gun on himself as a sign of capitulation and expiation. This is the first suicide in Capra's films; others will follow—real, attempted, or imagined. It provides a dramatic finale, in which the bad guy redeems himself when he discovers goodness and love. Handsome's suicide is a bitter form of catharsis. No one cares whether the blind girl and the good-looking pianist live happily ever after. Handsome is dead, making payment for his life as an outlaw, without reassuring the viewer.

The Way of the Strong leaves a strange feeling of discomfort. The gangster, now redeemed, turns the gun on himself after having looked at himself for the last time in the rearview mirror of his car (Handsome hates mirrors). This self-destructive gesture conveys a sensation of anxiety and a lack of identity that concern not only the villain, but the whole of contemporary society. As the villain is the real hero of the film, the viewer is forced to identify with him: Handsome involves the viewer by means of his apparent strength, which turns out to be weakness, and by means of the emotional charge of his desperation. Handsome is the monster in every man, in Capra's average man. A whole society lurks behind that hideous face, behind the suffering, unhappy mask of the bad/good hero. Like King Kong, Handsome combines infantile desires and bestial wickedness, becoming a monster of the American collective unconscious. Thus, *The Way of the Strong* may be taken as a pretext for reconsidering the convention of the happy ending in Capra's works.

The Obsession with Suicide

Handsome's suicide will be followed by others, real and symbolic, present like an obsession or a death wish. Capra's first film of 1930, *Ladies of Leisure*, tells the story of a painter, the son of a millionaire, who falls in love with a young woman from the lower classes, one of Capra's classic "screwball" themes. Behind the atmosphere of the bourgeois interior and the Bohemian life is a sensation of much deeper malaise, of a social distance between the protagonists that cannot be bridged. In fact, one might say that the film contains two endings. The story finishes with the attempted suicide of the woman, portrayed by Barbara Stanwyck, who jumps into the sea from the deck of a ship at the conclusion of her unhappy love affair, and the film does not seem to permit any other logical conclusion. But the "official" ending recovers her from the sea and also recovers its optimism, improbably rescuing the heroine and the whole story. The film ends with Stanwyck's character stretched out on a bed in an infirmary, surrounded by hopeful, reassuring faces, but one has the sensation that this is a tacked-on, falsely reassuring ending, an afterthought. The real ending is not at all happy; the real ending is death.

Capra's work contains a series of suicides, successful or interrupted at the last moment, that add a lot of wrinkles to the apparently reassuring face of his oeuvre. In addition to the protagonist of *The Way of the Strong*, one of the heroes of *Dirigible* (1931) tries to kill himself, although this is a sacrifice made to save his traveling companions. General Yen kills himself with "bitter tea," like Handsome redeeming with his death the blood he has shed and perhaps also the passion kindled in the breast of the missionary (Barbara Stanwyck again). His suicide disorients the heroine and interrupts the erotic tension. In deciding to commit suicide, General Yen accepts that such a transgressive, interracial relationship is still impossible.

In *Meet John Doe* (1941), according to the version with the tormented finale, Long John either commits suicide or attempts to do so. His only solution is to jump off a New York skyscraper when the crowd that had acclaimed him suddenly abandons him. George Bailey, in *It's a Wonderful Life*, also thinks about killing himself, tempted by the icy water of the river. The water into which Stanwyck's Kay Arnold throws herself in *Ladies of Leisure* is also icy. Careful analysis of the sequence of the "attempted" suicide supports the hypothesis that the final happy ending is a juxtaposed, false addition. The suicide jump is followed by a black fade-out. Then, with no music, none of the narrative tricks that usually trigger tears, the director fades in to Kay's frozen feet (the chill of death?). The camera then makes it clear that Kay has been saved. One sees her fiancé, Jerry, whispering reassurances, and another fade-out closes the little finale, added perhaps out of conviction or perhaps as a compromise.

The climax of *American Madness* (1932) is provided by a gun, when jealousy has broken down the final resistance of the banker, Thomas Dickson, who had managed to survive the loss of his financial assets. Here, too, is a hint of suicide. A tracking shot stops on the gun, suggesting the idea of death and creating suspense. This suicide is not physical, but moral and private, like the suicide of Lulu Smith in *Forbidden* (1932). Lulu kills and commits suicide metaphorically, refusing to accept the confession of the governor, Grover. Thus, she "annihilates" herself in the crowd, in anonymity. She kills herself by silence and oblivion.

Suicide runs through many of Capra's films of these years. It is undeniable that the idea of suicide represents the maximum moment of desperation, the peak of a drama that usually wends its way toward a happy ending, producing the comforting, moving "Capra effect," as in *It's a Wonderful Life*. Nevertheless, the dark leitmotif of a renunciation of life is an important clue to the climate of social despair that permeated the late twenties and the whole of the thirties.[24]

The Coming Catastrophe

During this period there is a feeling of catastrophe, different from that of McBride, that Capra clearly presents in both his more dramatic films with a social background and his lighter, apparently innocuous comedies. Here one needs to go back to Capra's partnership with Harry Langdon in *The Strong Man* (1926), an early film in which the private epic of the little hero becomes a communal epic, with the protagonist provoking a catastrophic catharsis, a destruction that purifies. In *The Strong Man* Langdon's character finds himself involved by chance, and for love, in a battle between Good and Evil, between the moralizers led by the heroine's father, the respectable, conventional good citizen, and the townspeople debased by alcohol and the temptation of the saloon. Langdon acts as a catalyst, and the ideological battle is transformed into a physical battle, a comic Western brawl in which the ingenuous hero in the unfamiliar role of the strong man ends up destroying the saloon. Good triumphs with a catastrophe, and the walls of Jericho, the name given to the walls of the awful saloon in the film, come tumbling down at the feet of the procession of reformers marching in front of this haunt of perdition. God, or respectability, makes use of the "boy" Langdon to enforce His will.

In this case the catastrophe is positive and prepares the way for the happy ending. At other times, however, it is less reassuring and leaves behind a sensation of anguish. An example is the thoughtful, ironic finale of *Rain or Shine* (1930), a film taken from a Broadway comedy but still full of apprehension. The circus has burned down, the fire caused by sparks created by the personal and social conflicts that have emerged in this microcosm. Now that the fire is over, Smiley, the star of the film, lights a cigar with a smoldering piece of rope, surrounded by a desert of destruction, and then the circus goes on its way, as it has done from time immemorial. But Capra shows us that the way is hard with a shot of a file of elephants marching through rain and mud.

The destruction of the circus in *Rain or Shine* is inevitably associated with the image of another "circus" that burns in a great, purifying bonfire, Florence Fallon's tabernacle-tent in *The Miracle Woman* (1931). The part of society shown in *The Miracle Woman* is dominated by an element of the irrational that perverts any attempt at conciliation. The film is about the psychology of the masses, about the gray mob that follows an opinion leader. This time the charismatic figure is a messianic evangelist (again, played by Barbara Stanwyck) whose religious mission is exploited for commercial ends to such an extent that the church ends up becoming a "circus." But the heroine, Florence, an anguished mixture of good and evil, finally realizes that she has become the victim of a perverse process, rather like John Doe ten years later. The only road to salvation is expiation and sacrifice; in the film's grand finale Florence's diabolical church is destroyed by a purifying fire, together with the ambitious plans of those who were exploiting her.

The Miracle Woman is a hallucinated, even macabre, film, with no hope and no utopia, even if Florence ends up in the Salvation Army (a much healthier organization) and there is a chance that a blind man will regain his sight. But the blindness of Mary (*The

Strong Man), of Nora (*The Way of the Strong*), and in this film of John (whose impaired corneas constitute an invitation to consider wider intentions of truth) clashes with the blindness of the ignorant masses and with the guilty, devilish blindness of the impresario. "It is not a church," Florence shouts to the faithful who have crucified her father, "it's a collection of hypocrites." The masses, therefore, are ignorant and hypocritical, as they are in *American Madness* and *Meet John Doe*, and Florence is the uncertain saint, the forerunner of the ambiguous Christ figure of *Meet John Doe*.

The films made by Capra during this period are studded with great and small catastrophes. The great catastrophes are the most shocking events, such as the recurrent fires or the equally frequent accidents: the airship destroyed by a storm in *Dirigible*, the accident involving the airplane that competes with the airship in the

3.2. Florence Fallon (Barbara Stanwyck) is carried on a stretcher to an ambulance after the climactic fire in *The Miracle Woman* (1931). (Museum of Modern Art/Film Stills Archive)

same film, the similar air accident in *Flight*, the breakdown in *Submarine*. Then there are the small catastrophes, such as the minor accident (highly significant in terms of the plot) in which George Bailey runs his car into a tree on Christmas Eve, just before his "nightmare." The loss of a wallet can be merely a narrative device, as it is in *That Certain Thing*, but the loss of a sum to be paid into the bank can provoke an apparently irreversible catastrophe in *It's a Wonderful Life*. These small and great catastrophes can be caused by a letter (*Dirigible*, *Forbidden*), by a pile of telegrams (*Mr. Smith Goes to Washington*), or, as will be seen, by simple suggestion or mass hysteria.

Family Conflicts

Catastrophe can also be caused by a party, that emblematic concentration of family and social dynamics. The party in *Lady for a Day* (1933) is a catastrophe because no one comes, and the party in *Platinum Blonde* (1931) is a castastrophe because too many people come, angering the wealthy, unpleasant character portrayed by Jean Harlow. Even the less catastrophic elements of the light comedies and social dramas show signs of a disaster in course. *Platinum Blonde* and *Forbidden* represent the other face of the Depression, in which the drama is more personal and more private, regardless of whether the solution is comic or tragic. These films show the middle class from the inside, the crises of the old values, and the decadence of a world riven by class distinctions and social paranoia. On the one hand there is the cold rejection of the upper classes faced with the new demands of the masses and, on the other, the perplexity of the ruling classes faced with private conflicts. The conflict, both private and public, emerges clearly in *Forbidden* (1932), the story of the forbidden love of a character played by Adolphe Menjou, torn between a successful career and his emotional inclination.

The family situations described by Capra are certainly not soothing. With the declared intent of seeking to resolve and heal their contradictions, Capra is forced to display and underline these contradictions. And what can be more conflict-ridden than the stereotype of the bourgeois family, whose apparently happy, calm surface can conceal chasms of incomprehension and alienation?

The films made by Capra during 1928–34 (and even the subsequent ones, from this particular point of view) display numerous indications of this type of family malaise. One sees a realistic picture of the respectable family that conceals deceit and adultery in *Forbidden* and the neuroses of wealthy families in *Broadway Bill* (1934) and in the later and more famous *You Can't Take It with You*. In *Broadway Bill* a stone thrown at the window of the dining room where the sacred family is gathered together is a liberating sign of revolt. In *You Can't Take It with You*, it is quite clear that the sound of a harmonica is not going to solve the class war, and yet one realizes that both families, rich and poor, create neuroses. A suggestion of shadow always lurks behind these apparently serene surfaces, as, for example, in the potential adultery of the banker's wife in *American Madness*.

Even the basic values of family solidarity, of inherited affections, are put in a position of crisis. These films show conflicts between the generations, from the one lightly sketched in *That Certain Thing* (1928) to the more dramatic and serious situation in *The Younger Generation* (1929). In the latter, all the problems of the institution of the family seem to be brought to the surface in the person of the ambitious son, Morris, who abandons the aging patriarch in the name of personal success and to make his way in society.

Social Conflicts

This family malaise, this individual and collective neurosis, conceals a much vaster folly. *American Madness* is emblematic of a generalized social malaise and is one of the more dramatic representations of the madness of a society during the early thirties. In spite of Capra's good intentions and notwithstanding his positive heroes, one detects a pessimistic vision of the masses grumbling and prevailing in the background. In *American Madness* and later in *Meet John Doe*, the mass of humanity is not the good neighbor, the trusting people who abound in the more usual Capra film; here it is an anonymous, savage crowd that can be manipulated and deceived.

In Capra's films, a telephone call, a word, a lie, or the name of a horse is enough to unleash a crowd with no powers of judgment and with no moral sense. This happens in *American Madness* and in *Broadway Bill*. The latter film is meant to be a comedy, but there is a bitter flavor to the ridiculing of the credulous crowd, based on the gag of Colonel Pettigrew, who spreads the word about a winning horse to obtain money for the protagonist of the film. In *American Madness* the crowd acts differently, in a perverse spiral, a maneuver that is intended to ruin the positive hero, the good financier played by Walter Huston. The sight of someone withdrawing his savings is enough to start a tragic run on the bank. Insistent long shots of frenzied crowds mimic the chaos of the Wall Street financial crash. Naturally, the positive hero, the good financier who lends money on trust, like Bailey in *It's a Wonderful Life*, wins out in the end. But he is shattered by the brutality of the social situation, notwithstanding the happy ending.

Another film whose "slips" (unconscious moments of denunciation of society) must be analyzed is *Lady for a Day*. In the innocuous, reassuring form of a farcical fable, this film shows some of the "real" people of the Depression: the gangsters, dropouts, outcasts, impotent politicians, and miserable tramps, of whom the star of the pathetic story, the apple-seller Apple Annie, is one. The story is a kind of fantasized realism that suggests parallels between the tramps of this film and those of Zavattini and De Sica in *Miracolo a Milano* (*Miracle in Milan*, 1950). Certainly, this film, too, includes a touch of consolation. You can be rich, if only for a day, if only in terms of affection. However, the hard fact still remains that there is a disquieting background to this fable: poverty, begging, the need for a moment of illusion, to be happy for just one day, in order to confront continuous despair. Cinderella does not, in fact, become a princess; this is the message. This is the reality conveyed by Capra's films, obscured under the more ingenuous, simple message. Without the fairy tale the Cinderella figures are destined to return to the ranks, as happened to Stew Smith, John Doe, Mr. Deeds, and Peter Warne in *It Happened One Night*.

Models and Crises of the System

What model of society was Capra displaying behind the conciliatory and corporative (to borrow a term used by the Fascists during these years) mask of his ideology in the films of this period? To answer this question one must go back to a minor, ingenuous film that is almost unknown but is full of social clues. *That Certain Thing* (1928) theorizes on the production methods of capitalism and on its possible contradictions.

The certain thing of the title is the secret of the sandwiches made by the heroine, Molly, who becomes a business woman for love. There are many reasons why this film can be considered a historical source, a document of the twenties. The male lead is a classic figure in the cinema of that period, the son of a millionaire. But the interesting feature is that this magnate's son falls in love with a working-class girl, marries her, and is disinherited by his father for doing so. This clash between the classes shows a picture of America that is certainly simplified to the level of a comic strip, but that is also indicative of a certain social climate. This permits the emergence of sketches of the various class protagonists: the trolley driver, the poor widow, the jealous neighbors, and the little dressmaker. The small, crowded, and noisy world of the working classes is contrasted with the sophisticated dining rooms of the upper classes.

In addition, *That Certain Thing* inserts a dominant motif into the classic theme of poor but beautiful against rich but lacking love, the motif of the emergence of the small entrepreneur, the legitimation of the self-made man. The self-made man is a woman in this particular case, the resourceful Molly, who, quite by chance, realizes that her sandwiches are good because they are popular with the workers of the company in which the young ex-millionaire is forced to work because he is penniless. Molly decides to start a business with her homemade sandwiches and succeeds in competing with the shark who owns the A.B.C. food chain, who just happens to be her millionaire father-in-law and who is taught a lesson by Molly and her husband.

Molly's very simple formula can be taken as an emblem of the neocapitalist system. The winning slogan of the younger generation is "cut the ham thick." The managerial approach of the neocapitalist entrepreneur is efficient, ready to invest, and non-parasitic. Thus, like Capra's more mature work, this symptomatic small film contains a picture of society, as well as a metaphor of the production methods of that society and an analysis of its ethics and its deepest workings.

One may take as an example the classic theme of the little people, the neighbors, a theme that was very dear to Capra. *That Certain Thing* presents a close-up of the neighbors who are good but can also be bad, as happens when Molly returns disappointed after her husband has been disinherited by his father and the neighbors become aggressive, vindictive monsters. As always, when the surface is scratched, good neighbors are capable of tearing each other apart: *homo homini lupus*. And forget about the "little man." Here, the man on the street is a repulsive trolley driver who courts Molly boorishly. There is even a touch of black humor in one of the earliest sequences, when an intertitle cynically says: "Maggie Kelly always told her husband where to go. One day he did and left her a widow." So much for the romance of the petit bourgeois family.

Off-Key Frames

As we see, Capra's films of 1928–34 can be read in a way that is anything but reassuring. In spite of the director's theoretical and poetic statements, despite his autobiography, against his will, unexpected surges of the collective unconscious emerge, indications of a reality that cannot be explained by the philosophy of Capra-corn. One finds a picture of an America in the throes of a radical transformation, in which the new imagery of the masses clashes against the old conflicts of the social situation. Modernism is achieved, but it creates friction with populism; efficiency and dynamism come into conflict with conservation and nostalgia. If Capra is the mythmaker of this America, he is also sometimes a potential destroyer of the myth, the ironic observer, the hidden accuser. His X-ray picture of American society captures the dynamics of the transformation: the newspapers, the telephones, the radio, the mass media—all bring civilization, but also corruption. The same is true of the means of transport that travel through the geography of Capra's films: cars, buses, helicopters, trains, submarines, dirigibles—all populated by contradictory personages. The trains carry carloads of tramps; poverty travels on the buses; when the cars stop, the passengers find a world of hunger.

It Happened One Night contains three extremely significant examples, three sequences that can be taken as emblematic cases of

Freudian slips. In the first, shortly after Peter Warne happily waves at a train at a level crossing, he discovers that dozens of tramps are crammed onto that train, as if to say that the Depression is passing through. The same sensation is produced in *It's a Wonderful Life* when Gower, the pharmacist, goes into Martini's bar during the nightmare sequence. With his emaciated look and his grimy clothes, the chill of the Depression seems to enter for a moment.

In the second emblematic Freudian slip in *It Happened One Night*, a mother faints on the bus where Ellie and Peter meet. She faints from hunger, at the end of her strength. Once again the subject of food comes up, a subtly obsessive factor in Capra's early films, even when it is made less dramatic by a touch of irony. *That Certain Thing* is definitely a film about food, as is *So This Is Love*, where food is a sign of love, but where there is also a desire for prosperity, a wish to satisfy real and symbolic hungers. *So This Is Love* starts with an amusing sequence in which the hero associates the image of a roast chicken with the face of the woman he loves; in the finale, the heroine makes sure that the hero wins a boxing match by stuffing his opponent with goodies until he almost explodes. And aren't Apple Annie's good-luck apple and the legendary doughnut of Gable and Colbert similar symbols?

The third emblematic slip in *It Happened One Night* occurs in the motel, when Ellie tries to take a shower, jumping a long line of disheveled women, and discovers a universe anticipating that of *The Grapes of Wrath* (1940). The reality of the Depression is shown in this fleeting image of poverty, a mixture of anguish and exhilaration. The image is even truer because it is given with a few, almost sublime brushstrokes.

Attention must be focused on these semi-unconscious messages when one reexamines Capra. By reading between the lines, one can transgress the rhetoric of the "populist" director or even show that he, in his turn, can be a "transgressive" director. In this way one will discover that the defender of faith in the American nation, the director who made the Why We Fight series for the U.S. Army, has some surprises in store.

In *Flight* (1929), a simplistic, rhetorical film about a revolution in Nicaragua, there are two small "slips." In one sequence the soldier Lefty tries not to vomit during the flag-raising ceremony; finally he does vomit, in front of the glorious Stars and Stripes.

Although the scene is meant to be funny, the result is desecrating. Another close-up shows the rough but good-hearted officer, Panama, spitting. Beginning with this spit and this vomit, one comes to understand that Capra-corn can be extremely bitter—and even lethal, like the potion drunk by General Yen.

Conclusion

Moments of tragedy, even if they are building blocks of comedy or narrative devices necessary to the structure of the story, cast new light on Capra's work. On these segments scholarly analysis must focus, without losing sight of the syntactic context in which they were conceived and placed.

This observation applies also to a "lost film," *The Matinee Idol* (1928), rediscovered in the early 1990s at the Cinématheque Fran-

3.3 Ginger Bolivar (Bessie Love) contends with theatrical producer Wingate (Ernest Hilliard) as blackface comedian Don Wilson (Johnnie Walker) looks on, in *The Matinee Idol* (1928). (Museum of Modern Art/Film Stills Archive)

çaise. Its story concerns an actor, Don Wilson, who has a hit on Broadway in the role of a blackface singer (a clear reference to Al Jolson in *The Jazz Singer* [1927]). One day, Wilson and his impresario happen upon a country company of amateur players run by the strong-willed Ginger Bolivar. The actor has himself cast by Ginger in a production of a Civil War drama; the need to substitute one of the players arises, and Don, without revealing his identity, steps in. But the drama is so poorly acted and directed that it becomes a refreshing event in the eyes of the impresario, who attends the show—a case, in short, of involuntary comicality. The impresario wants to reproduce the comic effect on Broadway and invites Ginger and her company to his theater. There Don will be forced into the classic double role with disguise—on one hand, as a character actor in the role of the blackface singer; on the other, as an actor in the company of inexperienced players—giving rise to the equally classic comedy of errors. Naturally, a disaster ensues: the drama presented by Ginger's company ends in laughter, and Don's identity and duplicity are discovered, triggering a crisis in her affection for him.

It is here, in these dramatic moments of climax, that one must seek the true nature of Capra's cinema. In a tragic subending, for instance, the desperate Ginger, conscious of the ruinous outcome of the piece, pays a visit to her father. The world has collapsed around her company; they have become aware not only of their illusions, but also of the crowd's lack of pity, of the nastiness and cynicism of a world that has not hesitated to exploit them wickedly. And, while the rain pours down, Ginger encounters Don, who tries to console her, but the raindrops wash away Don's blackface makeup and reveal his true face in a scene of high dramatic intensity and immense pathos.

Naturally, a happy ending will follow soon after. Again, drama is placed at the service of the comic solution. But it will seem artificial. The fact remains that even these early, minor films paint an interesting portrait of America from which, every now and then, Capra removes the makeup. This is an America of which Capra has often taken the pulse and to which he has certainly supplied many of his strong images in the double role of interpreter and creator of a collective imagination, a social mythology.

Notes

1. Andrew Bergman, *We're in the Money: Depression America and Its Films* (New York: New York Univ. Press, 1971).

2. Jeffrey Richards, "Frank Capra and the Cinema of Populism," *Cinema* (London) 5 (February 1970): 22–28, reprinted in Richards, *Visions of Yesterday* (London: Routledge & Kegan Paul, 1973), 234–53, and in *Movies and Methods: An Anthology*, ed. Bill Nichols (Berkeley and Los Angeles: Univ. of California Press, 1976), 65–77; *Business Week*, 13 March 1995.

3. Joseph McBride, *Frank Capra: The Catastrophe of Success* (New York: Simon & Schuster, 1992).

4. Although Capra's name rarely appeared in the French journal, Jean-Louis Comolli, in a retrospective symposium on the *politique des auteurs*, does say, "The battle has still to be fought as far as Lubitsch, DeMille, Capra and even Ford are concerned." See Jean-Louis Comolli, Jean-André Fieschi, Gérard Guégan, Michel Mardore, Claude Ollier, and André Téchiné, "Twenty Years On: A Discussion about American Cinema and the *politique des auteurs*," in *Cahiers du cinéma, 1960–1968: New Wave, New Cinema, Reevaluating Hollywood*, ed. Jim Hillier (Cambridge: Harvard Univ. Press, 1986), 205. Originally published in French as "Vingt ans après: le cinéma américain et la politique des auteurs," *Cahiers du cinéma* 172 (November 1965).

5. Vito Zagarrio, ed., *Accadde una notte: Frank Capra (1928–1934) e la Columbia (1934–1945)* (Rome: Di Giacomo, 1988), catalogue published on the occasion of the VIII Rassegna Internazionale Retrospettiva di Ancona, 3–8 December 1988, and the concomitant conference; Frank Capra, *Il nome sopra il titolo: Autobiografia*, trans. Alberto Rollo (Rome: Lucarini, 1989); *Frank Capra: Un italiano alla corte di Hollywood*, catalogue of the retrospective, Rome, 23 March–29 April 1995; *Da Bisacquino a Hollywood: Regie di Frank Capra*, catalogue of the retrospective, Bisacquino, 30 July–5 August 1997.

6. Jeanine Basinger, "America's Love Affair with Frank Capra," *American Film* 7, no. 5 (1982), 46–51, 81; *Meet Frank Capra: A Catalog of His Work* (Palo Alto and Los Angeles: Stanford Theatre Foundation and National Center for Film and Video Preservation, 1990); Raymond Carney, *American Vision: The Films of Frank Capra* (New York: Cambridge Univ. Press, 1986); Charles Wolfe, *Frank Capra: A Guide to References and Resources* (Boston: G.K. Hall, 1987); Michel Cieutat, *Frank Capra* (Paris: Rivages, 1988).

7. Vito Zagarrio, ed., *Studi Americani: Modi di produzione a Hollywood dalle origini all'era televisiva* (Venice: Marsilio, 1994), includes several essays by U.S. scholars in Italian translation.

8. See, for example, Donald Willis, *The Films of Frank Capra* (Metuchen, N.J.: Scarecrow Press, 1974).

9. The notion of the Freudian slip is used more broadly here than is customary in psychoanalysis. One might also use the expression *loss of control* to signify the moments when Capra relinquishes control of his ideology to build a dramatic climax. See also Sebastiano Timpanaro, *The Freudian Slip: Psychoanalysis and Textual Criticism* (London: New Left Books, 1976).

10. McBride, *Frank Capra*, 289–326, 311.

11. Ibid., 313; Charles J. Maland, *Frank Capra*, rev. ed. (New York: Twayne, 1995); McBride, *Frank Capra*, 312. Emphasis added.

12. McBride, *Frank Capra*, 312–13.

13. Ibid., 289.

14. See, for example, Lino Miccaché, ed., *De Sica* (Venice: Marsilio, 1991).

15. McBride, *Frank Capra*, 290–93.

16. Ibid., 290–91.

17. Carlo Ginzburg, *Ecstasies: Deciphering the Witches' Sabbath,* trans. Raymond Rosenthal (New York: Pantheon, 1991), 307, originally published as *Storia notturna: Una decifrazione del sabba* (Turin: Einaudi, 1989).

18. Thomas S. Kuhn, *The Structure of Scientific Revolutions* (Chicago; Univ. of Chicago Press, 1974); Carlo Ginzburg, "Clues: Roots of an Evidential Paradigm," in *Clues, Myths, and the Historical Method*, trans. John and Anne C. Tedeschi (Baltimore: Johns Hopkins Univ. Press, 1989), 96–126, originally published as "Spie: Radici di un paradigma indiziario," in *Miti emblemi spie: morfologia e storia* (Turin: Einaudi, 1986), 158–209. See also Robin W. Winks, ed., *The Historian as Detective: Essay on Evidence* (New York: Harper & Row, 1968).

19. I use the word *other* also in a psychoanalytic sense, after Melanie Klein. See Hanna Segal, *The Work of Hanna Segal: A Kleinian Approach to Clinical Practice* (London: Free Association Books, 1986).

20. See Adriano Aprà, ed., *Hollywood: lo studio system* (Venice: Marsilio, 1982), an anthology of articles prepared for a retrospective of and conference on Warner Bros. in the early 1930s, sponsored by the Mostra Internazionale del Nuovo Cinema.

21. Leland Poague, *The Cinema of Frank Capra: An Approach to Film Comedy* (South Brunswick, N.J.: A.S. Barnes, 1975). Poague offers a new perspective in a more recent study, *Another Frank Capra* (Cambridge: Cambridge Univ. Press, 1994).

22. Capra, *Il nome sopra il titolo*.

23. In restored prints of this film now circulating, the character's nickname has been changed to Pretty Boy.

24. See Bergman, *We're in the Money*, and Peter Roffman and Jim Purdy, *The Hollywood Social Problem Film: Madness, Despair and Politics from the Depression to the Fifties* (Bloomington: Indiana Univ. Press, 1981).

4

Capra and the Abyss: Self-interest versus the Common Good in Depression America

Charles J. Maland

The fantasy of goodwill . . . found its natural exponent in Frank Capra, considered by many to be the most capable director developed by the talkies.
Richard Griffith, *The Film till Now* (1949)

A movie depicts disturbing images. Torrents of water wash a crumpled poster, featuring a man's face, along a curb and down a storm drain. A dissolve reveals a close-up of the same man, looking gaunt and downcast, lit harshly from one side, walking forward. Superimposed is an image of a whirlpool swirling around his head. A newspaper headline rises from the bottom of the frame, proclaiming "FAKER." When the man reappears in a low-angle medium shot, he walks forward and raises his hand to his face. Simultaneously, faces dissolve in and out at various corners of the frame. The admonishing faces are delivering chiding rebukes: "fake," "racketeer," "liar," "cheat," "impostor." The haggard, tormented man contemplates suicide.

Or take another film: a man, frantic over economic problems, storms out of his house on Christmas Eve, stung with guilt after unjustifiably upbraiding his family. Nearly assaulted at a bar, he's

95

denied a loan by a business rival and then loses control of his car on a snowy evening, crashing into a tree. Leaving the scene, he's almost run over by a passing truck. The angry driver honks. The man stumbles through the snow to a bridge. Standing at its center, he gazes over the railing into the icy, roiling river waters below. He, too, contemplates suicide.

These scenes appear not in some somber film noir but in two movies directed by Frank Capra: *Meet John Doe* (1941) and *It's a Wonderful Life* (1946). The latter film, wrote William Pechter, is "one of the bleakest . . . films ever made."[1] Despite presenting such dark scenes in these and other films, however, Capra has often been dismissed (or celebrated) as a purveyor of Pollyanna platitudes, an American success who expressed his gratitude by making simple films that reaffirmed the American Dream. This view was perhaps captured most concisely by Richard Griffith when he stated that Frank Capra's movies are driven by a "fantasy of goodwill."[2]

How can we account for the persistence of this widespread view of Capra as a fantasist of goodwill, given the disturbing scenes of bleakness cited above? Some observers focus only on the happy endings of the Capra films, in which the hero, supported by his community, emerges victorious, with all narrative conflicts resolved, or nearly so. The celebratory atmosphere of the final scene in *It's a Wonderful Life* provides only the best-known example. Capra himself contributed to this popular image via his 1971 autobiography, *The Name above the Title*.[3] There, writing in the tradition of the mythic American success story, he portrays himself as the immigrant who made good despite the odds and then turned to fashion films that would be his way of thanking the country that had allowed him to succeed. In his autobiography Capra provided support for those who prize (or criticize) his films as simple and idealistic affirmations of the status quo.[4]

Yet the bleak scenes remain in the films, and Joseph McBride's corrective biography, *Frank Capra: The Catastrophe of Success*, challenges those who hold a blithely optimistic view of Capra and his films. In addition, recent work in cultural studies has encouraged us to focus not just on happy endings of films but also on the narrative conflicts that lead up to them. As one critic puts it, a popular film's "resolution may reinforce the ideology of the larger society, but the nature and articulation of the dramatic conflicts leading to that climax cannot be ignored." [5] If a film's happy ending points toward a culture's dreams, its narrative conflicts often insinuate cultural nightmares.

The nightmarish scenes in Capra's work are not limited to *Meet John Doe* and *It's a Wonderful Life*. They are both evident in his earlier work and central to the appeal of many of his best films. [6] In this essay I examine three of Capra's earlier films at Columbia— *American Madness* (1932), *Mr. Deeds Goes to Town* (1936), and *Mr. Smith Goes to Washington* (1939)—all of which present a hero who struggles with despair at crucial moments. Because attention to the happy endings of Capra's films has distorted the core of Capra's achievement and because I wish to interrogate the notion that movies provide one way for members of society to engage in and grapple with prevailing cultural tensions, I will focus particularly on the *moments of despair* in the films, as well as the way that narrative conflicts help generate that anguish. By looking at the narrative and stylistic features that lead the protagonists of these three films to the abyss and by subsequently connecting the texts themselves to American culture during the depression years and to Capra's own experience, I argue that the despair in his films arose from a tension, widely experienced in American culture and both central to American ideology and crucial in the depression decade, between private interest and pursuit of the common good.

Frank Capra directed twenty-five films at Columbia Pictures from 1928 to 1939, and his success in the 1930s was crucial in helping Harry Cohn's studio rise from a lowly producer of inexpensive quickies to one of Hollywood's eight major studios. [7] *American Madness* was the seventeenth film Capra directed at Columbia, *Mr. Deeds* the twenty-second, and *Mr. Smith* the last.

American Madness differs from the other two films in three ways. First, Capra made it at a faster pace: in the early 1930s, he was directing two or three features a year, compared to about one a year when he directed *Deeds* and *Smith*. Second, Capra was working with smaller budgets when he made *American Madness*, and it also had a correspondingly smaller gross. On that film he was working with less than $300,000. After the success of *It Happened One Night* in 1934, the director worked with more substantial budgets; *Deeds* cost a little over $800,000, and *Smith* cost nearly $2 million. Although *American Madness* did acceptable business for a Columbia film in the early 1930s, it could not compare to *Mr. Deeds*, which grossed about $1.15 million domestically in its first year and was among the top twenty grossing films of the year, and *Mr. Smith*, which was the second highest grossing film of 1939, finishing immediately below *Gone with the Wind*.[8] Finally, *American Madness* is a considerably shorter film, running only 76 minutes, whereas *Deeds* runs 115 minutes and *Smith* runs 125 minutes.

Yet all three movies share several elements. As with many classical Hollywood films, the character constellations of the films include a male protagonist, a romantic double, and an individual or group antagonist that creates obstacles for the protagonist. The function of the protagonist is split in *American Madness* between the banker Tom Dickson (Walter Huston) and the head teller Matt Brown (Pat O'Brien). In the other two films the protagonists are the small-town poet/businessman Longfellow Deeds (Gary Cooper) and the boy ranger leader turned senator, Jefferson Smith (James Stewart). The romantic doubles play significant roles, contributing in each film to the plot conflicts leading to the protagonist's moments of despair.[9] In *American Madness* two characters share this role: Tom Dickson's wife, Phyllis (Kay Johnson), and Matt's fiance, Helen (Constance Cummings). Two characters played by Jean Arthur embody the role in the other films: the newspaper reporter Babe Bennett in *Deeds* and the secretary Clarissa Saunders in *Smith*. The key antagonists in *American Madness* are the bank's board of directors and the bank employee Cluett, although for quite different reasons. In *Deeds* a variety of city vultures create obstacles for Deeds, among them the lawyer Cedar and his partners, the Semples, the poets, the Opera Board, and the newspaper reporters who make him an object of ridicule. In *Smith* the powerful magnate Jim Taylor and his subordinates, including Governor Hopper and Senator Paine, create difficulties for Smith.

All three films also function as genre films. Each contains elements of the social problem genre, while *Mr. Deeds* and *Mr. Smith* blend that genre with the screwball comedy, a popular form that

Capra helped to establish and popularize with *It Happened One Night*.[10] Like most films drawing on these two genres, all three have relatively closed endings. The fact that all draw on elements of the social problem genre is significant, for this form especially tends to center on concerns that related closely to ideological dilemmas in American culture.

Although sharing these similarities, each film presents its conflicts and moments of despair in distinctive ways. A careful look at the narrative and stylistic characteristics of these moments, as well as the way the narrative leads up to them and then moves toward the resolutions, gives us a firmer sense of Capra's perspective and the cultural significance of each film.

A Crisis of Faith

Released in August 1932 during the depths of the Depression, about three months before Franklin Delano Roosevelt was elected president, *American Madness* was surely, as the *Variety* reviewer put it, a "timely, topical" film.[11] A crucial sequence leading to Tom Dickson's moments of despair depicts the spreading rumors of the bank's insolvency the morning after a bank robbery and the subsequent run on the bank by worried depositors. By depicting the fear of bank failure, *American Madness* acknowledged public anxiety about the bank system. (Between 1930 and FDR's inauguration in March 1933 over five thousand banks—about a quarter of all the banks in the country—closed their doors.) Yet, by making a bank president and his chief teller the heroes, the movie was a challenge to sell to the public.[12]

Thomas Dickson plummets into the abyss in the midst of a run on his bank that occurs the morning after a bank robbery. Rumors have exaggerated the theft from the actual $100,000 to over $5 million, yet he fights valiantly to manage and control the run until he learns that one of his employees, Cyril Cluett, a man burdened with gambling debts, has helped arrange the theft and that his wife had been with Cluett in his apartment the previous night. Upon hearing this news, Dickson's will to fight is broken: he tells Helen and Matt not to call any other loyal customers for financial support and seems resigned to sell his stock and give up control of

his bank to the board of directors. Capra presents the depths of
the abyss in fifteen shots, lasting slightly over two minutes: [13]

1. MS (14 seconds), straight on (SO), Tom Dickson sits at
    office desk, reaches for picture of his wife on the desk, slowly
    picks it off his desk, looks at it briefly, then places it face
    down in the desk drawer, match on action to
2. MS (8 sec), slightly higher angle and perpendicular to the
    desk, camera dollies and tilts down to open drawer, ending
    on CU of Tom's hand next to a pistol.
3. MLS (8 sec), SO, board of directors' meeting room, Clark
    dictates agreement for Tom's stock sale to secretary, other
    board members look on in background.
4. ELS (3 sec), birds-eye angle, outside bank doors, crowd
    crushes way to entry (beginning in this shot and continuing
    through shot 11, noise of crowd clamor continues, the vol-
    ume varying depending on whether the shot includes indi-
    vidual dialogue).
5. MS (12 sec), SO, behind teller facing through window to
    customers, teller says he's out of money, tells them to go to
    another window, they begin to move left.
6. MCU (2.5 sec), SO, through iron divider between teller
    windows, a woman begins to be crushed by the crowd.
7. CU (3 sec), SO, same location, woman collapses, camera
    tilts down then back up after she moves below teller ledge.
8. MS (3.5 sec), SO, similar to shot 5 but different window,
    teller throws hands out to side and says, "That's all there is."
9. LS (4 sec), high angle, Phyllis Dickson climbs curved stair-
    case toward Tom's office door, security guard follows her,
    camera pans left and tilts up to reframe.
10. MLS (3 sec), SO, Phyllis knocks on door, asks guard if he's
    sure Tom is in there.
11. MCU (11 sec), SO, Phyllis knocks frantically on door, calls
    Tom's name, tries to force door open, finally asks guard if he
    has a key.
12. MLS (6 sec), SO, Phyllis gets key, unlocks door, opens it,
    match on action to
13. MLS (7 sec), SO, Phyllis steps into office, camera pans
    quickly right, then further right, then left back to her as she

stands by door. Closing door, she sees Tom standing isolated in LS, shoulders hunched and head bowed forward, in
front of a window; Phyllis comes to his side.

14. MS (16.5 sec), SO, Phyllis on left faces Tom (they're backlit with light from window in background the only significant light source), she pleads and tries to explain to him;
Tom remains motionless, riveted in same position as 13.

15. MCU (19 sec), high angle, Tom's head in upper right of
frame, Phyllis's in lower left, Phyllis continues to plead and
express her love for Tom; he remains stoic and untouched.

Capra intensifies the scene in several ways. One is through the
contrast between Dickson's immobility in these shots and the animated, confident bearing he has exhibited earlier in the film.[14]
Second, the silence and stasis in his office contrasts to the general
clamor and tumult outside it. Finally, two crucial shots define how
deeply Tom's spirit has sunk and generate narrative suspense. In
shot 2 the camera moves to frame tightly Tom's hand and the pistol lying beside it; as soon as the camera emphasizes the two images, Capra immediately cuts. The prospect of suicide is introduced, and while the pandemonium outside his office reigns from
shots 4 through 12, fears about Dickson's fate linger. Shot 13, although it initially focuses on Phyllis's entry into the office, introduces three quick camera movements that represent her perspective. The quick pan right from the mantel to Tom's desk, a pause,
the second quick movement past the desk to two chairs and a
globe in the corner, followed by a third pan left back to the mantel—these movements approximate Mrs. Dickson's sight lines as
she searches frantically for evidence of her husband. Only when
she swings the door further open to reveal him standing dejectedly by the full-length window is the fear of suicide allayed. In a
scene that points forward to George Bailey's emotional crisis and
the Pottersville sequence in *It's a Wonderful Life*, Capra forcefully
places his protagonist in the abyss.

The narrative conflicts established earlier help make Tom Dickson's crisis convincing. The film's working title, based on Robert
Riskin's screenplay, was "Faith."[15] That was an appropriate title,
for the film explores faith in relation to several people or groups:
Tom Dickson's faith in his bank, employees, wife, and the people

to whom he loans money on the basis of their character; the board of directors' faith in Tom Dickson's lending policies; and the depositors' faith in Tom and the solidity of the bank. From the start Dickson is portrayed as a man with faith in his employees and borrowers. Despite the gravity of the economic climate, he continues to make loans to those whom he considers good risks and refuses to foreclose on trustworthy borrowers experiencing economic strain during the hard times. This faith, however, leads to the first narrative conflict—the disagreement between Dickson and the board of directors, particularly Clark, about Dickson's lending policies. Complaining about the high number of "unsecured loans," Clark seeks to persuade his colleagues to call in all "doubtful loans" and approve a merger with the New York Trust, which will effectively deny Dickson his power to control loan policy. Al-

4.1. Banker Tom Dickson (Walter Huston, right) quarrels with the chairman of his board of directors, Mr. Clark (Edwin Maxwell), in *American Madness* (1932). (Museum of Modern Art/Film Stills Archive)

though the board believes that Tom should in these "precarious times" become much more conservative in his lending policies, he counters by arguing that their views intensify the economic downturn: "The trouble with this country today is there's too much hoarded cash. Idle money's no good to industry. Where is all the money today? In the banks, vaults, socks, old tin cans buried in the ground. I tell you, we've got to get the money in circulation before you'll get this country back to prosperity." This fundamental difference in lending policy during the Depression threatens Tom's position at the bank.

The second narrative conflict also relates to faith, in this case Dickson's faith in his employees, which resembles his faith in his borrowers. As he tells the board, "Before I take a man into this bank or before I extend credit to anyone, I satisfy myself on one thing: do I believe in him? So far my judgment's been right—100%." This faith in his employees is particularly exhibited in the case of the head teller, Matt Brown. Clark tells the other board members that Matt was caught breaking into Dickson's house, but because of Dickson's "hunch" that Brown could become a trustworthy employee, Tom hired him at the bank the next day.[16] Dickson also plans to promote Matt to assistant cashier and encourages him to marry his fiance, Dickson's secretary Helen.

The conflict arises when it appears that this faith in employees is misplaced. Cyril Cluett, Matt's superior and the bank's cashier, has suffered large gambling debts that he's unable to repay. When he is pressured by the gangster Dude Finley to set the bank vault timer for midnight so that Dude and his gang can rob the bank, Cluett reluctantly agrees. To establish an alibi, he asks Dickson's wife to go to the theater with him that evening. (Dickson has earlier hurt her feelings by planning a business meeting in Philadelphia that night and thus canceling their wedding anniversary plans.) Matt, who has accidentally seen Cluett making advances to Mrs. Dickson in his office, goes that evening to Cluett's apartment in hopes of confronting him about Cluett's actions and defending the Dicksons' marriage. When Cluett brings Mrs. Dickson to his apartment at midnight to establish his alibi, Matt is waiting there for him, and Mrs. Dickson decides to leave Cluett when Matt does.

Dickson plummets to despair the day after the robbery when it seems as if his faith in Cluett, Matt, and his wife has been misplaced. Because Matt is responsible for locking the vault and setting the timer for the next morning, he immediately becomes a suspect the morning after the robbery. By refusing to let investigators know where he was the previous evening, Matt hopes to protect Dickson from learning about his wife's apparent affair. Unfortunately, he also begins to seem suspicious, and Dickson wonders if Matt has betrayed his trust. Then, when Cluett confesses and accidentally tells Dickson that his wife was in his apartment the previous evening, the shaken Dickson calls Phyllis, who confirms her whereabouts the evening before. Dickson hangs up before she can explain. Faced with panicking depositors, two apparently dishonest employees, and a seemingly unfaithful wife, Dickson plunges into despair. The abyss is reached when the protagonist experiences strains in both his work and his private life, something that happens in both *Deeds* and *Smith* as well. As in many classical Hollywood films, a main plot revolving around the world of work is interspersed with a secondary plot revolving around heterosexual relationships.[17] When the two come together in *American Madness*, Dickson's faith in both spheres is tested, leading him to the abyss.

The narrative conflicts are finally resolved when Cluett is arrested, Matt and Mrs. Dickson explain that she was not unfaithful, and the small businessmen to whom Dickson has lent money come to *his* rescue after Matt and Helen call and implore them to bring in deposits to stem the bank run. The board of directors, who see that Dickson's trust in character does bear fruit, reluctantly agree to deposit some of their assets to help save the bank. The final sequence, only about two minutes long, takes place the morning after the bank run and two days after the narrative began. In it we learn that Matt receives his promotion to cashier, he and Helen are to be married, and Dickson, newly concerned about his wife, plans to take her on a cruise for a second honeymoon.

The Crush of City Cynicisms

Mr. Deeds Goes to Town appeared in April 1936, the year after the U.S. Congress had passed much of the legislation of the "second New Deal" and the year of President Roosevelt's landslide victory over Republican nominee Alf Landon. Like *American Madness*, *Deeds* contains elements of the social problem film, although *Deeds* blends this genre with conventions of the screwball comedy, a genre that had become popular in part because of the exceptional success of Capra's *It Happened One Night*. A central convention of the screwball comedy is the presentation of a comic yet at times stormy relationship between a heroine and hero, culminating in the romantic union of the couple in the film's resolution.[18] Drawing both on this convention and on the depiction of a difficult social problem endemic to the social problem genre, *Deeds* fashions some powerful moments of despair for the film's protagonist and title character, Longfellow Deeds.

The sequences of despair, however, are preceded by a comic set of conflicts between Longfellow Deeds and a variety of urban types after he inherits $20 million and travels to New York from his hometown of Mandrake Falls, Vermont. A pragmatic businessman, writer of postcard poetry, member of the volunteer fire department, and tuba player in the town band, Deeds is unimpressed with the inheritance, feels he neither deserves nor wants it, and determines to find a good use for the money. Yet, when he goes to the city near the beginning of the film, he is unprepared for the variety of chiselers interested in getting a piece of his action. The city dwellers he meets are greedy, unfeeling, elitist, and scornful. They include John Cedar and his law partners, who have held power of attorney over Martin Semple's fortune and have long been skimming from it. The members of the Opera Board ridicule Deeds's tuba playing, yet they expect him to subsidize the opera's debt as Semple had. Shirttail relatives of Semple hire Cedar to gain control of the fortune for themselves. The elite poets whom Deeds meets at "Tullio's—Home of the Literati" mock his sentimental greeting card homilies. Finally, a crack newspaper reporter, Babe Bennett (Jean Arthur), disguises herself as Mary Dawson, an unemployed woman faint with hunger, and plays on Deeds's sympathies in search of stories that will subject him to public derision. Coming into conflict with all these characters, Deeds is portrayed as good-hearted yet naive, altruistic yet unsuspecting, totally unprepared to cope with the wiles of city types. In fact, the film seems about to end as a fable of urban corruption versus small-town virtue as Deeds—pained upon learning of Mary Dawson's true identity—prepares to leave the Semple mansion and return to Mandrake Falls.

At this point the social problem genre bursts into the world of romantic comedy and moves Deeds toward the abyss. As he walks down the open staircase toward the spacious entry of Semple's mansion, Deeds hears a commotion by the front door and sees a bedraggled man being restrained by two butlers. Deeds tells them to let the man speak but, after hearing the man criticize him for his publicized actions, Deeds calls him a "moocher," someone who wants something like everyone else. The man persists, pulling a gun when the butlers try to close in and then denouncing Deeds's irresponsibility. Pointing his pistol at Deeds, he declares: "See what good your money's going to do when you're six feet underground. You never thought of that, did you? No, all you ever thought of was pinching pennies, you money-grabbing hick. You never gave a thought to all of those starving people standing in the bread lines, not knowing where their next meal was coming from, not able to feed their wife and kids, not able to . . ." With this, the man cracks, dropping his pistol and weeping. Shaken, Deeds befriends him, gives him a meal, and finally finds a cause for his altruism. He decides to distribute the bulk of his inheritance by giving nearly two thousand 10-acre "fully equipped" farms to unemployed farmers. However, as he works to administer his plan at the mansion, surrounded by hundreds of men applying for the farms, policemen take Deeds into custody on an insanity charge issued by Cedar on behalf of the Semples. It's the last straw. Deeds is stunned: "That's fine. Just because I want to give this money to people who need it, they think I'm crazy." Staring forward, head down, he's led through the crowd. The ensuing scene at the County Hospital presents Deeds at the nadir.

Capra dramatized the protagonist's anguish in two stages. The first came three scenes earlier, when Deeds learned that Mary Dawson was actually the reporter who had been writing stories ridiculing him as "the Cinderella man." As in *American Madness*, the hero moves to despair when he learns he has been betrayed by a woman. Although Babe tries to explain over the phone, as Phyllis had in *American Madness*, Deeds puts his bedroom phone in its cradle, and Capra presents the despair carefully:

1. MCU (15.5 seconds), SO, Deeds's face shadowed on left half. He looks down, despondent, looks up toward Cobb and tries to smile, looks back down, then begins to move. Match on action to

2. MLS (4 sec), SO, camera pans left as Deeds walks toward Cobb at screen left. Match on action

3. MLS (16 sec), SO, Cobb framed at the left edge of the frame. A large column is in the right background about a third of the way from the right edge of the frame. To its right is a full-length window and a curtain. Deeds walks left in front of the column, then moves right, behind it, ending in front of the window at the right edge of the frame. He's backlit and thus nearly dark on the side facing the camera. A butler asks if he should serve the squab, but Deeds, hunched forward, is silent.

4. MS (3.5 sec), SO, same lighting, with Deeds center frame, the column left, the curtain right.

5. MS (5 sec), SO, Cobb, who says, "If I knew you were going to take it so hard, I woulda kept my mouth shut."

6. MLS (8 sec), SO, similar to the framing and lighting in 4, but further away. Deeds looks up toward screen right and says, "Pack my things, Walter; I'm going home." Eyeline match to

7. MS (4 sec), SO, butler Walter, looking somber, says, "Yes, sir," and turns to the right. Wipe to next scene—unemployed farmer breaking into mansion.

This scene begins to establish Deeds's despair for, aside from Cobb and the butlers inside the mansion, who are paid to treat him well, Deeds receives kindness only from Mary. The lighting, framing, and Cooper's acting, along with Deeds's crucial silence, communicate how much he's been hurt by Babe's betrayal. Although the plan to give away the money puts his despair temporarily in abeyance, Deeds is plunged even further into the abyss after he's arrested and taken to the County Hospital to await his insanity hearing.

In a seven-shot scene, Capra portrays his protagonist in the County Hospital, so deeply depressed that he seems almost catatonic. After a shot of the County Hospital sign and two shots of

Babe trying to convince a guard to let her into Deeds's room, Capra presents the two key shots in the scene, both inside that room. The first begins in a long shot across the room. The room is dark, the only illumination coming from a window covered with woven wire. Deeds, thus backlit, sits in profile in front of the window, head leaning forward, silent. As Cobb tries to persuade him to get a lawyer, the camera dollies forward to a medium-long shot, then cuts after about sixteen seconds to a medium shot. In this framing, altered only slightly to reframe as Cobb moves from the left to the right of Deeds, Deeds's figure is outlined by the prison-like window. In a shot of fifty-eight seconds, Deeds remains in the center of the frame, immobile, seemingly oblivious to Cobb's entreaty: "Do you realize what's happening? They're trying to prove that you're nuts. If they win the case, they'll shove you in the bug house. The moment they accused you of it, they had you half-licked. You've gotta fight!" Silhouetted by the light coming through the window, Deeds seems entirely to have given up hope. Capra uses all the elements of cinematic style, particularly the effective use of mise-en-scène and framing, to intensify the hero's despair.

The scene ends with two more shots of Babe and Cobb in the hall outside the room. Babe begs Cobb for a chance to see Deeds and implores him to let her hire a lawyer for Deeds. When Babe says she's been trying to line up support for Deeds, Cobb cuts her off: "You're wasting your time. He doesn't want any lawyer. He's sunk so low he doesn't want help from anybody. You can take a bow for that. As swell a guy as ever hit this town and you crucified him for a couple of stinking headlines. You've done your bit. Now stay out of his way." As Cobb leaves to the left, he swings open a door with the same woven wire as on Deeds' window. It covers the left half of the frame as Babe, in medium close-up, looks concerned and dejected. Images of imprisonment and dejection thus end the scene as Capra dissolves into another documentary montage announcing the insanity hearing. The newspaper headlines read: "Cinderella Man Obstinately Refuses All Attempts at Defense"; "FARMERS AROUSED AT EFFORTS TO BALK THEIR BENEFACTOR"; and "POLICE SURROUND COURTHOUSE / ANTICIPATION OF OUTBREAK." Interspersed are shots of angry farmers and threatening policemen, accompanied by music on the soundtrack that suggests menace and disorder. The mood leading into the final scene is dark and ominous.

The film's conflicts are resolved in the final scene, the insanity hearing, which lasts slightly over twenty-nine minutes. For the first fifteen minutes, Cedar builds the case against Deeds, who, maintaining his silence, is often presented in medium shot or medium close-up, left hand on cheek, jaw resting on palm. Just as the judge is about to issue a decision against Deeds, however, Babe breaks in, declares her love for Deeds, and urges him to testify. Support from Babe's editor, from Cobb, and from the farmers in the gallery immediately follows. Deeds, vivified by both Babe's declaration and the broad support, defends himself (and the farmers' interests), systematically refuting those who testified against him. Emerging from the abyss by defending the need for altruism in times of social crisis, he makes his case convincingly.

4.2. Accused of insanity, Longfellow Deeds (Gary Cooper, center) is on trial in *Mr. Deeds Goes to Town* (1936). Press agent Cornelius Cobb (Lionel Stander) is at left, and Judge Walker (H. B. Warner) is in the right foreground. (Museum of Modern Art/Film Stills Archive)

The judge concludes that Deeds is "not only sane, but the sanest man that ever walked into this courtroom." Carried out of the courtroom by the elated farmers, Deeds returns later to lift Babe into his arms, the united couple embracing and kissing in the film's final shots. Yet it's hard to forget entirely the pain of Deeds's silence during the first half of the courtroom scene or the film's two darkest moments: the fifteen-second take of Deeds immediately after he learns that Mary Dawson is really Babe Bennett and the fifty-eight-second take of Deeds silent and immobile in the County Hospital. The despair resulting from a naive hero's confrontation with human betrayal, duplicity, and greed is powerfully presented.

The Boy Ranger's Despair

Mr. Smith Goes to Washington, which had its New York premiere on 19 October 1939, about seven weeks after World War II broke out, also takes its central character—young Senator Jefferson Smith (James Stewart)—to the abyss. Although the film was scripted by Sidney Buchman instead of Robert Riskin, the outline of its narrative structure is almost identical to that of *Mr. Deeds*.[19] In both films, an honest and relatively inexperienced man is taken from a small-town environment into a more complex world that tests and nearly shatters his world view. Threatened by men of power and wealth, the hero is supported at a crucial moment by the heroine. With her support and that of a benevolent authority figure and a large community of common people, the hero prevails. In contrast to *Deeds*, though, the villain in *Smith* is more focused on a single person, the magnate Jim Taylor (Edward Arnold), a businessman who commands his state's political machine and whose control extends to Joseph Paine (Claude Rains), the state's senior senator and an old friend of Smith's deceased father. The stakes in the film—manipulation of national government policy for private gain—are also larger than those in *Deeds*. And instead of the contrast between the virtuous small town and the corrupt city at the center of *Deeds*, *Smith* simultaneously poses two conflicts: political idealism versus political compromise, embodied in Smith's approach to politics versus Senator Paine's, and capitalist acquisitiveness versus pursuit of the common good, exemplified in Taylor's conflict with Smith. With Capra working at the height of his power, the film develops its conflicts skillfully and leads young Jefferson Smith to a crisis of despair.

That despair is presented most memorably in a scene at one of the film's most important settings, the Lincoln Memorial. Smith, a young patriot and leader of a group called the Boy Rangers, has been named U.S. senator to fill out the term of a man who has died in office. Upon arriving in Washington, he takes a bus tour that culminates at the Lincoln Memorial, which moves him deeply. When he inadvertently learns later of Taylor's corrupt scheme to benefit financially from a land deal buried in an appropriations bill, Smith is framed by Taylor's machine, Paine assisting, and is about to be expelled from the Senate. The evening after the hearing implicating Smith, the young senator, suitcase in hand, makes his last visit to the Lincoln Memorial before leaving town.

That scene presents Smith at his lowest point. It opens with a long shot of a part of the Gettysburg Address that is carved on a wall of the memorial, with the final three lines highlighted by brighter lighting: "and that government of the people, by the people, and for the people shall not perish from the earth." With background music playing, Capra cuts to two shots of Smith looking at the words, then up at Lincoln, followed by a low-angle, subjective long shot of the Lincoln statue gazing down toward Smith.[20] We cut back to a close-up of Smith, who smiles knowingly at his gullibility, after which he picks up his bags. A high-angle, extreme long shot cranes left to follow him as he walks to the left front, throws down his suitcases in a shadowed space to the left of one of the memorial's huge columns, and sits down dejectedly. The melody of "Oh, Bury Me Not on the Lone Prairie" begins to play on the soundtrack, and the rest of the scene takes place in this dark spot, with backlighting illuminating the stone wall behind Smith but keeping his face in low-key lighting. At the end of the long take, Smith puts his hands in his face and begins to cry. Saunders comes up next to the column and joins Smith when he notices her.

More than in either *American Madness* or *Deeds*, the hero's darkest moments—expressed in the next four shots—are conveyed by words as much as by the visual presentation of despair and are accompanied by constant background music. All four shots use the same low-key backlighting described above, as they follow Saunders's ironic observation that Jeff really *did* become a senator.

1. MCU (10 seconds), SO, Smith: "You sure had the right idea about me, Saunders: you told me to go back home and keep filling those kids full of a lot of hooey."

2. MS or slightly longer (53 sec), SO, Smith sitting at left of frame, Saunders on right: "Just a simple guy, you said, still wet behind the ears, lotta junk about American ideals . . . ya, it's certainly a lot of junk, all right." When Saunders tries to interrupt, he goes on: "I don't know; this is a whole new world to me. What are you going to believe in, when a man like Paine, Senator Joseph Paine, gets up and swears I've been robbing kids of nickels and dimes, a man I've admired and worshipped all my life? . . . I don't know. There are a lotta fancy words around this town; some of them are carved in stone. I guess the Taylors and Paines put them up there so suckers like me can read them. Then when you find out what men actually do . . . Well, I'm getting out of this town so fast, away from all the words and the monuments and the whole rotten show."

3. CU (6 sec), SO, Saunders: "I see. And when you get home, what are you going to tell those kids?"

4. MCU (8 sec), SO, Smith: "I'm going to tell them the truth. Might as well find it out right now as later."

Bitter, disillusioned, and aggrieved, Smith seems a destroyed man, resembling George Bailey when he storms out of his house in *It's a Wonderful Life*.

The narrative conflicts leading up to this point make the despair both understandable and profound. We have learned earlier in the film both of Smith's fervent idealism and of his deep respect for Senator Paine. That respect is rooted partly in the fact that Paine had earlier been a close friend of Jeff's father, when they worked together as a young lawyer and a young newspaperman, respectively, in challenging the power of a large mining concern. Together they had struggled in a "lost cause," Jeff's father even losing his life. Yet times have changed and, as the senior senator of

Jeff's state, Paine has long served under the shadow of Taylor's influence. Although he becomes a kind of surrogate father for Smith, Paine's affection for Jeff is undermined by his obligations to Taylor. When Jeff introduces his bill to build a boys' camp on same site as the dam that will enrich Taylor, the crisis hits, and both of the film's central conflicts come together. When Taylor offers to buy Jeff's cooperation in exchange for reelection or some other favor, telling Jeff that Paine has been under his thumb for twenty years, Jeff refuses to believe it and rushes to Paine's office. Paine tells Jeff that he's been living in a boy's world but that this is "a man's world, and you've got to check your ideals at the door." Taking the position that politics in the real world requires compromise, Paine defends his decision to "play ball" with Taylor and warns Smith not to object to the appropriations bill the following day. Yet Jeff rejects Paine's vision of politics as playing ball in favor of his own political idealism, for he believes that his bill supports the public interest while Taylor's dam will lead only to corrupt private gain.

When Smith rises on the floor of the Senate the next day to object to section 40 of the appropriations bill, the wheels of Taylor's machine quickly begin to turn: Paine, acting on Taylor's orders, rises to charge falsely that Smith owns the land on which the camp will be built and will profit if that bill passes. The ensuing scene, which precedes Smith's final visit to the Lincoln Memorial, is a brilliantly directed and cut hearing before the Committee on Privileges and Elections on the charges brought against Smith. In the first twenty-five shots of this forty-six-shot scene, three men charge that Smith owns the land around Willet Creek, and two of three handwriting experts agree that the signature on the land's deed is Smith's, not a forgery. Both Smith's impending disillusionment and Paine's eventual change of heart are set up after Paine takes the stand to accuse Smith. As Capra cuts from medium shots of Paine to long shots of committee members listening and medium close-ups of Smith reacting in astonishment, Paine callously charges that Smith owns the land. Completing his testimony, Paine walks past Smith on the way to his own chair, located right of the door, past several other chairs. Smith's eyes follow Paine as he walks. A brief sequence of shots, lasting only thirty-seven seconds and devoid of any dialogue by either Smith or

Paine, still manages to convey powerfully both Smith's despair and Paine's shame:

36. MLS (2.5 seconds), SO, Smith sits, looking toward Paine sitting down, and leans forward. Committee chair: "Senator Smith, please."
37. MCU (3.5 sec), Paine in profile, same as shot 15, looking down and guilty.
38. MS, (2 sec), SO, chair: "Will you . . . take the chair please?"
39. MS (7.5 sec) SO, Smith stands and moves toward Paine; camera reframes up and dollies right.
40. CU (2 sec), high angle, Paine in profile (Smith's point of view), looking straight forward, unable to meet Smith's eyes.
41. MCU/CU (4.5 sec), SO, Smith nearly gasps in pain, looks toward right when chair says off screen: "The committee is ready to hear you now, Senator Smith." Eyeline match to
42. LS (2 sec), high angle, chair and other senators looking up toward Smith.
43. MCU/CU (2.5 sec), SO, Smith, same as shot 41, turns left and begins to walk away toward door. Match on action to
44. LS (3 sec), SO, Smith walks out door as photographers outside snap flashbulbs. Paine is visible sitting in right foreground.
45. MS (2 sec), SO, reporters in back of committee room stand and make way toward door. Committee chair off screen: "Keep your seats, gentlemen."
46. CU (5 sec), high angle, Paine covers glasses with left hand and leans forward looking ashamed. Committee chair: "The committee is not adjourned yet. Please. Quiet." Wipe to next scene.

Both Smith's perspective and Paine's are important here. Although he's not the protagonist, Paine is framed more tightly than Smith in shots 37, 40, and 46. Significantly, the last two of those shots are from Smith's point of view, and Paine's eyes never meet Smith's, even though Smith looks in despair directly toward Paine in shots 36, 39, and 41. Neither character utters a word, yet Paine's facial expressions and refusal to meet Smith's gaze communicate his shame, while Smith's silence, shock, and refusal to testify indicate how much he has been hurt by Paine's betrayal. In this case expressions speak louder than words. Capra's direction here not only leads Smith to his moments of deepest despair but also motivates Paine's change of heart in the film's conclusion. *Mr. Smith* exhibits classic continuity editing at its highest level, and in some ways it's not surprising that Capra told Joseph McBride in 1984 that *Mr. Smith* was a better film than *It's a Wonderful Life*, the movie he regularly told interviewers and audiences was his favorite.[21]

Thus Smith is taken to the abyss. Yet at the Lincoln Memorial, following the four shots discussed above, Saunders convinces Smith to stay and fight by telling Smith that Lincoln had his Taylors and Paines, too, but refused to give in. In a scene parallel to the insanity hearing in *Deeds*, *Smith* concludes with Smith's filibuster, which he hopes will buy him the time to communicate with and win support from his state. Unlike Deeds, Smith speaks

4.3. Under duress, James Stewart as Jefferson Smith in *Mr. Smith Goes to Washington* (1939). (Museum of Modern Art/Film Stills Archive)

throughout the whole scene, but it begins to appear that Taylor's control of the newspapers and radio stations in his state makes Jeff's cause a lost one. The film is resolved only when Paine, watching Smith suffer in the second day of his filibuster and unable to bear his guilt any longer, rushes out of the Senate chamber, tries unsuccessfully to shoot himself, and then confesses Smith's innocence and his own guilt. The film ends with cheering in the Senate chamber, although the resolution may seem more tenuous than in either *American Madness* or *Deeds*, depending as it does on Paine's change of heart. Capra is careful to motivate Paine's actions, in both the hearing scene and others, as Smith's honesty and integrity affect him in much the same way as Deeds's goodness affects Babe Bennett and Corny Cobb in *Deeds*.

D riven to despair by both private and public disappointments, Capra's heroes are all retrieved from that despair when others provide support and encouragement at crucial moments. As I hope I have illustrated, the moments of despair in all three films are powerfully portrayed through effective depictions of narrative conflict and uses of cinematic style.

Private Interest and the Public Good in American Culture

These powerful representations of the abyss are related not only to the skillful manipulation of film form but also to the relationship between the representations and the culture in which the stories were produced and consumed. Cultural studies propose that movies provide one way for members of society to grapple with prevailing cultural tensions, and that is particularly true in these three films. The conflicts and anxieties leading to the abyss in these Capra films are rooted in a fundamental tension in American middle-class ideology, grounded in the American past. The tension was particularly wrenching during the Depression era, and Frank Capra, as a citizen who grew to adulthood in American culture, wrestled with it in his own personal experience. The tension, a key in helping to understand the abysses in and the appeal of Capra's films during the Depression era, concerns the conflict between private interest and the public good.

Many analysts of American society from the nineteenth century on have noted the polarities in American middle-class ideology between individualist and community values. One recent formulation, Robert McClosky and John Zaller's *The American Ethos*, helps us understand the cultural roots of despair in Capra films. Drawing on extensive surveys of American political attitudes and concerned with defining persistent values in American ideology, the authors argue that two dominant traditions of belief, which they label *capitalism* and *democracy*, have defined American political life since the establishment of nationhood in the eighteenth century and continue to shape it today. By *capitalism* the authors have in mind a set of beliefs and practices: private property, entrepreneurial pursuit of profit, and the right of unlimited material acquisition through economic activity. By *democracy* they refer to several principles and the actions that flow from them: that all people have equal worth and the right to select their leaders; that people deserve to be protected from arbitrary state authority; that freedom of speech, worship, assembly, and the press should be granted to everyone; and that all citizens are equal before the law and should enjoy both equal rights and equal opportunities.[22]

Anchored in part in the contrary pulls of libertarianism and egalitarianism embedded in the nation's founding, the traditions of capitalism and democracy share some values, although sometimes manifested in different ways. For example, both value freedom of exchange (of markets in the case of capitalism, of ideas in the case of democracy). Both resist impositions from above (capitalism, on what to produce or purchase; democracy, on what to think, read, or advocate). Both basically accept the concept of private property.[23]

Yet these two traditions have often clashed. The rapid industrialization of the United States in the late nineteenth century, which enabled some individuals and groups to amass enormous fortunes while others experienced poverty and powerlessness, exacerbated the tensions between capitalism and democracy. Defenders of the capitalist tradition during the Gilded Age justified this acquisition and concentration of wealth through the ideology of rugged individualism, which held that the greatest good would be served through laissez-faire economics: competition, however ruthless, would enable the fittest to survive and in the long run generate the most positive social benefits. Other citizens argued, however, that this concentration of wealth in the hands of the few violated the very spirit of democracy, for it gave the wealthy few a dispro-portionate influence on the political process and social polity. McClosky and Zeller observe that, "while democracy asserts the right of the people to rule, capitalism in effect limits this right by removing economic affairs from popular control." They add that, although tensions between the traditions may have abated some-what since the late nineteenth century, partly because of ex-pansion of the welfare state, they persist in part because "of the tendency for the material inequalities of capitalist society to un-dermine the democratic goals of equal opportunity."[24]

One strong impulse for reform during the Progressive Era came from those who sought to counter the untrammeled pursuit of economic self-interest with a concern for the public good and pro-tection of the victims of industrial capitalism. In fact, some Amer-ican historians have argued that the political and cultural climate in twentieth-century America has alternated between periods dominated by the reformist impulses of the democratic tradi-tion—the Progressive Era, the 1930s, and the 1960s—and peri-ods of reaction in which capitalism and the pursuit of self-interest have dominated—the 1920s, 1950s, and 1980s.[25]

In the 1930s Capra and the reputation of his films reached their zenith, while economic collapse led many Americans to criticize the abuses of the capitalist tradition from a democratic perspec-tive. In 1936, the year of *Mr. Deeds*, President Franklin D. Roo-sevelt issued just such a critique in his renomination acceptance speech in Philadelphia. Noting that in 1776 the American cause of freedom was hindered by eighteenth-century royalists, Roo-sevelt argued that in his day freedom was challenged by "eco-nomic royalists" who controlled the hours people worked, the wages they earned, and the conditions they experienced. "The royalists of the economic order have conceded that political free-dom was the business of the Government," Roosevelt contended, "but they have maintained that economic slavery was nobody's business." Some of his New Deal legislation established govern-ment intervention aimed at returning some basic economic rights to vulnerable citizens. The country, he argued, was fighting "a war against want and destitution and economic demoralization" that was also "a war for the survival of democracy."[26] The success of Roosevelt's appeal in that year is measured by his landslide victory over Alf Landon in the November election.

My contention here is that the abyss into which the Capra heroes fall in these three films can be understood in part as a despair resulting from the fear that democratic impulses, particularly pursuit of the common good, would be crushed in the Depression by the powerful forces of self-interest. The central narrative conflicts in each film emerge when the Capra hero, an advocate of what McClosky and Zaller term the *democratic tradition*, comes into conflict with a person or people who are animated by a concern for self-interest and private gain. In *American Madness* Tom Dickson shows consistent concern for the general welfare of two groups: his employees and those who do business at his bank (both the depositors and the borrowers). His speech to the board of directors, quoted above, shows that his concern extends to American society at large, for he believes that, if the wealthy would stop hoarding their money and start circulating it through investment, society at large would benefit.[27] When the bank robbery occurs, Dickson is even willing to put all his money into the bank to stave off the bank run. Yet the self-interested board of directors refuse when he proposes that they follow his lead. When panicked depositors, fearful of losing their money, rush in to withdraw their savings, Dickson himself fears that his faith in other human beings has been misplaced. This begins his slide to the abyss.

In *Mr. Deeds Goes to Town*, the same confrontation between concern for the common good and individual self-interest occurs. From the moment he inherits the Semple fortune, Deeds is unimpressed with the money; he quickly determines that he wants to put it to good use. Yet a number of people dominated by self-interest, particularly Cedar and the Semples, actively seek to gain control of the fortune for themselves. After the unemployed man breaks into Deed's mansion and excoriates him, Deeds commits to his good cause: giving away small farms to the struggling unemployed so they can survive the Depression. In the courtroom he uses two metaphors that define his concern for the common good. In the first, he likens his actions to a man whose car easily reaches the top of a hill while others can't make it, arguing that it's his responsibility to help those who can't reach the top of the hill. In the second he rhetorically asks if a lifeguard should throw a line to a drowning swimmer or someone in a rowboat who's just tired of rowing. Deeds's conception of the common good clearly animates his behavior, and he reaches his deepest despair when it seems to him that the system is too skewed in favor of the capitalist tradition to permit him to help others. His arrest in the mansion and incarceration in the County Hospital under charges of insanity create the conditions for his deepest despair.

Finally, *Mr. Smith* contains perhaps Capra's purest encounter between the capitalist and democratic traditions in the confrontation between Jim Taylor and Jefferson Smith. More overtly than Tom Dickson or Longfellow Deeds, Jefferson Smith identifies himself and his political beliefs with the American democratic tradition, particularly with Abraham Lincoln and the words of the Gettysburg Address.[28] Portrayed as a committed idealist who is still, in Saunders's words, "wet behind the ears," Smith exhibits devotion to the democratic tradition combined with naivete about the potential political influence of concentrated wealth. His plan to build a boys' camp that will help teach youngsters about American political ideals emerges from his conception of the common good, and his despair becomes most profound when that conception of the common good runs into Taylor's power like an egg crushed on a brick wall. The extent to which Taylor will exert force to protect his interests is shown not only by the orchestrated frame-up against Smith in the hearing but also after Smith, at Saunders's urging, decides to filibuster and take his case to the people. Taylor's control of the primary newspapers and radio stations in his state, as well as the willingness of his subordinates to use brute force to suppress political debate, disconcertingly depicts how the capitalist system, misused, can flout the values and practices associated with the democratic tradition. Ultimately, Smith can only counter that power in his filibuster through moral suasion, quoting the Bill of Rights and 1 Corinthians 13, urging his colleagues to stop Taylor's abuse of power.[29] Earlier, however, at the steps of the Lincoln Memorial, he can't even do that: at the abyss, convinced that his ideals are nothing but "junk," he just wants to get "away from all the words and the monuments and the whole rotten show." All three of these Capra films derive much of their power from the effective depiction of the tension between the democratic and the capitalist traditions so deeply rooted in the American experience. Their heroes fear that their efforts on behalf of the common good will be subdued by the powerful forces of private interest. Theirs was a widely shared American nightmare of the 1930s.

Capra and American Cultural Conflicts

America's nightmare was also, to some extent, Capra's. The depictions of the abyss so powerful in these three films were directed by a filmmaker who had his own demons. Although those demons may not be so evident in *The Name above the Title*, McBride's biography offers ample evidence of Capra's conflicts. Immigrating with his family to the United States from Sicily in 1903 at the age of six, Capra went from humble beginnings to the heights of prominence by the middle 1930s, and McBride, drawing on extensive interviews with Capra and those who knew him well, portrays a man whose "basic self-doubt was multiplied by his anxiety over the fact that he had to share his success with someone else." McBride even suggests that Capra may well have wrestled with what psychologists call "the impostor phenomenon": a "fear common to many high achievers that their success is actually based on a fraud." [30]

The darkness and self-doubt that McBride perceives in Capra's life are connected in part to the tension that many middle-class Americans experience between the conflicting dictates of the capitalist and democratic traditions. On the one hand, Capra possessed a burning ambition to succeed. Even granting that he carefully presents his life in *The Name above the Title* as a success story, it remains significant that Capra's first paragraph includes these sentences—"I hated being poor. Hated being a peasant. I wanted out. A quick out"—and that his first eight chapters are grouped under the heading, "Struggle for Success." [31] The craving to make something of himself clearly drove Capra.

However, Capra also had strong ties to family and to the ideal of democratic community in America. His marriage to Lucille Reyburn Capra lasted over fifty years, until her death in 1984, and McBride, quoting director John Huston's comment that Capra was "the most devoted husband I've ever known," notes that "the

Capras were one of the rare married couples in Hollywood about whom there never was any scandal."[32] And Capra's commitment to a conception of the common good can be linked, in part, to his roots in Italian and Italian-American Catholic culture. One critic has even suggested that the affirmations of family and community in Capra's films relate to a social ethic rooted in Italian Catholic culture and opposed to the unchecked pursuit of individual material gain.[33]

Capra's autobiography suggests that the tension between these two traditions—community and individualist, democratic and capitalist—was endemic to his upbringing: "I was born into a family that worshipped, first the Crucifix, and second, a coffee can stuffed with cash, preferably gold. God was our faith, but cash was our security." McBride's biography offers additional evidence of tensions and contradictions within Capra that help us understand the moments of abyss in his films. One of the threads running throughout McBride's book is Capra's frustration at never being fully able to please his mother. A strong and independent woman who helped keep the family together after they arrived in the United States, Rosaria Nicolosa Capra seemed never to have given her most famous son full approval. A telling anecdote is McBride's story that, after the proud Capra took his mother to the first studio screening of *Mr. Smith Goes to Washington*, he asked her what she thought, to which she replied, "Well, Frankie, when are you gonna get a job?"[34] Capra's desire to please his mother and her unwillingness to give him her full approval provide one reason for his burning ambition to succeed.

On the other hand, Capra's autobiographical accounts of his physical and psychological crisis after the success of *It Happened One Night* and of his "conversion" to committed filmmaking just before *Mr. Deeds* offer the most vivid example of how he was drawn, during the 1930s at least, to the democratic tradition. Although the story Capra tells in his autobiography about the little man berating him for his irresponsibility and egotism may be fictional, it does capture how a filmmaker who had earlier boasted that he could make a commercial film using the phone book as a script had come to view his vocation differently.[35] The combined influences of an Italian-Catholic upbringing, a physical and psychological crisis, and the democratic ethos of New Deal America led Capra toward a firmer conception of the common good.[36] And that conception at times waged war with Capra's own personal ambitions.

By the 1930s Capra had experienced both accomplishment and deep disappointment as he wrestled with the conflicting demands of achievement and commitment to others. He earned a bachelor of science degree in the face of financial and familial pressures that discouraged it, but Capra could not find work in that field following his discharge from the army after World War I. He made his way into the movies and worked his way up until he was directing successful Harry Langdon comic features during the middle 1920s, but he was unceremoniously fired by Langdon before the first preview for *Long Pants* and then had difficulty finding any work in his chosen career. Less than two months later, his deteriorating first marriage to Helen Howell Capra ended in divorce. McBride suggests that, in his acrimony toward her, Capra "may have transferred some of his feelings of helpless rage toward the other person he felt had betrayed him, Harry Langdon."[37] Capra's failed ambition seems closely tied to his personal problems here, just as the hero's deepest moments of abyss in the three films discussed in this chapter are fueled by the betrayal or suspected betrayal of a wife, a romantic partner, and a respected, even revered, surrogate father.

During the 1930s, as he was making the films discussed here, Capra's experience intensified his uncertainties and conflicts. The emptiness and fear actually grew after he scaled the heights of success and acclaim, winning the Oscar for best director for *It Happened One Night*. The fame and wealth that seemed assured after the Academy Awards ceremony in 1935 were accompanied by self-doubt, illness, and inactivity. Even with the successful "committed" films following the crisis—*Deeds*, *Lost Horizon* (1937), and *You Can't Take It with You* (1938)—Capra found that he was not insulated from pain. Capra was called away during the second reel of a successful press screening for *You Can't Take It with You* to learn that his son John, who had undergone a "routine tonsillectomy" that morning, had suddenly stopped breathing and died.[38] Success was undercut by human mortality.

Thus, despite the sunny and energetic portrait of a self-made man that emerges from his autobiography, Capra was a man who struggled with living, even during his period of greatest success. Chet Sticht, Capra's personal secretary for thirty-nine years, told McBride that Capra was a "complicated" man: "He was a brilliant guy in many ways, and yet subject to depressions. Being somewhat of an idealist, he may not have had enough faith in himself." [39] In this essay I have argued that we should not be blinded to this darker side of Frank Capra or of his films. Although the endings of Capra's films might lead us to believe that he was driven by a "fantasy of goodwill," the moments of abyss in his movies—not only in *Meet John Doe* and *It's a Wonderful Life*, but also in earlier Columbia films like *American Madness*, *Mr. Deeds Goes to Town*, and *Mr. Smith Goes to Washington*—should remind us that Capra was not as simple, optimistic, and uncomplicated as some suppose. These moments of abyss, so vividly and powerfully expressed, urge us to link these films and their filmmaker to the broader culture. The enduring tension in much American middle-class life between capitalism and democracy, self-interest and the common good, is dramatized continually in the films of Frank Capra. In the moments of abyss outlined here, we witness some of the most disturbing of our collective American nightmares.

Notes

1. William Pechter, "*American Madness*," in *Frank Capra: The Man and His Films*, ed. Richard Glatzer and John Raeburn (Ann Arbor: Univ. of Michigan Press, 1975), 182.

2. Richard Griffith and Paul Rotha, *The Film till Now: A Survey of World Cinema*, 2d ed. (London: Vision Press, 1949), 450.

3. Frank Capra, *The Name above the Title* (New York: Macmillan, 1971).

4. Charles Wolfe's excellent guide to Capra, *Frank Capra: A Guide to References and Resources* (Boston: G.K. Hall, 1987), contains hundreds of references to sources that take this optimistic view of Capra and his films, particularly after 1938, the year in which Capra's picture adorned the cover of *Time* magazine. Although some other critics note a dark side in Capra's life and movies, a browse through Wolfe's book shows that they are in a minority.

5. Joseph McBride, *Frank Capra: The Catastrophe of Success* (New York: Simon & Schuster, 1992); Thomas Schatz, *Hollywood Genres: Formulas, Filmmaking, and the Studio System* (New York: Random House, 1981), 35. Jackie Byars, in her insightful analysis of 1950s Hollywood melodrama, *All That Hollywood Allows: Re-reading Gender in 1950s Melodrama* (Chapel Hill: Univ. of North Carolina

Press, 1991), supports Schatz's view. She writes that improbable happy endings "call attention to the unsatisfactory nature of the dominant ideology's social 'solutions.' They highlight ideological contradictions, exhibiting and participating in constant renegotiation. The rhetoric of narrative resolution expresses both the dominant ideology and the contradictions that produce narrative conflicts" (131). One might add that, even if the happy endings are not improbable, the conflicts that lead to the resolutions point toward contradictions and tensions that are a fundamental part of social life. Cultural studies encourage us to look closely at narrative conflicts, not just narrative resolutions, because indicators of the culture's conflicts are more likely to reside there.

6. It may sound perverse, if not masochistic, to suggest that moments of despair or bleakness are a source of a film's appeal, but I believe that to be the case. Marcia Landy, in discussing the appeal of genre films, argues that popular films connect with audiences not just "in the interest of conformity" to society but also "as challenges to it." Movies thus create pleasures for the viewer stemming from "the validation of desires and the constraints placed on their realization." Landy, *British Genres: Cinema and Society, 1930–1960* (Princeton, N.J.: Princeton Univ. Press, 1991), 7, 8. We may find pleasure in the gratifying resolutions of movie plots, but we also derive satisfaction, I believe, from engaging imaginatively in the fictional depiction of conflicts and constraints that are connected to the real conflicts and constraints we experience in social life.

7. See Charles Maland, "Necessity and Invention: Frank Capra at Columbia," in *Columbia Pictures: Portrait of a Studio*, ed. Bernard F. Dick (Lexington: Univ. of Kentucky Press, 1992), 70–88.

8. For movie budgets see McBride, *Frank Capra*, 304, 346, 426. On the grosses of *Mr. Deeds*, see Frank Capra Archive, Wesleyan Cinema Archives, Wesleyan University, Middletown, Conn., box 3, folder 3. In early 1933, a *Variety* article noted that the average production cost of a Columbia feature was $175,000, the least of the major eight studios (3 January 1933, 4). *Variety* figures also indicate that *Mr. Smith* grossed more than that in its first two weeks in *one* theater alone, Radio City Music Hall—$199,000 (8 November 1939, 7). The difference indicates not only how much Capra's name had become a draw by the late 1930s but also how much more firmly established Columbia was as a studio by that time.

9. Leland Poague has also recently argued that *American Madness* contains important similarities to *Mr. Deeds*, emphasizing in particular how the portrayals of women in the run on the bank complicate any "simplistically populist reading" (111) of the film. See *Another Frank Capra* (Cambridge, England: Cambridge Univ. Press, 1994), 109–13.

10. Tino Balio notes that the social problem film and the screwball comedy were two popular genres among class-A features in the 1930s. See the chapter "Production Trends" in his *Grand Design: Hollywood as a Modern Business Enterprise*, vol. 5 of *History of the American Cinema* (New York: Scribner's, 1993), 268–98. Capra's blend, occasionally evident in films by other directors such as *My Man Godfrey* (Gregory LaCava, 1936), nevertheless became identified closely enough with Capra that Preston Sturges would satirize the type (and even mention Capra specifically in the dialogue) in *Sullivan's Travels* (1942).

11. Abel Green, "Review," *Variety*, 9 August 1932, 17.

12. McBride suggests that Thomas Dickson is probably modeled in part on A. H. and A. P. Giannini, brothers who were instrumental in founding the Bank of Italy and, in 1928, the Bank of America. Both followed Dickson's policy of lending to borrowers based on character, and Riskin reportedly visited A. H. Giannini when he was assigned to write the screenplay. Capra, on the other hand, claimed that A. P. Giannini was the model for Dickson. Because Columbia depended on the Bank of America for loans, *American Madness* can be looked at as part of what McBride calls "an attempt to propagandize for the liberal lending policies the Gianninis stood for and to help ensure that their bank would survive and maintain its character." McBride, *Frank Capra*, 249. See also Edward Buscombe, "Notes on Columbia Pictures Corporation 1926–1941," *Screen* 16, no. 3 (1975): 65–82, reprinted as chapter 9 of this book, for a discussion of the relationship between Columbia and the Bank of America, and John Raeburn's "*American Madness* and American Values," in Glatzer and Raeburn, *Frank Capra*, 57–67, which, like this essay, emphasizes the tensions in Capra's films and resists Griffith's formulation of Capra as a fantasist of goodwill.

13. The following abbreviations are used in shot analyses: ELS, extreme long shot; LS, long shot; MLS, medium long shot; MS, medium shot; MCU, medium close-up; CU, close-up; SO, straight on camera angle.

14. Raymond Carney writes perceptively of Walter Huston's performance in the film, particularly Huston's ability to "switch tones and styles" as he interacts with different people. Carney suggests that Huston's performance style depicts Dickson's capacity "to navigate through this institutional tangle of friendships, hierarchies, priorities, and employer-employee relationships and to do it all so masterfully." See *American Visions: The Films of Frank Capra* (Cambridge, England: Cambridge Univ. Press, 1986), 124, 127–28.

15. McBride, *Frank Capra*, 248. Riskin is clearly important in helping to define the concerns and issues in *American Madness*. This was the first time Capra directed a script for which Riskin received sole credit (he had shared credit with two others on *Platinum Blonde*), and Capra's sound mixer remembers that Capra was brought onto the film after four days of shooting, when Allen Dwan was replaced. Even though Capra started anew, his role in the original conception of the film is clearly less central than it was in either *Mr. Deeds* or *Mr. Smith*, and McBride uses *American Madness* as an example of Capra's refusal to give credit where credit was due (McBride, 247–63). Riskin was clearly important to Capra's career and, when one discusses films as the expression of the director, one must simultaneously acknowledge that film is a collaborative art form in which the director draws from many others in shaping the film's final form. Yet I also believe that McBride, striving to establish Capra's egotism, at times tries too hard to elevate the screenwriter's role in Capra's films. The fact that McBride also sometimes reads Capra's films as an expression of the director's inner conflicts reveals unresolved tensions in the biography itself.

16. This detail calls to mind Cotton Mather's account of the Puritan John Winthrop, who, when he learned that someone was stealing from his woodpile, decided to give the man wood to keep him from becoming a thief. Winthrop reasoned that, because he had more wood than he needed and the thief had none, the

contribution could make an honest man of the thief without unduly injuring himself. Mather's account, from *Magnalia Christi Americana*, is reprinted in the appendix of Sacvan Berkovitch, *The Puritan Origins of the American Self* (New Haven, Conn.: Yale Univ. Press, 1975), 192–93.

17. In *Narration in the Fiction Film* (Madison: Univ. of Wisconsin Press, 1985), David Bordwell argues that classical Hollywood narrative usually "presents a double causal structure, two plot lines: one involving heterosexual romance (boy/girl, husband/wife), the other involving another sphere—work, war, a mission or quest, other personal relationships" (157). *American Madness* actually contains both kinds of heterosexual relationships (Matt and Helen, the Dicksons), as well as Dickson's struggles in the world of work deriving from the economic downturn and the bank robbery.

18. William Leuchtenberg, *Franklin D. Roosevelt and the New Deal* (New York: Harper & Row, 1963), 162–66. *It Happened One Night* not only did exceptionally well at the box office for a Columbia film (it was the fifth-highest-grossing film of 1934, even though Columbia owned no theaters, as the big five studios did [see *Daily Variety*, 1 January 1935, 36]), but the film also was the first in Hollywood history to win the five major Oscars, for best film, direction, adapted screenplay, actor, and actress. Schatz, *Hollywood Genres*, 150–85.

19. For a more detailed comparison, see Charles J. Maland, *American Visions: The Films of Chaplin, Ford, Capra and Welles, 1936–1941* (New York: Arno, 1977), 256. Although Capra and Buchman borrowed the narrative structure from earlier Capra-Riskin collaborations, the overtly political rhetoric in *Mr. Smith* differs significantly from the urban vernacular so central to many of the Riskin-scripted films and is clearly related to the different screenwriter.

20. *Mr. Smith*, scored by Dimitri Tiomkin, contains much more background music than the other two films, which underscores how much more important the musical track became in emphasizing the mood of Hollywood films as the decade wore on. Tiomkin has written that film music is unobtrusive, "for being so is the primary characteristic of any movie score that is good. But screen music is now so artfully and effectively integrated with the script, direction, and the actors themselves, that it has come to be one of the means of storytelling" (quoted in Tony Thomas, *Film Score: The Art and Craft of Movie Music* [Burbank, Calif.: Riverwood Press, 1991], 123). Tiomkin scored all of Capra's features from *Lost Horizon* to *It's a Wonderful Life*, except *Arsenic and Old Lace*. He also served as musical director on the Why We Fight series. Particularly in the documentary montages of *Mr. Smith*, music provides the glue that holds together the rapidly changing images. On the function of film music in 1930s Hollywood, see David Bordwell and Kristin Thompson, "Technological Change and Classical Film Style," in Balio, *Grand Design*, esp. 115–16, 125.

21. McBride, *Frank Capra*, 413.

22. Robert McClosky and John Zaller, *The American Ethos* (Cambridge: Harvard Univ. Press, 1985), 2–3, 318, 320. Among many other works that discuss American culture as torn between individualist and community traditions, see Robert Bellah, Richard Madsen, William M. Sullivan, Ann Swidler, and Steven M. Tipton, *Habits of the Heart* (Berkeley and Los Angeles: Univ. of California Press,

1985); Michael Kammen, *People of Paradox* (New York: Knopf, 1972); and, in film studies, Robert Ray, *A Certain Tendency of the Hollywood Cinema, 1930–1980* (Princeton, N.J.: Princeton Univ. Press, 1985).

23. McClosky and Zaller, *American Ethos*, 163–67.

24. Ibid., 169, 171.

25. See Arthur Schlesinger, Jr., "The Cycles of American Politics," in *The Cycles of American History* (Boston: Houghton Mifflin, 1986), esp. 31–34.

26. Franklin D. Roosevelt, "Acceptance of the Renomination for the Presidency," in *The Public Papers and Addresses of Franklin D. Roosevelt* (New York: Random House, 1938), 233, 236.

27. By making this argument, Dickson resembles those wealthy Americans who did come to support Roosevelt in the 1930s. In his 1936 renomination speech, cited above, FDR distinguishes between the greedy and powerful "economic royalists" and what he calls "honest and progressive-minded men of wealth, aware of their obligations to their generation" (232).

28. However, both Dickson and Deeds also identify themselves with American political and cultural traditions: in his battles with the board of directors, Dickson cites Alexander Hamilton, and Deeds rhapsodizes about equal opportunity in America as he stands before Grant's Tomb. Deeds also alludes to Thoreau's observation that creating good people is more important than constructing big buildings. Raymond Carney, in particular, has explored the connections between Capra's films and the American romantics of the middle nineteenth century (in *American Visions*).

29. By urging others to exhibit and practice basic human charity, both Deeds and Smith use rhetoric that resembles Roosevelt's in the same era. In the speech cited above, FDR urges his audience to practice "faith, hope, and charity" and to see them not as "'unattainable ideals' but as stout supports of a Nation fighting the fight for freedom in a modern civilization" (235). Both the film and Roosevelt's acceptance speech provide good examples of what commentators have called American *civil religion*.

30. McBride, *Frank Capra*, 312.

31. Capra, *Name above the Title*, xi.

32. McBride, *Frank Capra*, 266.

33. See Lee Lourdeaux, *Italian and Irish Filmmakers in America: Ford, Capra, Coppola, and Scorsese* (Philadelphia: Temple Univ. Press, 1990). Comparing Capra's work to John Ford's, Lourdeaux writes: "As for a resemblance to Ford's work, Capra's films often relied on communal values and family scenes. But whereas Ford wrestled with age-old Irish conflicts or their multiethnic equivalents in America, Capra asserted positive Italian virtues to revitalize Anglo America; his big mild-mannered men, typified by James Stewart and Gary Cooper, encourage a subtly Italian familial vision based on immediate compassion and a long-suffering nature" (130).

34. Capra, *Name above the Title*, 112; McBride, *Frank Capra*, 270.

35. Capra, *Name above the Title*, 172–82. McBride, *Frank Capra*, 317–26, fills out the story of Capra's illness, suggesting that most of the story about the little man berating Capra about his irresponsibility is fiction, but adding that Capra *was* gravely ill after two operations in late 1934 and then fell ill enough in

March 1935 to be forced home from work into April. McBride also suggests that Capra, because of the illnesses following his almost undreamed-of success, "was engaged in a desperate search for a social message big enough to justify, to himself and to the world, his new status as something more than a mere commercial director" (322). The story of the little man, if nothing else, serves as a dramatization in the autobiography of Capra's search.

36. McBride suggests that screenwriters like Riskin and Sidney Buchman helped push Capra toward a more liberal perspective. He also argues, however, that Capra became more connected with audiences as he understood the Depression better and that his active involvement in Directors Guild politics contributed to making him "more open to progressive ideas than at any other time in his life" in the later 1930s. McBride, *Frank Capra*, 411.

37. McBride, *Frank Capra*, 170–71.

38. McBride, *Frank Capra*, 395–96; Capra, *Name above the Title*, 242.

39. McBride, *Frank Capra*, 321.

5

It Happened One Night:
The Recreation of the Patriarch

Richard Maltby

Standards of Entertainment

The total mythos of comedy, only a small part of which is ordinarily presented, has regularly what in music is called a ternary form: the hero's society rebels against the society of the *senex* and triumphs, but the hero's society is a Saturnalia, a reversal of social standards which recalls a golden age in the past before the main action of the play begins. Thus we have a stable and harmonious order disrupted by folly, obsession, forgetfulness, "pride and prejudice," or events not fully understood by the characters themselves, and then restored. Often there is a benevolent grandfather, so to speak, who overrules the action set up by the blocking humor and so links the first and third parts.[1]

On 10 February 1930, the Association of Motion Picture Producers debated the adoption of an internal system of film censorship. They had before them two documents. One, written by Irving Thalberg, supplied the basic list of prohibitions and restrictions that were included in the code they adopted on 17 February 1930.[2] Thalberg expressed the common attitude among producers that "there is a very general tendency to overemphasize the moral and educational influence of the motion pictures . . . The motion picture does not present the audience with tastes and manners and views and morals; it reflects those they already have . . . The motion picture is literally bound to the mental and moral level of its vast audience." His argument, however, omitted any justification of censorship beyond the merely pragmatic response to the activities of existing state censor boards and what Thalberg called "recognized social improvement groups." [3]

The other document discussed by the Association of Motion Picture Producers was written by Father Daniel A. Lord, S.J., editor of *The Queen's Work* and the leading figure in the revival of the Catholic Sodality youth movement. It provided a rationale for proscription that, in broad outline, expressed the concerns of the various religious, educational, and civic groups anxious for reform of the movies.[4] Although Father Lord left the meeting confident that his code had been accepted by the producers, the arguments he offered in favor of the regulation of entertainment were not included in the code published by the Motion Picture Producers and Distributors of America, Inc. (MPPDA) on 31 March 1930.[5]

Lord and Thalberg disagreed over the necessity for censorship and over its severity, but perhaps most fundamentally they disagreed over its justification. Thalberg was a leading proponent of the position that the film industry should be regarded as comparable to the press and preferably be given the protection of the First Amendment. In his document he asserted that

> the commercial picture can only be regarded as entertainment. It cannot be considered as education or as a sermon or even indirectly as an essentially moral or immoral force. It should be kept in mind that there is a vast populace whose taste is pleased only by entertainment of a very simple and vigorous sort. If not satisfied by motion picture entertainment, this audience will seek other sources. In its endeavor to produce higher grade entertainment the industry must take care not to lose this tremendous audience.[6]

Lord, on the other hand, offered a much more instrumentalist view of culture, which emphasized the industry's responsibility for the moral correctness of the entertainment produced: "The moral importance of entertainment is something which has been universally recognized. It enters intimately into the lives of men and women and affects them closely; it occupies their minds and affections during leisure hours; and ultimately touches the whole of their lives. A man may be judged by his standard of entertainment as easily as by the standard of his work."[7]

In the spring and early summer of 1934, the MPPDA's much-publicized negotiations with the Catholic Church hierarchy produced one significant alteration to the text of the code: the inclusion of much of the Lord document within it, as the "Reasons Supporting the Code."[8] This amounted to a concession on the part of the producers to the definition of the movies' cultural function propounded by their critics. Although Lord's notion of "correct entertainment" as that "which tends to improve the race, or at least to recreate and rebuild human beings exhausted with the realities of life," undoubtedly fitted into a Catholic tradition, it was also the common assumption of all the groups concerned with reforming the movies in the early 1930s. In practice, the censorship activities of the Studio Relations Committee (SRC), precursor to the Production Code Administration, had since 1930 operated under the constraints of this instrumentalist definition, if only on the pragmatic grounds that the industry had to defend itself on its opponents' terms. The most commonly identified "Menace of the Movies" was that, as Fred Eastman put it, "they are educating millions of young people daily in false standards of taste and conduct, false conceptions of human relationships."[9] The Payne Fund Studies and other media research in the early 1930s were primarily concerned with the effects of movies on juvenile attitudes to legal and familial authority.[10] In his discussions with the Association of Motion Picture Producers, Father Lord had enlarged on his definition of *recreation* to describe it as "the period in which a man rebuilds himself after his work . . . during which he gets the chance to rebuild himself physically . . . morally, spiritually, and intellectually."[11] The proper purpose of recreation, then, according to Father Lord, was the reconstruction of the male self.

Columbia and the Code

With the completion of their distribution network, Columbia Pictures joined the MPPDA in November 1930, the last of the major studios to do so. They had, however, been cooperating with the Production Code before that, and the company was not noticeably troublesome to the Studio Relations Committee.[12] The only Columbia picture to cause the industry serious difficulty in the early 1930s was *So This Is Africa*, a Wheeler-Woolsey comedy produced in late 1932, one of several instances during the 1932–33 production season in which the SRC miscalculated the extent to which state censor boards were becoming increasingly illiberal in their decisions. Accepted by the SRC in December 1932, it was rejected both by the New York Censor Board and, unusually, by the National Board of Review because of the vulgarity of its comedy sex situations. In working with the New York office of the MPPDA to produce a version of the film that was satisfactory for general release, Columbia was certainly much more cooperative than Howard Hughes was proving to be over the development of an acceptable version of *Scarface*.[13]

Columbia's generally cooperative attitude toward the SRC may well be explained by Harry Cohn's desire for a status comparable with that of the major studios.[14] Given that desire, Cohn would hardly be likely deliberately to pursue a policy of antagonistic relations with the MPPDA, an organization that was at the same time the majors' "club" and an extremely powerful force within the industry. Moreover, Columbia's distribution pattern relied heavily on playing to the lower-run theaters in neighborhood, small-town, and rural venues, whose management and clientele were unenthusiastic about the "sophisticated" and explicit movies that caused the SRC most concern. Columbia's distribution policy meant that it had a much less strong interest in making such pictures than, say, MGM or Warner Bros. As a result, the overall content of Columbia's films provided few occasions for the studio to choose to be uncooperative.

Even in those instances (including several directed by Capra) where Columbia's films might cause problems, the studio seems to have adopted a general policy of playing safe. Although *Platinum Blonde* was released in November 1931 without the final print having been seen by the SRC, the film was discreet enough to be granted a Production Code Administration Seal for reissue in August 1935, at a time of much more restrictive internal censorship, when several of Jean Harlow's later MGM films were being firmly refused certificates for re-release.[15] Typically for Columbia's output during this period, *Platinum Blonde* borrowed its inspiration from other films. Its title came from the advertising campaign used for Harlow's first appearance in Howard Hughes's *Hell's Angels* (1930), and its representation of the newspaper office had its source in Hughes's version of *The Front Page* (1931). But Capra's film took neither the risks of *Hell's Angels* in Harlow's décolletage (she is fully covered and fairly firmly holstered throughout), nor those of *The Front Page*'s suggestiveness and vulgarity in dialogue.

An MPPDA document detailing the Production Code's first year of operation cited the SRC's work on Capra's *The Miracle Woman* (1931) as an example of its effectiveness. The film's obvious references to the Angelus Temple of Aimee Semple MacPherson undoubtedly made it potentially dangerous, but the SRC clearly thought that they had contained the risks. Before production, they had obtained "advice from religious leaders for the guidance of the studio," which led to significant changes in the script. These included the removal of several drinking scenes and "everything sacrilegious or blasphemous, . . . the elimination of any suggestion that the woman evangelist might be engaged in illicit love affairs," and the insertion of a speech "making it perfectly clear that the woman had firmly regained her faith and that she intends to live accordingly in the future."[16]

In his autobiography Capra takes responsibility for most of these insertions and blames himself, and them, for the movie's failure.[17] The SRC report, however, indicates the extent of Columbia's cooperation with the SRC. The lack of major censorship difficulties over the content of any of Capra's films, including *It Happened One Night*, suggests that he may have been viewed with particular favor by the SRC. Certain producers and directors, such as Ernst Lubitsch, were regarded as being especially adept at handling "difficult" material "delicately."[18] The SRC's reactions to *The Bitter Tea of General Yen* (1933) and *American Madness* (1932) offer confirmation of the favorable treatment they afforded Capra's projects. Despite its dangerous theme of miscegenation and the problems attached to any film that represented the Chinese, *The Bitter Tea of General Yen* underwent only minor alteration to produce a version acceptable to the Chinese chargé d'affaires in Washington. The SRC argued that "the story is in fact a eulogy of the Chinese philosophy, fair dealing, morality and graciousness."[19]

Columbia received several plaudits for its treatment of the banking crisis in *American Madness*. Colonel Jason Joy, head of the Studio Relations Committee, wrote to Will Hays in March 1932:

> The bank stories I think are all right from a policy standpoint and will even do good by helping rebuild confidence in banking institutions. In fact one of them, a Columbia story tentatively called *Faith* ought to be seen by all the bankers themselves for, in script form at least, it is a strong preachment of principles I know you thoroughly believe in, namely enough confidence by bankers in human nature to allow them to take leadership and help cure these screwy times . . . Incidentally, the dialogue very strongly points out the bank's importance as well as its duty. There is a realization in the studios of a responsibility not to impair confidence in banks and I foresee no danger of their doing so.[20]

Two months later, A. H. Giannini, chairman of the Bank of America, financial supporter of Columbia, and possibly the real-life model for bank manager Tom Dickson in the film, wrote to Harry Cohn about the same movie: "I have just had the pleasure of seeing your *American Madness*. I believe that this photoplay, which should be exploited by the leading theaters of this country, will do more than any other single agency to stop runs on banks which are started by false or malicious rumors. I hope it achieves the success it so richly deserves."[21]

By November 1933, when the script of *It Happened One Night* was considered by the SRC, the fact that Capra was directing it counted in its favor. Commenting on the script in a letter to Cohn, Joseph Breen noted: "While a few of the situations will need careful handling, we feel sure that under Mr. Capra's direction, they will be treated in such a way in the finished picture as to be not only satisfying under the Code, but free from danger of censorship." The censorship history of the film was uneventful. On completion of the film, Breen confirmed his original opinion, calling it "a very distinguished achievement, unquestionably one of the finest pictures we have seen in many months," and this endorsement permitted him to treat leniently such normally censorable details as Gable's nose-thumbing gesture, which Breen regarded as being "not offensive."[22] Various state and foreign censor boards made minor deletions, including Ohio's elimination, in the final scene, of "all scenes where blanket is shown, of it falling down and lying on floor."[23]

The Legion of Decency was less convinced of the merits of the film than was Breen. During the early months of the Legion's operation, a jurisdictional dispute arose between the archdioceses of Chicago and Detroit over the publication of lists of recommended films. Together with the Shirley Temple vehicle *Little Miss Marker* (1934), *It Happened One Night* was placed on the Detroit Recommended list, but on the class B list ("pictures in this group may be considered offensive because they are suggestive in spots, vulgar, sophisticated or lacking in modesty," but not prohibited) by Chicago in July 1934. By September, Detroit had demurred to

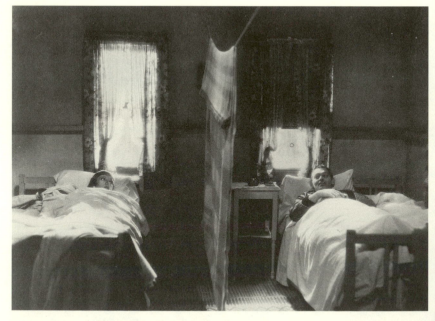

5.1. Ellie Andrews (Claudette Colbert) and Peter Warne (Clark Gable) with the "wall of Jericho" between them, in *It Happened One Night* (1934). (Museum of Modern Art/Film Stills Archive)

the Chicago classification and now regarded both films as "defective or offensive in spots, and although they are not forbidden for adults they are not . . . suitable for children or for adolescents."[24]

Patriarchy in Depression

The crisis of the early 1930s should be seen in a social and cultural context as well as an economic one; that is, it needs to be seen not only as a crisis in capitalism but also as a crisis in other social and cultural institutions, particularly in the institutions of patriarchy. Analysts of melodrama have frequently pointed to the representation of the family as a paradigm of social relations, in which the figure of the Father is equated with the Law. Although this critical territory has been most extensively explored in relation to domestic melodrama in the 1950s, the deployment of the family as a legitimizing metaphor for the social order has a much longer history in representation. As David Rodowick has pointed out, social and psychic determinations intersect

> in the figuration of patriarchal power as an overdetermined instance in the representation of social power per se. As the lynch-pin on which narrative conflict must turn, the problem of familial authority and stability therefore establishes a frame of reference against which the logic and order of the representations of social relations are measured. It was, indeed, the movies' representation of the crisis of capitalism as a crisis of patriarchal order that led to many of the specific problems over censorship that films incurred.[25]

It is not hard to discover evidence of the perception of a crisis in patriarchal authority within the family in the early 1930s. Robert Lynd and Helen Merrill Lynd noted changes in Muncie, Indiana, when they returned for a second investigation in 1935:

> A person long in close and sympathetic professional contact with Middletown's high-school students . . . commented: "Our high-school students of both sexes are increasingly sophisticated. They know everything and do everything—

openly. And they aren't ashamed to talk about it." In the early 1930s the situation became so acute, according to one of the city's businessmen, that it "got away from the high-school authorities. There was much drinking and immorality in the high school . . . The schools are inclined to trace a number of their problems in the depression back to the parents."[26]

In Middletown, as elsewhere, those who did not blame the parents often blamed the movies. Alterations in traditional standards of behavior were not, however, restricted to what one Middletown minister called "the growing irresponsibility of our young people," nor did these alterations begin with the Depression. The Lynds quoted a local businessman:

> Drinking increased markedly here in '27 and '28, and in '30 was heavy and open. With the depression, there seemed to be a collapse of public morals. I don't know whether it was the depression, but in the winter of '29–'30 and in '30–'31 things were roaring here. There was much drunkenness— people holding these bathtub gin parties. There was a great increase in women's drinking and drunkenness. And there was a lot of sleeping about by married people and a number of divorces resulted.[27]

The Lynds also saw evidence that the traditional male role was seriously disrupted by the Depression. The growth of employment opportunities for women and the developing consumer culture of the 1920s had induced rapid changes in women's roles, but the cultural conflicts they provoked had remained largely latent during the prosperity of the 1920s. The Depression brought these conflicts into sharper focus, heightened by the bruising economic effects of the slump, which put a quarter of Middletown's families on relief:

> The narrowed role of the male, so largely confined to moneymaking, took the brunt of the shock . . . With the man's failure of role went . . . inability to marry in many cases and the postponement of children. Men's and women's roles

have in some cases been reversed, with the woman taking a
job at whatever money she could earn and the man caring for
household and children; all sorts of temperamental variations have appeared, with women showing perspective and
steadfastness under stress and men sometimes dissolving
into pettiness and personal rancor. In many cases the wife
has had to support not only her own morale but that of her
husband as well. One may hazard the guess that it is the
world of male roles that has been under most pressure in
Middletown in the depression, and that for women the years
following 1929 may even in some cases have brought temporary easement of tensions.[28]

As Middletown went, so went the movies. From a number of
perspectives, and particularly from a patriarchal one, the movies of
the early 1930s might best be seen as texts of Dystopia. What
Robert Sklar has called Hollywood's "Golden Age of Turbulence"
in the early 1930s constituted, among other things, a series of attempts to explain the crisis of American capitalism, but the explanation was indirect, displacing economic anxieties into emotional
terms.[29] Hollywood's history of the previous decade was not a history of speculation on Wall Street and insecure construction in the
fortresses of finance capital, but rather a history of speculation
about sexual difference and insecure construction in that other
fortress (as David O. Selznick described it in the opening titles of
Since You Went Away [1944]), the American home.

A disturbance in the sphere of economics presented the Dream
Factory with an intolerable contradiction. How could you represent a crisis of capitalism entertainingly? What suitable images
could a capitalist industry find to represent and reassure the economic neuroses of Depression America, when its self-definition as
entertainment prevented it from representing the sphere of disturbance? Hollywood's account of a "disturbance in the sphere of
sexuality" as an explanation of the social conditions of the early
1930s conformed exactly, if inversely, to Freud's use of the idea
of censorship to describe the process by which unconscious
thoughts that cannot emerge directly into consciousness emerge
in a distorted form.[30] Dreams are a prime site for such distortions,

displacements, censorships. Hollywood the Dream Factory, the manufacturing plant for public rather than private fantasies, engaged in different forms of censorship and repression, but the mechanism of censorship—displacement for the production of a distorted meaning—was essentially the same. The unrepresentable disturbance in the sphere of economics provoked a neurosis in the system of representation. The neurotic symptom emerged via censorship as a distortion in the production of the patient's discourse, as a disturbance in the sphere of sexuality. And that, in turn, contributed to the widespread cultural anxiety of the early 1930s over control of the institutions of representation and, in particular, Hollywood.

A more complete discussion of the film industry's representation of the patriarchal family as social microcosm must await a more lengthy opportunity;[31] here, related phenomena can merely be briefly noted. Certain stories, certain plot devices, and certain characters apparently became unavailable to movies during the worst years of the Depression. Most notable and perhaps least surprising was the absence of the patriarchal hero. During the three production seasons from 1930 to 1933, there were few successful businessmen and few successful fathers in movies. The family without a father was a commonplace; it was almost a sine qua non of the gangster movie. The Oedipal trajectory of *The Public Enemy* (1931) is an oft-told early-Depression tale: the younger son of a fatherless family is led astray; the elder son fails adequately to fill the restraining patriarchal role.[32] *American Madness* traverses similar terrain, if to a more optimistic conclusion. The patriarchal Tom Dickson (Walter Huston) is crushed into immobility not by the run on his bank, but by his suspicion that his wife has been unfaithful. Matt Brown (Pat O'Brien) declares at one point in the movie that Dickson has been "like a father to me." Cyril Cluett (Gavin Gordon), the bank treasurer whose alibi for the robbery is Dickson's wife, has the same filial connection with Dickson. As Leonardo Gandini has pointed out, the revelation takes place in the private, domestic space of Dickson's office, where he retreats from the public arena of the bank floor, preoccupied with familial concerns.[33] In the scene that follows, Dickson, alone in his office, puts his wife's picture away in a drawer, looks at the pistol he finds there, and, it is implied, contemplates suicide. A suspected infidelity threatens the local economy with collapse; it is not Dickson the impotent patriarch, but his "elder son" Brown who succeeds in restoring confidence.

Parallel with the failures of the patriarchal hero was a crisis in the representation of romantic heroism. The Lynds had noted the way in which Middletown's typical male moviegoer "may have felt new inadequacies as a husband and a lover in these days when grand passions are paraded nightly before Middletown in the movies."[34] The passionate, melodramatic male sexuality of Rudolph Valentino and John Gilbert proved vulnerable to the dictates of a sound cinema intolerant of its feminization of the male as erotic object.[35] Joel McCrea, John Boles, Lew Ayres, and Robert Montgomery were hindered by an absence of assertiveness often attached to an effete aristocracy in the "drawing room" genre borrowed from Broadway. In an article on Gable in *Modern Screen*, Faith Baldwin suggested that "the feminine public is wearying of rather pretty and too polished young men," but few acceptable alternatives emerged. The three top male box-office stars of the early 1930s were Will Rogers, Eddie Cantor, and Wallace Beery.[36] Warners' urban ethnics—Cagney, Muni, Robinson—were seldom more than peripheral romantic leads. Baldwin went on to complain that "since the world war there has been a demand for charm, for romantic charm. It is beginning to lessen. There are far too many young men of romantic charm and not much else, in life as well as on the screen. There seems to be something of a reaction against them. The average fan is beginning to call for men of action, men whom the old trite term, 'he-man,' fits like a glove." Gable, she proposed,

> has a manner which indicates that while he might kiss a woman's lips he might also under provocation slap her face, and with perfect ease . . . [He] is not particularly mysterious, neither is his vogue. He is simply an unusual looking young man, with danger as his password, and women have always loved danger. They may choose security, in the long run, for their life motto, but they haven't forgotten danger. And that is why they will flock to see Mr. Gable . . . in order to forget

their personal security while they live, for an hour, and quite vicariously the exciting, the sometimes brutal and the always interesting life which Mr. Gable appears to embody.[37]

Like that of Victor McLaglen and Gary Cooper, Gable's representation of masculine sexuality was tainted with a disturbing brutality. His treatment of Norma Shearer in *A Free Soul* (1931), for example, was comparable with Cagney's now more celebrated treatment of Mae Clarke in *The Public Enemy*. At one point in the movie, Shearer tells him, "You're swine walking with swine." "You're talking to the man you love," he replies. On another occasion, Gable shoves her back into a chair, saying "Sit down and take it and like it . . . You're an idiot—a spoiled, silly brat that needs a hairbrush now and then."[38]

Alongside the crisis in the representation of the masculine was the prevalence of "fallen women" and "prodigal daughter" cycles, replete with the anxious representation of female sexuality as socially disruptive.[39] A worried Colonel Joy informed Hays that a quarter of all movies in production in September 1932 were concerned with "illicit sex relations."[40] The basic plot structure of these films militated against the positive representation of their male leads, and the SRC's increasingly strict insistence on a moral resolution made it difficult for them to end in scenes of reconciliation. In their failure to conclude with a reconstruction of the family, Capra's *Ladies of Leisure* (1930) and *Forbidden* (1932) are typical of the cycle. Such impairments were in part responsible for the often unsatisfying narratives of early 1930s movies. The problem arose from the studio's attempts to circumnavigate the Production Code by constructing narratives that took advantage of Father Lord's distinction that "sympathy with a person who sins is not the same as sympathy with the sin or crime of which he is guilty." For instance, in September 1931 MGM released a Helen Hayes vehicle, *The Sin of Madelon Claudet*, in which, as Joseph Breen's secretary Olga Martin explained, "a mother had an admirable aim and motive—that of providing education for her son—but sought to fulfill it by means of prostituting herself."[41] Similarly, Joy justified the plot of *Blonde Venus* (1932) by arguing that, "while the woman is admittedly unfaithful to her husband, she is motivated only by a desire to save his life."[42]

Casting desirable stars as social outcasts located them as sites of ideological contradiction not only within the narrative trajectory but also in terms of potential audience response. The Production Code insisted that wrongdoing must be shown to result in suffering for the perpetrator and must lead either to punishment or regeneration, conclusions that denied the audience a unified affective experience in which an attractive character achieved a socially acceptable and emotionally rewarding resolution. The insistence on adhering to what Breen referred to as the "spirit" of the code (usually referring to the "Reasons" when he did so) grew increasingly vehement after Breen's own involvement in SRC activities in March 1933,[43] but the same arguments, including the requirement for there to be a "voice of morality," had frequently been used earlier by Joy.[44] Although the major companies abandoned the production of gangster movies in November 1931,[45] the "fallen woman" cycle continued, although its plot development was increasingly hindered by overt denunciations of its leading characters' immoral conduct. Motherhood, in particular, became an occasion of suffering. If earlier Depression films had justified prostitution (or rather, some unnamed activity akin to it) by motivating it through maternal love, the half-hearted family reconciliation scene at the end of *Blonde Venus* had by late 1933 been replaced by a conclusion in which an unfit mother renounced her right to her child. A late instance of the cycle, Twentieth Century's *Born to be Bad*, is so hedged around with moral caveats that it must interrupt its plot on eight occasions for characters to denounce the female protagonist (Loretta Young) for her failings as a mother. Under such relentless pressure she eventually succumbs and achieves a degree of moral redemption in the only way possible to her, by surrendering her child to a more fit substitute mother. The film asserts a bourgeois patriarchal norm (in the form of Cary Grant), prescribes a restricting definition of the maternal within patriarchy, and badgers Young until she acquiesces in her own containment. Hamstrung in its narrative structure by the requirements of censorship, *Born to be Bad* demonstrated the debilitation of the cycle into narrative incoherence, without managing to rescue itself from the reformers' criticism that it provided evidence that Hollywood was failing properly to fulfill its role as recreation. The review of the film in *Selected Motion Pictures*, published by the MPPDA itself, described it as

> a thoroughly maudlin and objectionable melodrama with
> story material that is unbelievable, immoral, vulgar and thor-
> oughly distasteful. It concerns a young unwed mother so
> embittered at what life has done to her that she trains her
> child in delinquency to harden him against the suffering she
> has endured. The effort to make something out of a group
> of unpleasant characters results in a complete waste of time,
> thought and talent. Decency comes to the unnatural mother
> too late in the story to convince anybody of her sincerity.
> Protested and not recommended for anyone.[46]

Gable

> Comedy usually moves toward a happy ending, and the nor-
> mal response of the audience to a happy ending is "this
> should be," which sounds like a moral judgement. So it is,
> except that it is not moral in the restricted sense, but social.
> Its opposite is not the villainous, but the absurd . . . Happy
> endings do not impress us as true, but as desirable . . . The
> action of the comedy thus moves towards the incorporation
> of the hero into the society that he naturally fits. The hero
> himself is seldom a very interesting person: in conformity
> with low mimetic decorum, he is ordinary in his virtues, but
> socially attractive.[47]

It Happened One Night is a film produced at the moment of the
restoration of order. By late 1933 the worst of the slump had
passed, and with it the fear of immediate collapse. The "alphabet
agencies" of Roosevelt's Hundred Days at least ensured that the
bleakest hardships of the previous winter were not repeated on the
same scale, while the slight signs of optimism in the economy in
the summer of 1933 indicated that the Depression might have
bottomed out, allowing the National Recovery Administration
(NRA) to lead the process of recovery.[48] The NRA Code of Fair
Competition for the Motion Picture Industry, the longest and

most comprehensive of any of the NRA industry codes, was drafted and redrafted through the fall of 1933; while public attention was directed at excessive salaries in production, the NRA Code consolidated the major companies' control of the industry in large part by not taking a position on the most contentious disputes between them and independent exhibitors.[49] Although the stage-managed public performance of the crisis over censorship was yet to come, the MPPDA's internal mechanisms for self-regulation were established and operational.[50] Theater receipts, which had fallen during the summer of 1933 to half their level in January 1931, were beginning to pick up again, and the trend of improvement was more marked in neighborhood and outlying theaters than in the downtown first-run houses.[51]

It Happened One Night was a product ideally suited to these conditions. For at least two years, nonmetropolitan exhibitors had been lobbying against the sophisticated, gangster, and "drawing-room" type movies in favor of what they termed "simple romances."[52] The increasing pressure of the censorship lobbies both inside and outside the industry and the box-office successes of such films as *Lady for a Day* (1933) and *Little Women* (1933) endorsed such a shift in content. The *Variety* review of *It Happened One Night* noted, significantly, that it demonstrated that "a clean story can be funnier than a dirty one."[53]

According to Capra's autobiography, we owe the success of *It Happened One Night* and what Clark Gable, in the film, calls its "simple story for simple people" to Myles Connolly's critique of a script draft:

> Your leading characters are non-interest-grabbing. People can't identify with them. Take your girl: a spoiled brat, a rich heiress. How many spoiled heiresses do people know? And how many give a damn what happens to them? . . . Don't let her be a brat because she's an heiress, but because she's bored with being an heiress. More sympathetic. And the man. Forget that panty-waist painter. Make him a guy we all know and like. Maybe a tough, crusading reporter—at outs with his pig-headed editor. More sympathetic. And when he meets the spoiled heiress—well, it's *The Taming of the Shrew*. But

the shrew must be worth taming, and the guy that tames her must be one of us.[54]

It is not possible to piece together a chronology of the scripting process from Capra's account and therefore to know whether this alteration came before or after Louis B. Mayer proposed Clark Gable as an alternative male lead to Robert Montgomery.[55] The adaptation of the story better to suit its audience and to accommodate Gable was crucial to the film's success. At the same time, the movie effectively shifted Gable's public persona. Although a valuable studio property, rated in 1933 in the lower half of the top ten box-office attractions and the highest-rated male romantic lead, Gable's commercially successful formula, with Harlow in *Red Dust* (released in November 1932), for instance, was becoming increasingly problematic. Images of aggressive male sexuality were at least as troubling as images of aggressive female sexuality, and among male stars Gable was the one most regularly criticized in the early 1930s for his overt expressions of sexuality. Father Lord described him, in a letter to Hays, as "a menace to morals."[56] Gable's sexual violence was recognized as particularly dangerous. What a later biographer called the insinuation that Gable "had a power to give orgasms, even to a generation of women who were not too sure whether they were supposed to have them,"[57] was described more circumspectly, and with less certainty that it represented a desirable condition, by contemporary fan magazine writers:

> Mr. Gable's brilliant mixture of suavity and brutality, his quite magnificent physique and his effect of arrogance, which is not the usual "debonair" arrogance, are some of the reasons why frail women swoon with admiration and strong men curse with envy when his name is mentioned . . . Women, today, are "independent," they rejoice in their personal and economic freedom, they demand equal rights. But they remain women, for all that; or the majority of them do; and this majority remains susceptible to the extremely masculine.
>
> Mr. Gable, on the screen, gives one the impression that while he might adore the current heroine to the point of madness, he might also, if sufficiently exasperated, give her a

very good beating—and get away with it . . . He appears to regard women as conveniences rather than idols. Women may resent this but they respond to it . . . This lack of romantic emotion which is so dominant in his screen works makes him doubly interesting to all the women in his audience . . . There are probably thousands of women in the country today who, having seen Gable, have left the theatre thinking, if only I had the chance to reform him! For a man to inculcate in women the desire to turn loving reformer is a sure sympton [sic] of his popularity.[58]

A strange phenomenon of feminine psychology, the almost instantaneous success of this new type of lover. Note that I did not use the word "hero." For Clark Gable's popularity does not rest upon the foundation of noble deeds, tender passion, nor self-sacrifice. As a lover he begins with indifference, demands utter submission, and ends with either complete and uncompromising domination or defeat . . . The characters which he plays today would have been repugnant a few years ago. With one exception, he has played hard-boiled guys, and his success has been based on those parts. Is it not possible that the long series of gangster pictures, making heroes of underworld characters (pardon, Mr. Hays), has led up to a tolerance, then an acceptance, of such men. And, without any intent to discuss anything political or topical, may there not be an unconscious glorification of the man who, in utter disregard of all law, goes out and gets what he wants at the risk of his neck?[59]

Such a public image became increasingly untenable as censorship pressures mounted. MGM was experimenting with Gable's persona in 1933, in *The White Sister* and *Night Flight*,[60] and this experimentation provides a much more likely motivation for Mayer's agreeing to loan Gable to Columbia than does the Capra-derived story that Gable was sent there as a punishment for expressing displeasure at "his typecasting in brutish roles."[61] Loan-outs of stars became common in 1932,[62] and, because of their longer contract roster, MGM initially engaged in it more than other studios. Gable had been loaned out to First National for *The*

Finger Points in 1931 and to Paramount for *No Man of Her Own* in 1932. Early in 1935, before winning the Oscar for *It Happened One Night*, he was loaned out to Twentieth Century for *Call of the Wild*. In accord with the general pattern of loan-outs, his role in *It Happened One Night* was further from his established persona than those variants tested in his own studio, so that the larger box-office risk was pushed off onto another studio.[63] The film he made for MGM immediately after *It Happened One Night*, *Men in White*, similarly experimented with a less aggressive persona. After the success of *It Happened One Night*, the studio next cast him in two comedies, *Forsaking All Others* (1934) and *After Office Hours* (1935).

The exhibition history of *It Happened One Night* corresponds to the pattern of the market in early 1934. The film received only moderate attention and did satisfactory but unremarkable business at its New York opening. Its big box-office success was in the neighborhood theaters, where it attracted repeat bookings all year and eventually gained the critical attention that resulted in its Oscars and a Broadway revival a year after its initial release. A more detailed knowledge of the terms of Columbia's exhibition contracts might establish whether favorable rental fees had something to do with the film's success, but the fact and the location of that success are as clear as is contemporary critics' bafflement at its unexpected nature.[64]

The Rediscovery of Order

What normally happens is that a young man wants a young woman, that his desire is resisted by some opposition, usually paternal, and that near the end of the play some twist in the plot enables the hero to have his will. In this simple pattern there are several complex elements. In the first place, the movement of comedy is usually a movement from one kind of society to another. At the beginning of the play, the obstructing characters are in charge of the play's society, and the audience recognizes that they are usurpers. At the end of the play the device in the plot that brings hero and heroine together causes a new society to crystallize around the hero, and the moment when this crystallization occurs is the point of resolution in the action, the comic discovery, *anagnorisis* or *cognito* . . . The appearance of this new society is frequently signalized by some kind of party or festive ritual, which either appears at the end of the play or is assumed to take place immediately afterward. Weddings are most common . . . In the movie, where darkness permits a more erotically oriented audience, the plot usually moves toward an act which, like death in Greek tragedy, takes place offstage, and is symbolized by a closing embrace.[65]

It Happened One Night inverts the class affiliations of hero and heroine from the pattern that had dominated the "kept woman" cycle; unlike *Ladies of Leisure* or *Forbidden* or *Red-Headed Woman* or *Baby Face*, *It Happened One Night* is a romance across class lines in which the heroine is upper class and the hero is middle to working class. The entire emphasis of the story changes as a result, permitting the shift from melodrama to comedy that Thomas Schatz describes in chapter 1 of this volume. Where the lower-class heroine can demonstrate her worth only by sacrifice and thus becomes the victim of the plot, the lower-class hero demonstrates his worth by overcoming class obstacles to the romance. In this *It Happened One Night* resembles the "fairy tale musical" featuring Maurice Chevalier and Jeanette MacDonald that Rick Altman identifies as a major subgenre of the musical in the early 1930s. Altman argues that the fairy-tale musical modifies the system of New Comedy by locating the obstacle to the lovers' union not in another character but "within each lover, in the form of pride or vanity." The system of New Comedy, in which the lovers are a unified couple pitted against the world, is turned sideways by having the lovers oppose each other, a maneuver that "permits the introduction of diametrically opposed values or value systems which are 'carried' by the would-be lovers. The resolution of the love plot thus assures not only the coupling and marriage of the lovers but the merging of cultural values once defined as mutually exclusive."[66]

As Altman observes, the parallel development between the fairy-tale musical and the screwball comedy has been inadequately observed because of the relative rigidity of categorization within genre studies. Clearly, Peter and Ellie's union is a marriage of opposing values, and it is now a critical commonplace to identify Peter's assertion of bourgeois values in the restoration of harmony. However, it is worthwhile examining the relationship of *It Happened One Night* to the conventions of New Comedy in some greater detail to identify some of the text's undercurrents. In his account of the mythos of comedy, Northrop Frye proposes that "the theme of the comic is the integration of society, which usually takes the form of integrating a central character into it." [67] In *It Happened One Night* the character integrated into society is not, as might be conventional, the hero, Peter, but the heroine, Ellie.

In a way quite different from *Born to be Bad*, *It Happened One Night* describes, quite overtly, the containment of the heroine under patriarchy. The film opens with Ellie's defiance of her father— a defiance staged over her fitness to marry (i.e., to enter the world of adult sexuality) and the fitness of her choice of patriarchal re-

5.2. At the bus station in *It Happened One Night* (1934). (Museum of Modern Art/Film Stills Archive)

placement. We see a newspaper headline that reads, "Ellen Andrews Escapes Father."[68] Initially, she wants to replace her father with a Bad King, King Westley, the "high-flying" autogiro pilot who might have been the hero of a drawing-room romance. The course of the movie will ensure that she marries the Good King, King Gable, a king of the people.[69] However, before she can enter into the world of adult sexuality in her prescribed role as consort to the king, Ellie must be reduced by Peter to the condition of a child and brought up again—reeducated—to assume her proper place, her place as property. In their first encounter on the bus, Peter claims his right of possession over her: "That which you are sitting on is mine." Having taken possession of her ticket at Jacksonville, he again claims possession of her as an act of protection, telling Shapely that she is his wife. After this encounter, he reduces her to a state of financial dependence by taking her money from her. At the first auto camp, he once more protects her—this time from her father's detectives—by claiming her as his wife. Later, he quite accurately tells Shapely that he has kidnapped her.

Altman notes the way in which the fairy-tale musical develops, during the 1930s, away from the overt emphasis on the sexual implications of courtship evident in the Chevalier-MacDonald-Lubitsch films. Instead, the rituals of courtship are enacted "through antagonistic dialogue and especially through the characteristic plot construction whereby sexual energy is transmuted into quarreling and the progression of romantic attachment is made, paradoxically, to parallel the intensification of the conflict between the two would-be lovers."[70] In *It Happened One Night* the enactment of this process becomes an exercise in the expression of control over Ellie's sexuality. On each occasion that she seeks to assert her independence, she is punished for it. On the bus, when she leaves Peter's seat, she is accosted first by the fat man and then by Shapely. In the first auto camp, when she tries to argue with Peter, he threatens her with the sight of his sexuality by undressing; her adult resistance dissolves into a childlike response, and she runs away, an action that obliges her to accept Peter's terms over "the walls of Jericho." In the hitchhiking scene, she proves, as she says, that "the limb is mightier than the thumb," but then they are robbed by the driver who picks them up, and she again has to be protected by Peter.

On several occasions Peter and Ellie enact her childlike dependence on him, and gradually they discover that both of them enjoy and desire it. The first morning on the bus she is shown sleeping with her head on his shoulder, clutching his lapel, in the pose of a child. Shortly afterward, he tells her, "You're as helpless as a baby." In her conversation with Peter, she reveals her inexperience with men, which Peter translates as childishness. He begins to assume the role of the authoritative father, teaching her how to dunk doughnuts. Throughout the movie, Peter constructs the rules of the childish world he has created: what to do with money, how to dunk doughnuts, what is and is not piggybacking, the walls of Jericho. In this world Peter assumes, and learns, the role of the authoritative father, to the point of hitting Ellie when she argues with him, repeating the action of her father that led her to run away at the outset. Now that she has acquiesced in his construction of her, however, she does not try to escape again. As a vestigial remnant of Gable's persona in *Night Nurse* (1931), Peter displays a noticeable enthusiasm for doing violence to children. When Shapely demands half the reward, Peter threatens him with violence to his children if he tells anyone. Later, he tells Ellie's father that "what she needs is a guy that will take a sock at her once a day whether it's coming to her or not. If you'd had half the brains you're supposed to have, you'd have done it yourself long ago." Peter not only disapproves of her father, he usurps his role, expressing patriarchal anger whenever Ellie provokes another man's desire. When she wants to gold-dig Danker for a meal, Peter threatens to break her neck.

For both Ellie and her father, Peter's desirability is established by his attitude to the necessary use of violence in the operation of patriarchal authority rather than by the display of the male body as an object of desire. The movie successfully contains the explicit violence of Gable's sexuality within the acceptable bounds of a reestablished patriarchal family. At the first auto camp when, for the benefit of her father's detectives, Peter has apparently reduced Ellie to hysterical tears by his shouting and threatening to hit her, the camp owner tells the detectives, "I told you they were a perfectly nice married couple."

By the time of the haystack scene, Peter has reduced Ellie to a condition of complete childish dependence on him, a condition that now begins both to annoy him and to pose him problems. Ellie behaves like a child, petulantly complaining that she is scared and hungry. He leaves to find her some food. Unaware that he has left, she declares that she can look after herself and then discovers that she is alone. Filled with the panic of an abandoned and helpless child, she screams. When Peter returns, she refuses the carrots he has brought her, saying she is too scared.

She is, perhaps, too childish to eat Peter's carrots.[71] The movie, with Peter, solves "the problem" of female sexuality by rendering it childlike, but that does not solve its, and Peter's, other problem: that of male desire, as he experiences it in the hayfield. Even (or perhaps especially) in the childish world he has created, a father cannot sleep with his daughter, as Peter realizes when he covers her with his coat in imitation of the walls of Jericho.[72]

Now Peter must confront the consequences of his own education. At the start of the film, he is also at odds with a father figure, Joe the editor, and the adult nature of his behavior remains in doubt for much of the movie. In the hitchhiking scene the morning after the hayfield, Ellie refuses another carrot ("I hate the horrid things"), and Peter responds with a braggadocio display of his prowess: "It's all in that old thumb, that old thumb never fails . . . Keep your eye on that thumb, baby!" His adolescent attitude to sexual display is rewarded with failure: no cars stop, and he is reduced to thumbing his nose in the way Joe Breen found "not offensive." Ellie seizes the opportunity to assert her independence and sexuality again, and it is not until the more dangerous consequences of that action manifest themselves, when the driver robs them, that Peter can once again restore his patriarchal authority and order. Then, on their last night together, Peter confronts a further stage in his own education. Ellie is seduced into his adolescent fantasy of escape to a Pacific island, as she has been seduced into childish dependence in Peter's artificial world of auto camps and studio hayfields. If he is to realize his fantasy, Peter must return from the transient Utopia of his own invention to negotiate his rights of patriarchal possession. At first, he seeks to negotiate with his own patriarchal figure, the editor, but Joe cannot give him Ellie.

It is at this point in the action that the movie's relation to the conventions of New Comedy develops a further intricacy, as we recognize a further displacement from its patterns. At the outset of the movie, Mr. Andrews seems to be the "*senex iratus* or heavy father . . . with his rages and threats, his obsessions and his gullibility,"[73] presenting an obstacle to the romance of Ellen and King, and he remains cast in this role in relation to that romance throughout. However, from the second scene in the movie the audience recognizes—from King's absence but more insistently from Gable's presence—that this is the wrong romance and that the characters are in the wrong relationship to each other. The course of the movie is occupied with establishing the proper comedic pattern among the characters. The obstacles to the lovers are found in misrecognitions by the characters of the proper situation (which is known to the audience all along by the casting). First, Peter and Ellie have to recognize that they are the lovers in this comedy. This process occupies most of the movie, reaching its "discovery" in their discussion of "escape" on the third night. The discovery is, however, made separately by the two characters: by Ellie first, in her breaching "the wall of Jericho," and then by Peter after Ellie has fallen asleep—providing the opportunity for a further misrecognition that will permit the final, necessary discovery. This takes place between Peter and Mr. Andrews, in which Mr. Andrews recognizes that the proper romance is between his daughter and Peter and then assumes his proper place in relation to it, a role closer to that of an occasional New Comedy character, the benevolent grandparent "who overrules the action set up by the blocking humor."[74] Mr. Andrews recognizes the virtues of his younger self in Peter and thus identifies him as a fitting man to whom he can hand over possession of his daughter. No longer a *senex* figure, the patriarch has become the benign disposer of wisdom. "The tendency of comedy is to include as many people as possible in its final society: the blocking characters are more often reconciled or converted than simply repudiated. Comedy often includes a scapegoat ritual of expulsion which gets rid of some irreconcilable character, but exposure and disgrace make for pathos, or even tragedy."[75] The "blocking humor" in the proper romance thus turns out to be King Westley, playing the role of braggadocio with his autogiro, who is expelled by being bought off. King is irreconcilable less because he is the rejected lover (he has occupied that role only vestigially) and much more because he represents the "merry-go-round" of the previous decade: the stiff collars, cocktails, and stunts for the tabloid press of a circular and unproductive existence.

The scenes after Ellie's return disclose how dystopic the world of sophisticated, drawing-room drama with King Westley would be for a woman who has been changed as much as Ellie by Peter's education. The remainder of the movie is concerned with Mr. Andrews's machinations to ensure that his daughter is given to the right man. It is the presence of this figure that permits the full restoration of order at the movie's close, when the patriarch permits his daughter's entry into the realm of adult sexuality as the legal possession of a suitable substitute for himself. He exactly occupies the role that was absent from the "sophisticated" plots of the early 1930s.[76] Referring to Aristophanes and Shakespeare, Frye observes that "the theme of rebirth is not invariably feminine in context"; it also embraces "the rejuvenation of the *Senex* . . . the healing of the impotent king."[77] The crippled patriarch seeking to achieve national recovery is a central figure in the iconography of the New Deal.

It Happened One Night enacts the restoration of social order in its establishment of proper, and proprietorial, relations between the sexes. The film charts the distance between wedding and honeymoon and directly depicts the father giving his daughter as an object of male sexual desire to another man—the man in question changes as the movie progresses, from a figure of disapproval to one of approval. The process of approval or disapproval is related to class. King is presented as a figure of the frivolous and dissipated aristocracy, who has nothing to do but fly around and who is clearly identified with the values of the previous decade through the metaphor of the merry-go-round that goes nowhere. Peter, on the other hand, represents the solid middle-class virtues of a work ethic, even if his work is the writing of stories, and in this case the creation of a fantasy that comes true (we are, after all, in Hollywood, where work cannot be represented).

Peter's middle-class virtues have to do with not accepting or expecting charity, living within your means, and not taking something for nothing. These are the bourgeois virtues of dealing with money, and it is Peter's attitude to money that convinces Mr. Andrews that he is a suitable recipient for the other form of property,

Ellie. Peter is not in rebellion against society; he wishes to restore order. Order has been disrupted by the "screwball" behavior of the rich, by the characters of the drawing-room comedies on their merry-go-rounds. Peter is an archetype of middle-class male normality who restores order and conventionality. As the screwball comedy established its own more certain generic conventions—in *My Man Godfrey* (1936), for instance—the behavior of the rich became less unpleasant and more absurd, less recognizably a hangover of the 1920s as the audience grew chronologically more distanced from that decade. More characters could, in consequence, be included in the final inclusive comedic celebrations.

In *It Happened One Night* the ineffectual matriarchy of the early 1930s is removed altogether, the absent father is replaced by the benign patriarch, and female sexuality is contained within an account of it as childishness. It is worth remembering that the female box-office phenomenon of the mid-1930s was Shirley Temple and that her films, too, deal extensively with the amorous relations between father and daughter and with the reconstruction of families. Like Tom Dickson and Shirley Temple's father, Mr. Andrews is a banker. Although any discussion of what appealed to audiences about a film now more than fifty years old can offer no more than a hypothesis, it is possible to see in *It Happened One Night* the representation of a return to older, more ordered values at a moment when such a representation might seem both attractive and plausible, particularly to the audience to whom it seems predominantly to have appealed.

Acknowledgments

Much of the research for this essay was undertaken in the academic year 1983–84, during which I held an American Studies Fellowship from the American Council of Learned Societies. Further research has been facilitated by awards from the British Academy and the University of Exeter. I am greatly indebted to James Bouras of the Motion Picture Association of America for permitting me to consult documents in the MPAA archive in New York; to Father William Barnaby Faherty, S.J., and Mrs. Nancy Merz of the Jesuit Missouri Province Archives, St. Louis, Missouri; and to Sam Gill, archivist of the Margaret Herrick Library of the Academy of Motion Picture Arts and Sciences, Los Angeles. Matthew Bernstein generously consulted the Production Code Administration Case File on *It Happened One Night* for me. This chapter has benefited greatly from discussions with other contributors to this book at the VII Rassegna Internazionale Retrospettiva in Ancona, Italy. My greatest debt is to Ruth Vasey, for sharing her ideas, her editorial advice, and everything else.

Notes

1. Northrop Frye, *Anatomy of Criticism* (Princeton, N.J.: Princeton Univ. Press, 1971), 171. Following Stanley Cavell at a respectful distance but in only partial agreement, I seek to use Frye in this essay to elucidate relationships between New Comedy as the restoration of patriarchal order in the guise of romance, *It Happened One Night*, and the New Deal.

2. *A Code to Govern the Making of Talking, Synchronized and Silent Motion Pictures*, Association of Motion Picture Producers, 17 February 1930, Motion Picture Association of America Archive, New York (hereafter cited as MPA).

3. "Principles to Govern the Preparation of a Revised Code of Ethics for Talking Pictures," reporter's transcript, 10 February 1930 (1930 Production Code File, MPA), 136–43.

4. "Suggested Code to Govern the Production of Motion Pictures," reporter's transcript, 10 February 1930 (1930 Production Code File, MPA), 116–35. On Father Lord's activities, see Sister Mary Florence, *The Sodality Movement in the United States, 1926–1936* (St. Louis: Queen's Work, 1939), 38.

5. Father Daniel A. Lord to George, Cardinal Mundelein, 14 February 1930 (Folder, Movie Production Code, 1929–30, Father Daniel Lord Archive, Jesuit Missouri Province Archives, St. Louis [hereafter cited as Lord Archive]). The Production Code was published in a variety of inconsistent forms. A pamphlet published by the MPPDA under the title *A Code to Maintain Social and Community Values in the Production of Silent, Synchronized and Talking Motion Pictures* and dated 31 March 1930 did contain a section called "Principles Underlying the Code," which quoted two paragraphs from Lord's document while omitting the preamble to the Association of Motion Picture Producers' *Code to Govern the Making of Talking, Synchronized and Silent Motion Pictures*. However, Lord's document was otherwise unpublished until June 1934. For a fuller discussion of the various drafts of the Production Code, see Richard Maltby, "The Genesis of the Production Code," *Quarterly Review of Film and Video* 15, no. 4 (March 1995): 5–63.

6. Irving Thalberg, "Principles," reporter's transcript, 10 February 1930 (1930 Production Code File, MPA), 136–43.

7. Reporter's transcript, 10 February 1930 (1930 Production Code File, MPA), 116.

8. They were appended in three sections entitled "Reasons Supporting Pre-

amble of Code," "Reasons Supporting General Principles," and "Reasons Underlying Particular Applications." *A Code to Govern the Making of Motion and Talking Pictures, the Reasons Supporting It and the Resolution for Uniform Interpretation* (New York: Motion Picture Producers and Distributors of America, 13 June 1934) (hereafter cited as Code 1934).

9. Code 1934, 8; Fred Eastman, "The Menace of the Movies," *Christian Century*, 15 January 1930, 77.

10. See, for example, Charles C. Peters, *Motion Pictures and Standards of Morality* (New York: Macmillan, 1933); Alice Miller Mitchell, *Children and Movies* (Chicago: Univ. of Chicago Press, 1929).

11. Reporter's transcript of meeting of the Association of Motion Picture Producers, 10 February 1930 (1930 Production Code File, MPA), 11.

12. The SRC director, Colonel Jason Joy, did on one occasion early in 1932 complain to MPPDA President Will Hays that "there has been little inclination over there to bother with the Code," but the remark was made in relation to one of the relatively few Columbia pictures to experience extensive problems with the state censor boards. Joy to Hays, 15 February 1932, Production Code Administration (PCA) *Love Affair* Case File, Margaret Herrick Library, Academy of Motion Picture Arts and Sciences, Los Angeles, Calif. My thanks to Robert Sklar for this information.

13. PCA *So This Is Africa* Case File. For an account of the discussions between the MPPDA and Hughes over *Scarface*, see Richard Maltby, "Grief in the Limelight: Al Capone, Howard Hughes, the Hays Code and the Politics of the Unstable Text," in *Movies and Politics: The Dynamic Relationship*, ed. James Combs (New York: Garland, 1993), and "Tragic Heroes? Al Capone and the Spectacle of Criminality, 1948–1931," in *Screening the Past: VI. Australian History and Film Conference Papers*, ed. John Benson, Ken Berryman, and Wayne Levy (Melbourne: La Trobe Univ. Press, 1995), 112–19.

14. Anecdotal evidence for Cohn's concern over status is provided in Neal Gabler, *An Empire of Their Own: How the Jews Invented Hollywood* (New York: Crown, 1988), 169, 173; for an account of the economic rationale behind Cohn's ambitions, see Tino Balio, "Columbia Pictures: The Making of a Motion Picture Major, 1930–1943," in *Post-Theory: Reconstructing Film Studies*, ed. David Bordwell and Noël Carroll (Madison: Univ. of Wisconsin Press, 1996), 419–33.

15. Reports, 4 November 1931, 29 August 1935 (PCA *Platinum Blonde* Case File).

16. Memo, Colonel Jason S. Joy to Hays, 1 March 1931 (1931 Production Code File, MPA).

17. Frank Capra, *The Name above the Title* (New York: Macmillan, 1971), 131—in which, incidentally, he misremembers the ending of the film.

18. See, for example, the PCA Case File on *One Hour with You*.

19. Memos, Frederick L. Herron to Hays, 1 January 1933, and John V. Wilson to Hays, 21 January 1933 (PCA *The Bitter Tea of General Yen* Case File). Despite these precautions, the film was banned in parts of the British empire, although not in Britain itself. When Columbia sought to reissue the film in August 1950, the PCA was adamant that its characterizations of Americans and Chinese and a scene in which the heroine offered herself to the general were both "very questionable," and the film was not re-released.

20. Joy to Hays, 21 March 1932 (PCA *American Madness* Case File).

21. Edward Buscombe: "Notes on Columbia Pictures Corporation, 1926–1941," *Screen* 16, no. 3 (1975): 65–82, reprinted as chapter 9 of this volume; Giannini to Cohn, 28 April 1932 (PCA *American Madness* Case File).

22. Breen to Cohn, 9 November 1933 (PCA *It Happened One Night/You Can't Run Away from It* Case File). *You Can't Run Away from It* was the title of the 1956 remake. Breen to Cohn, 8 February 1934 (PCA *It Happened One Night/ You Can't Run Away from It* Case File). Memo, Breen to Maurice McKenzie, 8 March 1934 (PCA *It Happened One Night/You Can't Run Away from It* Case File). There is a barely visible deletion from the final release print, of what Breen referred to as "the toilet joke" in the scene of the passengers leaving the coach at the first rest stop.

23. State Censor Board record (PCA *It Happened One Night/You Can't Run Away from It* Case File).

24. *Harrison's Reports* 16, no. 27 (21 July 1934), sec. 2; 16, no. 36 (9 September 1934), sec. 2.

25. David N. Rodowick, "Madness, Authority and Ideology: The Domestic Melodrama of the 1950s," in *Home Is Where the Heart Is: Studies in Melodrama and the Woman's Film*, ed. Christine Gledhill (London: British Film Institute, 1987), 271. The essays by Thomas Elsaesser, Nick Browne, and Richard de Cordova in the same volume provide discussions of the patriarchal family as social metaphor. For an instance of such representation in the early 1930s, see Richard Maltby, "*Baby Face*, or How Joe Breen Made Barbara Stanwyck Atone for Causing the Wall St. Crash," *Screen* 27, no. 2 (1986): 22–45.

26. Robert Lynd and Helen Merrill Lynd, *Middletown in Transition* (New York: Harcourt, Brace, 1937), 170–71.

27. Ibid., 172.

28. Ibid., 178–79.

29. Robert Sklar, *Movie-Made America: A Cultural History of American Movies* (New York: Random House, 1975, 1994), 175 ff.

30. Sigmund Freud, *The Interpretation of Dreams*, trans. James Strachey (Harmondsworth: Penguin, 1975), 224. Originally published as volumes 4 and 5 of *The Standard Edition of the Complete Psychological Works of Sigmund Freud* (London: Hogarth Press, 1953).

31. See Richard Maltby, *Reforming the Movies: Politics, Censorship, and the Institutions of the American Cinema, 1908–1939* (New York: Oxford Univ. Press, forthcoming).

32. Tom Powers's policeman father makes one appearance in *The Public Enemy*, when he beats the child Tom. That the father is dead is established immediately after the first crime Tom commits, which ends in the death of a cop. *I Am a Fugitive from a Chain Gang* (1932) provides another example of the role of the elder brother.

33. Leonardo Gandini, *L'immagine della citta americana nel cinema hollywoodiano 1927–1932* (Bologna: CLUEB, 1994).

34. Lynd and Lynd, *Middletown in Transition*, 177–78.

35. The myth of John Gilbert's "feminine" voice is the most obvious instance of this; see Kevin Brownlow, *Hollywood: The Pioneers* (London: Collins, 1979), 192–94, for an account of Gilbert's career decline. Miriam Hansen, "Pleasure,

Ambivalence, Identification: Valentino and Female Spectatorship," *Cinema Journal* 25, no. 4 (1986): 8–10, provides a theoretical basis for the discussion of sexual mobility and the temporary slippage between gender definitions. See also Gaylyn Studlar, *In the Realm of Pleasure: Von Sternberg, Dietrich, and the Masochistic Aesthetic* (Urbana: Univ. of Illinois Press, 1988), and Studlar, *This Mad Masquerade: Stardom and Masculinity in the Jazz Age* (New York: Columbia Univ. Press, 1996).

36. *Motion Picture Herald*, 6 January 1934.

37. Faith Baldwin, "Why All the Mystery about Gable's Appeal," *Modern Screen*, March 1932. Reprinted in *The Best of Modern Screen*, ed. Mark Bego (London: Columbus, 1986), 46, 48.

38. Quoted in David Shipman, *Caught in the Act: Sex and Eroticism in the Movies* (London: Hamish Hamilton, 1985), 58; quoted in Lyn Tornabene, *Long Live the King* (New York: Putnam's, 1976), 134.

39. For a comprehensive account of the cycle, see Lea Jacobs, *The Wages of Sin: Censorship and the Fallen Woman Film, 1928–1942* (Madison: Univ. of Wisconsin Press, 1991).

40. Memo, Joy to Hays, September 1932 (1932 Production Code File, MPA).

41. Code 1934, 10; Olga J. Martin, *Hollywood's Movie Commandments: A Handbook for Motion Picture Writers and Reviewers* (New York: H.W. Wilson, 1937), 103. Martin cites *The Sin of Madelon Claudet* as an instance of a film condoning wrongdoing by supplying an admirable motive. The PCA file, however, reveals that the film was extensively revised after Joy discussed it with Thalberg, and it met few difficulties with state censor boards on its initial release.

42. Joy to John Hammell of Paramount, 16 September 1931 (PCA *Blonde Venus* File).

43. For example, Breen's report to Dr. James Wingate, SRC director, 5 May 1933, on RKO's *Ann Vickers* (RKO Production File, *Ann Vickers*, RKO Corporate Archives, Los Angeles). For an account of Breen's activities during this period, see Maltby, "*Baby Face*."

44. For example, Joy to Darryl Zanuck, 1 December 1931, over *The Mouthpiece* (Warner Bros. Production File, *The Mouthpiece*).

45. An account of the censorship history of gangster films is found in Maltby, "Grief in the Limelight."

46. *Selected Motion Pictures*, July 1934, 9. *Selected Motion Pictures* contained the "estimates" of the Previewing Committees of seven national organizations, including the General Federation of Women's Clubs, the Congress of Parents and Teachers, the Women's University Club, and the National Council of Jewish Women. They were published on a monthly basis by the MPPDA and distributed to their membership at the MPPDA's expense.

47. Frye, *Anatomy of Criticism*, 167, 170, 44.

48. Robert S. MacIlvaine, *The Great Depression: America 1929–1941* (New York: Times Books, 1984), 152–60.

49. *Motion Picture Herald*, 29 July 1933 to 6 January 1934, passim. See also Douglas Gomery, "Hollywood, the National Recovery Administration, and the Question of Monopoly Power," in *The American Movie Industry: The Business of Motion Pictures*, ed. Gorham Kindem (Carbondale: Southern Illinois Univ. Press, 1982), 205–14.

50. Access to the PCA files has made possible a revision of the "official" histories of the Production Code in Raymond Moley's *The Hays Office* (Indianapolis: Bobbs-Merrill, 1945), on which most earlier accounts have depended. As well as works previously cited, recent scholarship making use of the PCA Archive includes Lea Jacobs, "Industry Self-regulation and the Problem of Textual Determination," *Velvet Light Trap* 23 (1989): 4–15; Garth S. Jowett, "Moral Responsibility and Commercial Entertainment: Social Control in the United States Film Industry, 1907–1968," *Historical Journal of Film, Radio and Television* 10, no. 1 (1990): 3–31; Leonard J. Leff and Jerold L. Simmons, *The Dame in the Kimono: Hollywood, Censorship and the Production Code from the 1920s to the 1960s* (New York: Grove Weidenfeld, 1990); Ruth Vasey, *The World According to Hollywood, 1918–1939* (Madison: Univ. of Wisconsin Press, 1997); Frank Walsh, *Sin and Censorship: The Catholic Church and the Motion Picture Industry* (New Haven, Conn.: Yale Univ. Press, 1996); Gregory D. Black, *Hollywood Censored: Morality Codes and the Movies* (Cambridge: Cambridge Univ. Press, 1994); special issue on Hollywood, Censorship and American Culture, *Quarterly Review of Film and Video* 15, no. 4 (March 1995); *Movie Censorship and American Culture*, ed. Frank Couvares (Washington, D.C.: Smithsonian Institution Press, 1996); Richard Maltby, "The Production Code and the Hays Office," in Tino Balio, *Grand Design: Hollywood as a Modern Business Enterprise, 1930–1939*, History of the American Cinema, vol. 5 (New York: Scribner's, 1993), 37–72. Several of these accounts suggest that the changes brought about in 1934 were more sweeping and more directly attributable to Joseph Breen than was in reality the case. An account of the history of self-regulation during the period 1930–34 and of the negotiations between the MPPDA and various reform groups will appear in Maltby, *Reforming the Movies*.

51. *Motion Picture Herald*, 14 September 1933, 23; ibid., 16 June 1934, 9–11.

52. For example, *Motion Picture Herald*, 16 April 1932, 9–11.

53. *Variety*, 27 February 1934, 17. See also editorial, "Good Pictures Pay!" *Christian Century*, 27 June 1934.

54. Capra, *Name above the Title*, 164.

55. Capra's account suggests that the script was rewritten before Gable was cast, but his version cannot be relied upon. Gable's casting in *Night Bus* was announced in *Motion Picture Herald* on 28 October 1933. Geoffrey Shurlock of the SRC read the script on 2 November, and the comments transmitted by Breen to Cohn on 9 November referred to the rewritten and final version of the script. The best reason everyone concerned had for not casting Montgomery was that he was already involved in another movie featuring a cross-country bus journey, *Fugitive Lovers*, released by MGM in January 1934. It would be extremely improbable for the script not to have been modified to accommodate Gable, and thus the most reasonable assumption must be that negotiations over Gable's casting were agreed between the studios earlier in October, while the final version of the script was being drafted.

56. "Personally I should not like to be responsible for turning loose upon the public a menace to morals like Mr. Clark Gable, and I frankly fail to understand how Mr. William Powell could allow his wife [Carole Lombard, co-starring with Gable in *No Man of Her Own*], taken so recently in a much popularized wedding, to appear in a rapid succession of plays all of which appear to be equally filthy."

Lord to Hays, 20 February 1933, Lord Archive. Another figure similarly denounced by Father Lord was "the unspeakable Constance Bennett." Lord to Joy, 15 December 1932 (1932 Production Code File, MPA). Bennett was at one time considered for the female lead in *It Happened One Night*.

57. Rene Jordan, *Clark Gable* (New York: Pyramid, 1973). Quoted in Clyde Jeavons and Jeremy Pascall, *A Pictorial History of Sex in the Movies* (London: Hamlyn, 1975), 57.

58. Baldwin, "Why All the Mystery," in Bego, *Best of Modern Screen*, 46, 48.

59. James R. Quirk, "Why Women Go Crazy about Clark Gable," *Photoplay*, November 1931, reprinted in *The Talkies: Articles and Illustrations from a Great Fan Magazine, 1928–1940*, ed. Richard Griffith (New York: Dover, 1971), 45, 278.

60. An unenthusiastic commentary on this experimentation in his recent performances is provided in two "Open Letters to Clark Gable from his Former Wife," Josephine Dillon, in *Motion Picture Magazine*, July 1933, quoted in Tornabene, *Long Live the King*, 166–67.

61. Ephraim Katz, *The International Film Encyclopedia* (London: Macmillan, 1979), 469. Capra's account is in *The Name above the Title*, 164–65.

62. *Motion Picture Herald*, 2 July 1932, 36.

63. See Cathy Klaprat, "The Star as Market Strategy: Bette Davis in Another Light," in *The American Film Industry*, ed. Tino Balio, 2d ed. (Madison: Univ. of Wisconsin Press, 1986), 351–76.

64. *Variety* declared the film the fifth biggest money-maker of 1934. *Variety*, 1 January 1935, 36. *Harrison's Reports* 16, no. 22 (2 June 1934), sec. 2, suggests that Columbia's rental rates to independent exhibitors were sufficiently lower than those of the majors to justify block booking the studio's films, despite their overall poor box-office performance. If a repeat booking of *It Happened One Night* was available as a substitute for one of Columbia's other films in the block, it would undoubtedly have proved more profitable. More definite knowledge may well have to await access to Columbia's distribution archives.

The reviews written at the time of the film's New York opening were politely complimentary, with several of them noting Capra's direction but not making great claims for the film. The *New York Sun*, for instance, noted that "it's not a picture that bears much description. Its values are mainly cinematic, quick inconsequential bits of nonsense and drama" (23 February 1934). By the end of the year, however, critical comment had become much more favorable; by 10 April 1935, William Troy was describing it in the *Nation* "as one of the few potential classics of the recent cinema." By then, too, magazine articles extolling Capra as a "director's director" had appeared, coinciding with the release of *Broadway Bill* in November 1934. A digest of contemporary reviews is provided in Charles Wolfe, *Frank Capra: A Guide to References and Resources* (Boston: G.K. Hall, 1987), 204–10. Troy's review and Otis Ferguson's review in the *New Republic*, 9 May 1934, are both reproduced in *American Film Criticism: From the Beginnings to Citizen Kane*, ed. Stanley Kauffmann with Bruce Henstell (New York: Liveright, 1972), 299–301.

65. Frye, *Anatomy of Criticism*, 163–64.

66. Rick Altman, *The American Film Musical* (Bloomington: Indiana Univ. Press, 1987), 144, 145.

67. Frye, *Anatomy of Criticism*, 43.

68. Although the film's plot follows quite closely its source, a short story by Samuel Adams Hopkins called "Night Bus," Ellie's conflict with her father in the original has to do with her going on an expedition with King Westley, not marrying him, and Peter's infantilization of Ellie and his critique of her upbringing are also script additions. "Night Bus" is reprinted in *Stories into Film*, ed. William Kittredge and Steven M. Krauzer (New York: Harper & Row, 1979), 32–91.

69. In his first scene, after his telephone argument with his editor, Peter is cheered by the crowd, who call him the "king." Later in the decade, Gable acquired the title as his conventional nickname.

70. Altman, *American Film Musical*, 168.

71. "My feeling about the carrot is that we have no more use for making its phallic symbolism explicit than Ellie and Peter would have—I mean at the time she accepts it in the car, on the way to their third night together. Surely we do not need to be told that their relationship has sexual overtones or undercurrents. To discover this together, and acceptably is, rather, exactly their problem. And to suppose that this comes down to discovering the carrot's symbolism strikes me as denying the dimensions of significance I have traced in the carrot—its place as a food, uncooked, and as a gift, from a father." Stanley Cavell, *Pursuits of Happiness: The Hollywood Comedy of Remarriage* (Cambridge: Harvard Univ. Press, 1981), 93. I note in passing the masculine nature of Cavell's metaphor when he observes that "one does not want to penetrate the sexual censoring too soon or tactlessly, pull the blanket down before it has done its work, by screening, of forming hope—to create the reality of disillusionment before honoring the truth of illusion. The timing of explicitness is a place at which comedy and farce and melodrama will find their differences. I am saying that explicitness poses analogous issues for criticism. An interpretation offered at the wrong place, in the wrong spirit, is as useless, or harmful, as a wrong interpretation." My analysis of the film differs from Cavell's in its interpretation of Peter and, in particular, in our assessments of the maturity of his sexuality.

72. This is a gesture repeated from *Ladies of Leisure*, where Jerry Strange (Ralph Graves) covers Kay Arnold (Barbara Stanwyck) with a coverlet when she stays overnight in his studio. *Ladies of Leisure* is another instance in Capra's films of a man—in this case a "pantywaist painter" who might well have been the prototype for Capra's first version of Peter Warne—taking possession of a woman and constructing her in the image of his desire.

73. Frye, *Anatomy of Criticism*, 172.

74. Ibid., 171.

75. Ibid., 165.

76. For example, *Ladies of Leisure*, where the final scene of Jerry's declaration of love for the corpselike Kay fails to resolve the narrative precisely because it does not incorporate the larger family, and particularly his father, into the reconciliation. This figure is, incidentally, also absent from the early 1930s Chevalier-MacDonald-Lubitsch fairy-tale musicals.

77. Frye, *Anatomy of Criticism*, 183.

6

Roosevelt, Arnold, and Capra, (or) the Federalist-Populist Paradox

Giuliana Muscio

The main argument of this essay deals with the complex interaction between politics and communications—especially cinema—in the United States during the 1930s.[1] In the thirties, both the function and methods of politics were modified by contact with modern systems of communication. Politics transformed its public into spectators of new secular mass ceremonies and rituals at the same time that cinema, becoming more aware of its ideological function, attempted to transform its spectators into a public, mainly through the implementation of the Hays Code.[2] Thus, the New Deal is not simply a historical background for a segment of film history; its interaction with Hollywood classical cinema requires a reexamination.

To understand this process one must focus on the peculiar relation between socioeconomic conditions and ideological processes during the 1930s. As Warren Susman has written:

> It is possible to suggest that the newly developed media and
> their special kinds of appeal helped reinforce a social order
> rapidly disintegrating under economic and social pressures
> that were too great to endure, and helped create an environ-
> ment in which the sharing of common experiences, be they
> of hunger, dustbowls, or war, made uniform demand of

action and reform more striking and urgent . . . Whatever
else might be said about the New Deal, its successes and failures, it is obviously true that it was a sociological and psychological triumph.[3]

The socioeconomic, cultural, and emotional needs of Depression
America received, indeed, an overall satisfactory response from the
political establishment through communications. In the 1930s,
a political leadership that competently used the media in all these
three directions worked together with cinema—the key mass
medium during this period—to stabilize society and revitalize
Americanism.

When discussing ideology, means of communication, and New
Deal politics, it is necessary first of all to reconsider some definitions—the antinomic pairs that often recur in this chapter: fed-
eralism/populism, liberalism/conservatism, reformism/restora-
tion.[4] These terms identify ideological areas that, in theory, do not
overlap. Was the New Deal exclusively federalist, or does there exist a populist image of the New Deal? This question of definitions
is not a minor one, inasmuch as contemporary revisionist historiography has concentrated for the most part on the reinterpretation of these terms in relation to the New Deal.[5]

Populism can be associated with terms such as *rural, diffusion
of power, nativism*, and, in a broader sense, *isolationism* and *antimonopolism*.[6] Its individualism is tempered by good-neighborliness. In its political manifestations, it demonstrates a rebellious
tendency and phobic attitudes. It has therefore been interpreted
as a conservative movement, nostalgic for a better past.[7] Its typical mode of expression was demagogic oratory (i.e., soap-box
rhetoric). By the 1930s populism was not limited geographically
to rural areas; it attracted instead the recently urbanized lower
middle class, and it dwelled in the comfortable dimension of the
small town. Federalism is usually associated with *urban*, even metropolitan, values: finance and industry, *concentration of power*,
partisan political machines, political and *industrial organization*,
and the myths of the frontier and of private initiative, with an optimistic outlook and a tendency toward the future.

These two contrasting ideological nuclei were typical of a
prevalently WASP America in a regime of private enterprise and an

economy of production. With the migratory waves of the 1910s and 1920s, the urbanization of rural population, and the more advanced and complex developments of the economic system, these two ideological poles were modified in the context of the emergence of a reformist middle class. Progressivism brought about a form of individualism tempered by self-regulation. The reformist spirit was often closer to Christian charity than to social justice.[8] Expressive manifestations of progressive reformism were muckraking journalism and the realistic novel—that is, the written word.

Reformism and populism overlap historically and ideologically in their paternalistic attitudes and in a didactic spirit toward the masses, within a framework of a decline of rural values in favor of small-town, lower-middle-class values. These ideological formations reacted to a social and economic situation—subsequent to World War I—in which the myths of success and prosperity were as yet intact. These myths were articulated in two possible trajectories—"from rags to riches" and "from a log cabin to the White House"—and in a series of mythic figures: Jefferson as the symbol of equal opportunity, Jackson as that of individualism, and Lincoln as that of enterprise. The objective of reformist and populist movements was the removal of possible obstacles on the road to individual success, given that a certain degree of social equality and a fair minimum of subsistence seemed to be guaranteed.

The Depression deeply undermined this socioeconomic structure; even physical survival was threatened by the explosion of irreconcilable contradictions between overproduction on the one hand and hunger and unemployment on the other. Traditional ideologies no longer seemed capable of suturing this conflict. The "Revolution"—a socioeconomic change of great impact—seemed inevitable. But, as Lawrence Levine argues in his essay, "American Culture and the Great Depression," the country was paralyzed by fear, shame, and confusion.[9] The Revolution did not take place. However, neither can one say that the irreconcilable contradictions of the socioeconomic system were resolved. The crisis of the Great Depression found a paradoxical answer in the New Deal, a peculiar mixture of renewal and tradition, of federalism and populism—of irredeemable polarities.

Arnold, who, in his own time, was an expert on paradox, perceived the necessity of this very paradox—of federalist contents expressed in populist terms—when stating that "a new idea must appear to be an old idea before it will work at all."[10] Here we are not referring to the Arnold of Capra's films—the actor Edward, embodiment of the evil, cigar-smoking capitalist and perfect antagonist to the Capran hero—but to Thurman W. Arnold, the genial intellectual of the 1930s and perhaps not by chance the head of the Antitrust Division that filed the Paramount case in 1938 (Supreme Court case, *United States v. Paramount Pictures, Inc., et al*). Through his peculiar fusion of social sciences, juridical thought, and sarcastic criticism of contemporary social and economic institutions, Arnold studied "the folklore of capitalism" and "the symbols of government," as read the titles of two of his most famous books. With incredible timing and acute observation, Arnold perceived that the essential problem of the New Deal was its difficulty in being accepted by the people, due to its innovativeness.

> In order to solve the pressing problems of waste of labor and national resources, new organizations were sorely needed; yet there was no logical place in the mythology of government to which they could be assigned. The social needs were felt by everyone, but the slogans which the new organizations used had a queer sound. Therefore, the spirit of the Constitution, the traditional symbols of economics, and the general picture of a "rule of law" as opposed to "bureaucratic control" were all arrayed against them . . .
>
> This phenomenon always occurs whenever new types of social organization are struggling to arise to fill the gaps left in an old order . . . Today there is a great pressure on the government to take over the techniques of bankers, to form government corporations, to use government credit to promote the distribution of goods as bankers had used it and even directly to distribute the goods themselves. Such new activities, of course, meet the same kind of theological opposition as met by the growth of private banking in the Middle Ages. They are immoral; they will cause the ruin of national character; they will break up the home: they will destroy freedom.[11]

According to Arnold, "high ideals" and absolute values did not make sense anymore in the "era of the Organization," but, at the same time, techniques and organization alone were not sufficient in resolving the problems of society, if they could not be adapted to fit the emotional needs of the people. Recognizing a need for rituals and ceremonies even in modern society, he indicated that the government had to learn to communicate with the people's deeply rooted ways of thinking. He pointed out that:

> 1. Institutions are like personalities playing a dramatic part in society. They are to be judged by their utility in the distribution of physical comforts and in development of an atmosphere of spiritual peace.
>
> 2. When institutions fail to function, reforms must be attempted with something like the same point of view with which a trained psychiatrist reforms an individual. That point of view must recognize that an institution has something which may be called a subconscious mind. This means only that its verbal conduct must be calculated to inspire morale and not to describe what it does.
>
> 3. Law and economics are the formal language of institutions on parade.[12]

Arnold, a second Machiavelli, added that "every governmental creed must represent all the contradictory ideals of a people if it must be accepted by them"—a statement that emphasized the ability of ideology to contain contradiction.

Arnold's social and ideological work of deconstruction stressed the eminently spectacular and ritual content assumed by politics in a mass society:

> Men are coming to realize that political government is necessarily a dramatic spectacle, that games are really important in the growth and development of institutions, and that these games can be controlled . . . A most useful social philosophy for the future is one which recognizes the functions which dramatic contests of all sorts perform in giving unity and stability in government. The most primitive type of such

contests is war. The most civilized types are games and judicial trial. The frank recognition of this fact is the beginning of knowledge of social institutions. It gives us an understanding of the part that football teams play in the growth and tradition of a college, and the similar part that such an institution as the Supreme Court of the United States plays in the growth, tradition, and unity of a nation.[13]

Arnold explained and justified the need for showmanship in politics, the new ritual and symbolic requirements for sociopolitical organizations, exactly in the moment in which this evolution was taking place—during the 1930s.[14]

The dialectics between idealism and pragmatism, between the old and the new, or, rather, between traditional and progressive values, between the individual and the masses, are central to Arnold's reflection. They were synthesized in the elaboration of his "project"—the concept of "political dynamics"—a pragmatic method of politics that recognized the symbolic and emotional needs of the masses, on the one hand, and the social and economic necessities of renewal on the other.

This transformation of the interaction between politics and communications happened within a wider cultural struggle. In *Culture as History*, Warren Susman maintains that the greatest conflict of our century is that between a "puritan-Republican, producer-capitalist culture and a newly emerging culture of consumption."[15] Arnold, Roosevelt, and Capra played key roles in this clash between old and new, between WASP culture and the culture of mass consumption. They cannot be identified either with one of the above-mentioned positions (with populism, federalism, or progressivism) or with the two contrasting cultures. They orchestrated instead a mediation, a form of "political dynamics." Arnold, apparently a federalist,[16] had a progressive outlook and a didactic intent, albeit sui generis, of populist flavor. He has been defined, in fact, as a cross between Voltaire and a cowboy because of the Western traits that he maintained behind the guise of the pragmatic, sophisticated Eastern lawyer.[17] FDR and Capra also embody the interaction of politics and communication, in the specific historical formation it assumed in the 1930s, which

mediated crucial cultural transformations by infusing new meaning into traditional attitudes and by dressing up new institutions
in old costumes.

The somewhat mechanical parallelism that we are proposing
between Capra and Roosevelt (and the New Deal)—which would
be vehemently contested by the film director—encourages a re-
consideration of the relationships they entertained with the public. According to our hypothesis, their publics were practically
identical. Especially during the first years of the New Deal, President Roosevelt enjoyed great popularity: his public was a com-
pound of all social classes—a mass audience. Even if there is no
doubt that the main beneficiary of the New Deal was the middle
class and that FDR elected the "average man" as his privileged interlocutor, it was, however, among the lowest classes that his popularity was greater.[18] Analogously to FDR, the movies aimed at a
large public, identified in terms of "people," rather than "masses."
And, as with FDR, the movies enjoyed their greatest popularity
with the less-well-to-do classes.

According to a widely accredited hypothesis, elaborated by
Margaret Thorp,[19] classical cinema elected the middle class as its
preferred audience because in those years people who were unemployed or penniless could not afford going to the movies. On
the contrary, during the Depression everyone went to the movies.
Cinema was recognized as a necessity by the Hoover administration, which, in the midst of the crisis, distributed food, clothing,
and tickets to the movies to keep people off the streets and to give
them comfort and refuge—*panem et circenses*.

Owners of small theaters realized that the movies were the answer to the Depression of the American housewife (before Woody
Allen did, with *The Purple Rose of Cairo*). Therefore, they gave
away china sets as gifts or raffled off tickets, aiming at the impoverished middle class, which needed material incentives to quiet its
Puritan sense of guilt, provoked by such a "superfluous" consumption as going to the movies. The invention of the double bill,
of "two films for the price of one," during the crisis—an innova-
tion that radically transformed the production and marketing
strategy of cinema—corresponded to this idea of "movies for
everyone." This enormous number of tickets at a low cost was not,
perhaps, the kind of profit that the industry was most interested

in, in that it drew its largest and most rapid profits from first-run theaters. If the movie industry took on the burden of this market, despite its modest income, it was because the studios considered it a social function.[20] However, we must mention the case of Columbia Pictures, which concentrated its productive activity in this market—the neighborhood theaters and the B portion of the double bill—and built its fortune on it, during the 1930s, thanks to its main director, Capra.

Beyond these commercial considerations, it is from the ideological point of view that the cinema of the 1930s offered itself to *all*, in a universality of social classes and ideological values, expressed by the Hays Code. Within 1930s popular cinema, Capra was the director par excellence, given his great commercial, critical, and professional success, as testified by the number of Academy Awards he won, by his role in the Academy, and, in general, in the affirmation of his role as author and director.[21] His "popularity" is constantly stressed in the literature about his work, and it is often used to indicate his significance in the American culture of the era.

Individual/Masses

Notwithstanding the fact that Roosevelt is commonly identified with the imposition of the modern model of political, economic, and social organization, both the content of his speeches—for example, of his "fireside chats"—and his rhetorical and stylistic apparatus have populist undertones. They constantly refer to the interlocutor as an individual, part of the "people," of the "nation." Roosevelt concocted complex communicative strategies to maintain direct contact with the American people. They consisted of traveling, monitoring the press, reading the correspondence addressed to the White House, and paying attention to a series of reports that he received from numerous "special reporters," such as his wife and his collaborators. This strategy made him aware of what the American people thought of his programs and of his reforms; it allowed him to create a public opinion in support of his politics in Congress and to be informed of the needs and the mood of the people. These letters and reports, furthermore, contributed to the repertoire of human examples and personal touches that colored his oratory with humanitarian participation. FDR constructed the image of a leader who was close to his people by using the radio to its fullest advantage, through his simple way of speaking that reduced even the most complex and innovative economic reforms to a question of good sense, linking them to deeply rooted American traditions such as good-neighborliness. The tones and themes of these radio chats repositioned the individual away from the public sphere, placing him in a community, in a more relaxed atmosphere, within the comfortable walls of domesticity, or, more exactly, in front of a fireplace.

Capra, too, opposed the concept of the "mass," to the point of declaring that *Mr. Deeds Goes to Town* was "the rebellious cry of an individual against being trampled to an ant by massiveness—mass

6.1. A 1934 publicity portrait of director Frank Capra. (Museum of Modern Art/Film Stills Archive)

production, mass thought, mass education, mass politics, mass wealth, mass conformity."[22] His hero was not an isolated individual; he was presented as being part of a community. As the beginning of *The Miracle Woman* shows, this community is not good in itself; on the contrary, it can be ungrateful, even moblike, until it learns, through the teachings of the hero, to love its neighbor unselfishly and to give the hero the necessary help. Individual and community together form an interdependent whole: they are reciprocally indispensable. Capra's heroes are often born and live in a small community, in a village or neighborhood in which everybody knows everybody else by name (this holds true not only for Deeds and Smith, but also for the protagonists of one of Capra's first films, *The Younger Generation*). When they "go to the city," they carry with themselves the values and the ethical resources with which they have grown up. Initially these values constitute a cumbersome baggage among the throng of a city that is ready to deride these attitudes, which it considers naive and out of date. But when the hero, in a sort of ritual sacrifice, seems about to immolate himself for the good of—or because of the indifference of—the community,[23] the mechanism of a collective redemption is released; life returns to shine for all, as in the ending of *It's a Wonderful Life*, a clear demonstration of a hero and a community that are absolutely indispensable to each other.

Urban/Rural

The assumption that we should identify FDR with the metropolitan world and Capra with rural romance is erroneous. We refer to George Mosse for an acute analysis of the role of agrarian and populist imagery in the rhetoric of the political systems of the 1930s, from Fascism to the New Deal.[24] The majority of Capra's early films produced by Columbia Pictures offer a representation of society in perfect alignment with the so-called culture of abundance and with the progressive image of a city at once dynamic and corrupt (as in *Ladies of Leisure* and *Platinum Blonde*). In a brilliant analysis of the iconography of *It Happened One Night*, Susman emphasizes the nearly obsessive presence of means of communication and transportation in this film, which perfectly embodies the myth of social mobility.[25] As a matter of fact, many of Capra's early films are dedicated to various means of transportation (*Dirigible*, *Submarine*, *Flight*), represented with a strong tension of the engineering imagery of the director. Camera movements, means of transportation, and social mobility: the work of this director seems to propose energy and movement on every level. The consideration that this stylistic and thematic peculiarity was in itself a therapeutic answer to the paralysis—both psychological and economic—that froze America after the Great Depression cannot but strike one.

The countryside is remarkably absent from Capra's cinema, being reduced to the farms that Deeds wants to distribute to the poor or to the rural background of *It Happened One Night*—not by chance an environment in which the protagonists, typical representatives of the urban world, are not at all at their ease. From the beginning of the twentieth century, the populist ideal had moved from the rural community to the small town. Capra's films are exemplary of this populist shifting, to the point that the Mandrake Falls of *Mr. Deeds* and the Bedford Falls of *It's a Wonderful Life* have become mythical images of the provincial American small town.

The contrast between the values of the small town and the absence of values of the metropolis is represented with particular vividness in the sets of *The Miracle Woman*, which juxtapose the "good" drawing room, decorated in typical "Old American" style, that belongs to the blind musician with Florence's apartment, furnished with modernist taste. Likewise, the transfer from the warm surroundings of the Jewish ghetto to the cold marble of the Fifth Avenue living rooms in *The Younger Generation* takes place within the sphere of the decor: monumental fireplaces that give off no heat, long tables around which no communication can exist.

On the other hand, the "agrarian" was Roosevelt, who was truly interested in the conservation of the land, to the point of creating the Civilian Conservation Corps, an *ante litteram* "ecological guard." Exemplary of Roosevelt's rhetorical use of rural imagery was a fireside chat of 1936, in which he described a visit to the Dust Bowl. He constructed an analogy between the Dust Bowl and the Great Depression, thereby strengthening the association between his programs of reform and the salvaging of the

American land. The text of this speech is, in a sense, the virtual script of Pare Lorentz's government-produced documentary film, *The River*.[26] Roosevelt was a gentleman farmer; his agrarian spirit is expressed by the constant use of metaphors and images referring to the earth. For Capra, the rural was instead associated with agricultural work—a nightmarish image from which his family had attempted to escape.

As Capra expressed a neopopulist tension in the image of the small city, so the New Deal did not propose an anachronistic return to the land but a new synthesis of city and country that was encompassed in the Greenbelt Towns and in the attempt to manage agricultural activities with instruments and methods typical of the modern entrepreneur.[27]

Enemies

From *Mr. Deeds* onward it is evident that Capra's demonology was typically urban. As Andrew Bergman observes in *We're in the Money*,[28] under fire were the metropolitan cynics, the reporters in search of a scoop, high society, corrupt lawyers—all those who, to pursue the ideal of a false success, betrayed the values of the small town. Edward Arnold, the classic Capran villain, replicated rather closely the typical profile of the antagonist of the progressives: big business, the professional politician, corrupt and corrupter. Roosevelt, too, in his famous speech on the bank "holiday," attacked the "money changers," Wall Street finance, which had been responsible for the Great Crash, a traditional target of the anger of the American public because of the Puritan tradition linking economic success to productive labor rather than to speculation.

In 1936 and 1937, during an economic recession that was malignly coined "Roosevelt's Depression," the honeymoon between FDR and the country came to an end. The president was confronted by a growing wave of populist demagogy in the persons of Huey Long and Father Coughlin, both of whom posed a serious threat to Roosevelt's popularity and, consequently, to his reforms, which, until then, had been successful because of their popular support. At this point, to steal the thunder from Long's rhetoric, which proposed redistribution of wealth, FDR imposed the "wealth tax," which alienated the sympathies of the social class from which he came and transformed personalities such as Hearst from supporters into bitter critics of the administration. Roosevelt was convinced that the press, under the control of conservative capitalism, opposed and purposely distorted his politics. He relied more and more on the radio as the means to maintain direct contact with the people, delivering periodic attacks against the fourth estate—attacks that were not dissimilar in tone and in character from populist rhetoric and, in particular, from Capra's attitude in the *Mr. Deeds, Mr. Smith*, and *Meet John Doe* trilogy. Analogously, the director, in these films, attacked newspaper ownership, not the function and role of those journalists who were in contact with the authentic values of the American tradition.[29]

The Crisis of 1937 induced Roosevelt to adopt a neopopulist policy against the trusts. "Big" industrial structures, which had been practically sanctioned by the NRA, came under attack during this period. Among the main antimonopoly cases filed by the administration was the *Paramount* case, which questioned the entire structure of the film industry. The charge of monopoly was based both on vertical integration (the major production companies owned both distribution and exhibition) and on such trade practices as block booking, which limited the freedom of choice of the theater owner and sanctioned market control by the majors, obstructing the activity and, in a certain sense, the expressive autonomy of the smaller companies—the independent producers.

Among the personalities that the Antitrust Division, headed by Thurman Arnold, intended to call to the witness stand was Frank Capra, who seemed to represent the point of view of these smaller companies and of the industry's most pugnacious technical and creative staff. He was, in fact, particularly sensitive to the themes of independence, as demonstrated not only by his films, but also by his activities within the Directors Guild and by his legendary battles with Harry Cohn regarding the paternity of the films—"the name above the title." But Capra had "recently made arrangements with one of the big producers," according to the correspondence files of the *Paramount* case, and was therefore rejected as a witness.[30]

Success

Both Capra and FDR represent the typical American success story, although they came from situations poles apart. Roosevelt, who was "born with a silver spoon in his mouth," came from WASP stock of long standing. He was a "patrician," as Hofstadter defined him, who demonstrated a precocious gift for politics and administration in the navy and in the Democratic Party. After this initial personal success, he was paralyzed by an attack of polio in the fullness of his family, professional, and political life.[31] Roosevelt was able to overcome this terrible test with great inner strength and character (i.e., with ethical qualities and individual initiative). As a result of this difficult experience, he developed a strong sense of Christian charity toward his suffering neighbor.

Capra came from a poor family that had known only privation, tribulation, and hard work in Sicily and, as if in a nightmare, had found these same things in California, to the point that young Capra hated the American Dream of recent immigrants.[32] Through education (at Cal Tech) and work, but especially through individual enterprise (he did not disdain employing unorthodox methods of obtaining wealth, e.g., selling mining shares of dubious value to poor farmers or cheating at cards), Capra was able to make a success of himself. He most of all made money, which represented for him, as he repeats throughout his autobiography, a very important accomplishment. Later he was able to achieve success in his professional field by conducting a protracted and victorious battle against the studio system—the Hollywood machine that suffocated individual creativity. This image of Capra, as a romantic and somewhat of a screwball hero, similar to his protagonists, is, at the very least, incomplete. We must cast our minds instead to the likable scoundrels of his first films: urbane, disenchanted, and absolute individualists. "Get rich, get famous, get even" is the motto proposed in *The Miracle Woman*, and it can as well represent Capra's attitude toward life.

In an era when, within the criteria of social evaluation, personality and image were gradually taking the place of character (the individual identified with his ethical qualities),[33] Capra and Roosevelt functioned as intermediate models of transition. Both were,

6.2. Actors James Stewart and Guy Kibbee with Frank Capra on the set of *Mr. Smith Goes to Washington* (1939). (Museum of Modern Art/Film Stills Archive)

in fact, public personalities, orchestrators of the media, and, themselves, images constructed by the media. And yet, behind their image shined their character, the determination and the ethical qualities that characterized their success.

Past and Future

Populist ideals are usually identified with nostalgic attitudes—the dream of an impossible return to a mythically idyllic past—whereas the New Deal, with its emphasis on novelty, seemed to point straight toward the modern and toward the future. Capra's mid-1930s films, in addition to being a hymn to the virtues of an America of times gone by, constituted an authentic saga of American mythology, reviewing a vast repertoire of monuments (Grant's Tomb, the Lincoln Memorial) and of highly significant names (such as Longfellow Deeds and Jefferson Smith). "Things like that can only happen in a country like America," says Deeds, in front of Grant's Tomb, citing that particular version of the myth "from a log cabin to the White House," which saw the poor farmer from Ohio become a great soldier and then president. This is not a minor historical detail added by Capra for color: it is a deeply felt declaration of faith in the America of equal opportunity, the America that, by offering him success, had "redeemed" Capra. The historical and monumental references are never secondary in these films. They are placed instead in the moment of social catharsis for the hero and the community—a moment directly linked to the happy ending and to the sanction of the hero's success. Lawrence Levine has noted that "Capra is an important reminder that the reiteration of the traditional American creed emanated not just from defensive old-stock Americans but often issued in its most dynamic and aggressive form from converts to Americanism." Capra himself defined his work as "films that would be my way of saying, 'thanks, America.'" For Capra, the past was not just an inventory of intact traditions and on-going myths. It was a social force that he was able to salvage. Levine writes, "Capra is struggling to understand how traditional American values and means could be made to work in contemporary America": this refunctionalization came about through his films.[34]

Analogous historical, rhetorical, and monumental paraphernalia were mobilized by the New Dealers, especially after 1936. In the volume published for the Philadelphia Democratic Convention of 1936, during a delicate phase for Roosevelt's popularity and for the fate of the New Deal, this effort by the New Dealers to create a past for themselves, rooting themselves more deeply in the history of American institutions, becomes particularly evident. The cover is dedicated to Independence Hall; there is a photostatic reproduction of the American Constitution (but also an article by Charles Beard, author of a fundamental study on the economic matrix of this document). The history of the White House is narrated by parading the wives of past Democratic presidents.

Quotations by Jefferson, Wilson, and FDR are inserted at regular intervals. Even the advertisements in the volume continually recall the great traditions of the past, the myths of progress and success the "American way."[35] An account of Roosevelt's life written in typical *Reader's Digest* style, entitled "A Study in Backgrounds," attempts to explain his success by referring to his ancestral roots, to the persistence of a Dutchman accustomed to the battle to tame Nature.

This political document is not, therefore, a return to the past. In a quotation Franklin Roosevelt states, for example, that "democracy is not a static thing." This "usable past" is in fact instrumental in constructing the future. As Arnold noted, to guarantee its own acceptance the New Deal needed to assure people of its legitimate ascendancy. In the background we can trace the great debate between those who defended the sacredness—and therefore the immobility—of the Constitution and the New Dealers, dedicated to proving that their reforms were not unconstitutional (as the Supreme Court had ruled in reference to the NRA), but rather attempts to update the spirit of that document.

This operation of historical legitimation of the New Deal had vast implications. The New Deal administration created regional art repertories and centers of American history, organizing a rediscovery and a revitalization of American culture and traditions. In the 1930s the redefinition of Americanism involved not only conservatives and those nostalgic for the past, but also the Left, to the point that American Communists proclaimed to represent twentieth-century Americanism. (*Native Land*, the 1942 documentary on union rights by Leo Hurwitz and Paul Strand, functioned also as a lyrical and passionate appropriation of the American past).[36]

Fear

In assuming his office, Roosevelt proclaimed, "The only thing we have to fear is fear itself." According to Levine, the dominant character of American culture in the 1930s was fear—and the attempts to overcome that fear. Both Capra and FDR gave security and comfort to the Depressed Americans through a special touch of humanity in an almost instinctive recognition of the affective and emotional needs of the people. Roosevelt knew how to reassure the American people, not merely with his reforms, but also with his warm and calm tone of voice, with simple words, with the exemplary tales he used to simplify the real and to make plausible, nearly achieved, the impossible. FDR's speeches skipped the rational level and substituted it with common sense, with the education of the public, in pragmatic terms. His oratory contained profoundly ethical and religious terms and continually recalled society's and the individual's obligation not to forget the struggle of the forgotten men or the suffering of that "one third of a Nation ill-nourished, ill-clad, ill-housed." [37]

Christian solidarity as a response to the economic and social tensions of the time was typical of both Capra and Roosevelt, but in both this position underwent some transformations. Roosevelt, the patrician, went from a purely Christian perception of his fellowman to the idea of social justice and from welfare state to economic democracy. This democracy was not of an agrarian-populist form, but it had a redistributive model, which included antimonopolism, in order to guarantee economic freedom [38]—a project that would have been approved by the John Doe Clubs. The films by Catholic (though sui generis) Capra went from a phase in which the wealthy resolved the situations with their providential intervention (as in *It Happened One Night* and *You Can't Take It with You*) to one in which the collaboration of the people saved the hero and allowed his Utopia to come true.

Capra knew how to reassure the American lower middle class, in content by making use of the theme of solidarity and stylistically through his "Capra touch": the contagious humor of his comedies, the winning attitudes of his characters, the happy ending of his tales of social mobility. His optimism was actually forced and, in a sense, false, but it was necessary then.

The director gave voice to the fear that the institutional transformations imposed by the New Deal might be too radical or authoritarian—a fear particularly diffused among middle-class America after the reforms of 1937 and the Supreme Court crisis. In his essay on the representation of American politics in the cinema of the Depression era, Levine deals mainly with Capra, stressing how the director approached this fear of an authoritarian threat by pointing out the increasingly serious risks for American democracy: Deeds clashes with the snobbery and the cynicism of the metropolis, Smith with corrupt political power, Doe with a media tycoon who proposes himself as a sort of fascist dictator. It became increasingly difficult for Capra to react to these sociopolitical risks with a positive solution, as can be seen by the complex gestation of the five endings of *Meet John Doe*.[39]

Critical commentary holds that such films directed by Capra as *Mr. Smith* and *Meet John Doe*, with their paranoid representation of American politics, attack the New Deal, its institutional reforms, and Roosevelt's political leadership. Capra instead opposed false leaders, that is, those who manipulated social control to affirm their own power. He never opposed those leaders who received their investiture from the masses and who then represented the people. (However ably FDR manipulated the media and controlled public opinion, he was not a dictator. He achieved this result within consensus—created and maintained, but consensus just the same.)

Furthermore, Capra's characters usually win their battles through the use of oratory, a typically populist expressive form, whereas the "wicked" are associated with the written word. (Here the parallelism with FDR arises spontaneously.) Capra often deals with the control and function of mass media. Newspapermen are recurrent figures in his films. In *Meet John Doe* he expresses the fear of a possible monopolization and manipulation of the media by unscrupulous petty politicians. From a thematic point of view, politics and communications are represented in a manner that is anything but reassuring, but in the end a deeply rooted democracy always triumphs.

At this point one could pose the problem of how cinema represented all other media. Capra was, in fact, not simply a witness, a narrator, of the relationship between communications and politics. He was a key protagonist in this process. The way in which Capra described the power of cinema was symptomatic: "I never cease to thrill at an audience seeing a picture. For two hours you've got 'em. Hitler can't keep 'em that long. You eventually reach more people than Roosevelt does on the radio."[40] In a certain sense, Capra saw his films as being in competition for the president's audiences; he took for granted the similarity of film public and political audience that we postulated at the beginning of this chapter.

Capra's films are a decisive incursion by Hollywood cinema into the territory of political commitment—a commitment that the director assumed in full during World War II, supervising the Why We Fight series for the U.S. Army: Mr. Smith left Hollywood to go to Washington. It was not altogether an easy transfer; the concept that Hollywood could or should address politics was not generally accepted. Among the opponents to this involvement were, perhaps unexpectedly, the heads of the Office of War Information, who found Capra's series too full of propaganda and too "Hollywoodish." The Office of War Information criticized the series for its manipulative use of the spectator's emotions and for its simplification of the issues.[41] This criticism was not shared by other authorities; as far as the army and Roosevelt were concerned, during the war Hollywood was the ideal instrument for American propaganda, at home as well as abroad, and Capra its prophet. Sharing the vision of the world supported by the government, Hollywood and Capra wore their uniforms with a due sense of responsibility and with notable ease.

In the end, the paradox discussed in the introduction to this essay seems less implausible. In the New Deal, as in the films by Capra, pragmatism and utopian idealism joined forces. In an attempt to reconcile the irreconcilable, Roosevelt's fireside chats stimulated interest in the concrete results achieved by the New Deal, spinning a success story of his reforms—a story that was equally as improbable, but just as reassuring, as the happy endings of Capra's films. The New Deal made an effort to transform itself into a sort of federalism with a humanitarian face. Roosevelt added the appropriate rhetoric to an authentic spirit of solidarity, associated with the pragmatism of these reforms. He evoked a new spiritual force that the old Puritan ethic, so profoundly individualistic, had lost under the ruins of the Crash. The post–World War I migratory waves, in addition to corroding the monolithic superiority of WASP culture, had forcefully introduced other religious faiths, particularly Catholicism. In the 1930s this religion was receiving political and social legitimation in the United States. An important study of the New Dealers stated that:

> Together with Farley and Flynn, [Frank Walker] is a tacit reminder that Roosevelt's strongest single element of strength is the Catholic Church, infused with a new and dramatic spirit of liberalism by the great humanitarian, economic encyclicals of Pope Pius XI. The individualism of Protestantism has run its economic course to social confusion; the collective principles of Catholicism have been reaffirmed, after a lapse of four centuries, and are becoming a real force in American politics.[42]

The history of the writing of the Hays Code emphasizes how, even on this front, American Catholics affirmed not simply their cultural power, but also the force of their reforming ethic.[43] As far as Capra is concerned, even though he defined religion as "peasant stuff," his protagonists, humble and offended, often recall the figure of Christ. In his autobiography, Capra explained his "conversion" to a cinema of greater social commitment, after the success of *It Happened One Night*, with an authentic angelic apparition, similar to those in *It's a Wonderful Life*.[44]

Both Capra in his films and Roosevelt in his speeches appealed to the American tendency—of Puritan origin—to personalize conflict and to internalize the faults of society, searching for the origins of evil not within the system, but within the individual. If the causes of evil were within the scope of individual responsibility, they were controllable, easier to take care of, by appealing to the resources of the nation's moral forces. Virtues such as courage, faith, and enterprise guaranteed the redemption of the country. These could not be the same virtues as had existed in the past, in their populist version. The injection of Catholicism could be particularly productive in a moment of such crisis.

Even leaving aside this ideological Catholic element, the New Deal, in the person of Roosevelt—and Capra in popular culture—tried to react to the emotional needs of the community. In describing what he was trying to do with his films, Capra said, "The world was hungry for a lift; hungry for quickening examples of how individuals overcome the dreads of their environment. That was my needed job: lift the human spirit."[45] While Roosevelt tried to reassure the people with his fireside chats, transmitting human warmth directly, using radio waves to reach the people in their living rooms, Capra addressed his audience in the movie theaters, and yet they both communicated with the individual, positioned in the domestic community.[46] To accomplish this task they used the media—radio and the silver screen—demonstrating how these means of communication could transmit not only messages, but also emotions. They dreamt of an organic relationship between the individual and society—a relationship, as Arnold had indicated, in which the one recognized not only the material necessities of others, but also their characteristics and emotional needs: a dream in which the means of communication had an essential role.

Capra had trouble with the ending of *Meet John Doe* and in general with the endings of the Deeds-Smith-Doe trilogy because it was difficult to suture social contradictions in the comforting closure of a narrative structure. It was especially difficult to exorcise the dark ghost of self-destruction, which seemed to return inexorably in many of his films. But Capra always found a happy ending for his stories, which, beyond rational logic, comforted his audience, with a shifting into the world of magic—of achieved utopias. It is not out of place, then, to remember that Roosevelt had given specific instructions to his ghost writers to conclude his speeches on a high note—epic, edifying, and, above all, reassuring.

Notes

1. This interaction has been examined in my book, *Hollywood's New Deal* (Philadelphia: Temple Univ. Press, 1997). On communications see Daniel J. Czitrom, *Media and the American Mind: From Morse to McLuhan* (Chapel Hill: Univ. of North Carolina Press, 1982), and Warren I. Susman, *Culture as History: The Transformation of American Society in the Twentieth Century* (New York: Pantheon, 1984).

2. The political articulation of classical Hollywood cinema, in addition to being registered in its "constitution," the Hays Code, is evident (1) in the way this cinema elaborated social conflict, through the very structure of the classic narrative; (2) in the connections between the film industry and the administration (e.g., in the case of such personalities as Joseph Kennedy, Raymond Moley, and Frank

Walker); and (3) in the politicization—and unionization—of the Hollywood community in the 1930s.

3. Susman, *Culture as History*, 159.

4. "At the core of the New Deal was not a philosophy (FDR could identify himself philosophically only as a Christian and a democrat), but an attitude." Richard Hofstadter, *The Age of Reform: From Bryan to FDR* (New York: Knopf, 1955), 323. Hofstadter's interpretations, both of the New Deal and of the reform movements, were influential in the writing of this essay. On New Deal ideology see Howard Zinn, *New Deal Thought* (Indianapolis: Bobbs-Merrill, 1966). On the New Deal in general, see William E. Leuchtenburg, *Roosevelt and the New Deal* (New York: Harper & Row, 1963); Arthur Schlesinger, Jr., *The Age of Roosevelt*, 3 vols. (Boston: Houghton Mifflin, 1957–60); and Frank Friedel, *Franklin D. Roosevelt*, 4 vols. (Boston: Little, Brown, 1952–73).

5. Significant revisionist interpretations of the New Deal, which emphasize the continuity with a reformist past, include *Towards a New Past*, ed. Barton Bernstein (New York: Pantheon, 1968); Gabriel Kolko, *Main Currents in Modern American History* (New York: Pantheon, 1975); and *The Rise and Fall of the New Deal, 1930–1980*, ed. Gary Gerstle and Steve Fraser (Princeton, N.J.: Princeton Univ. Press, 1989). Both Leuchtenburg and Hofstadter play important roles in the revisionist field, as well.

6. In addition to Hofstadter's work on populism, see Alan Brinkley, *Voices of Protest: Huey Long, Father Coughlin, and the Great Depression* (New York: Knopf, 1982). Jeffrey Richards, "The Ideology of Populism," in *Visions of Yesterday* (London: Routledge & Kegan Paul, 1973), introduced the identification of Capra with populism.

7. Recently there has been a revision of the interpretation of populism and of its conservative nature. In their introduction to *The New Populism: The Politics of Empowerment*, ed. Harry C. Boyte and Frank Riessman (Philadelphia: Temple Univ. Press, 1986), the editors argue that "populism grows from the life of actual communities that seek to control the forces that threaten to overwhelm them" (4) and thus challenges the conventional Left and Right. An important contribution to this reinterpretation is Craig Jackson Calhoun, "The Radicalism of Tradition," *American Journal of Sociology* 88, no. 5 (1983): 886–914.

8. On reformist movements see Eric Goldman, *Rendezvous with Destiny: A History of Modern American Reform* (New York: Knopf, 1954), and Richard Hofstadter, *The American Political Tradition and the Men Who Made It* (New York: Knopf, 1948).

9. Lawrence Levine, "American Culture and the Great Depression," *Yale Review* 74, no. 2 (1985), 196–223.

10. Arnold wrote an extremely ironic chapter on the antitrust laws in *The Folklore of Capitalism* (New Haven: Yale Univ. Press, 1937). The book was a best-seller during the 1930s; shortly after its publication, Arnold was nominated as head of the Antitrust Division. On Arnold, see Gene M. Gressley, ed., *Voltaire and the Cowboy: The Letters of Thurman Arnold* (Boulder: Colorado Associated Univ. Press, 1977), and Edward N. Kearny, *Thurman Arnold, Social Critic: The Satirical Challenge to Orthodoxy* (Albuquerque: Univ. of New Mexico Press, 1970). The

quoted passage is from Arnold, *The Bottlenecks of Business* (New York: Reynal & Hitchcock, 1940), 96.

11. Arnold, *Folklore of Capitalism*, 2–3.

12. Ibid., 137–38.

13. Ibid., 343–45.

14. As Richard Westbrook writes, "Nineteenth-century partisan culture fostered an active, rich symbolic experience of community, ethno-religious, and class solidarity, while for the modern American voter electoral politics has, by virtue of its transformation into an exercise in mass marketing, come to share with other spheres of experience the peculiar features of the culture of consumption: passivity, atomization, and spectatorship." Richard Westbrook, "Politics as Consumption," in *The Culture of Consumption*, ed. R. Wightman Fox and T. J. Jackson Lears (New York: Pantheon, 1983), 151.

15. Susman, *Culture as History*, xx.

16. Hofstadter remarks, "Arnold's work, with its skepticism about right-thinking citizens, its rejection of fixed moral principles and disinterested rationality in politics, its pragmatic temper, its worship of accomplishment, its apotheosis of organization and institutional discipline, and its defense of political machines, may exaggerate the extent of the difference between the New Deal and pre-war Progressivism, but it does point sharply to the character of that difference." *Age of Reform*, 321–22.

17. Cf. the title of Gene M. Gressley's edition of Arnold's letters, *Voltaire and the Cowboy*.

18. According to a Gallup Poll of 14 August 1938, quoted in Robert S. Fine, "Roosevelt's Radio Chatting" (Ph.D. diss., New York University, 1977). On FDR's relationship with public opinion, see E. E. Cornwell, *Presidential Leadership of Public Opinion* (Bloomington: Indiana Univ. Press, 1965), and Richard W. Steele, *Propaganda in an Open Society: The Roosevelt Administration and the Media 1933–1941* (Westport, Conn.: Greenwood Press, 1985).

19. Margaret Thorp, *America at the Movies* (New Haven: Yale Univ. Press, 1939). On cinema audiences see Leo Handel, *Hollywood Looks at Its Audience* (Urbana: Univ. of Illinois Press, 1950), and Garth Jowett, "Giving Them What They Want: Movie Audience Research before 1950," in *Current Research in Film: Audiences, Economics, Law*, vol. 1, ed. Bruce A. Austin (Norwood, N.J.: Ablex, 1985).

20. See the following congressional hearings on motion picture trade practices: House Committee on Interstate and Foreign Commerce, Subcommittee, *Motion-Picture Films: Hearings before a Subcommittee of the Committee on Interstate and Foreign Commerce*, 74th Cong., 2d sess., March 1936; Senate Committee on Interstate and Foreign Commerce, *Motion-Picture Films: Hearings before the Committee on Interstate and Foreign Commerce on S. 280*, 76th Cong., 1st sess., April 1939; House Committee on Interstate and Foreign Commerce, *Motion-Picture Films (Compulsory Block Booking and Blind Selling): Hearings before the Committee on Interstate and Foreign Commerce on S. 280*, 76th Cong., 3d sess., pt. 1, May 1940; House Committee on Interstate and Foreign Commerce, *Motion-Picture Films (Compulsory Block Booking and Blind Selling): Hearings before the*

Committee on Interstate and Foreign Commerce on S. 280, 76th Cong., 3d sess., pt. 2, May-June 1940.

21. My approach to Capra is based, for the most part, on his autobiography, *The Name above the Title* (New York: Macmillan, 1971), and on viewing of his films. See also *Frank Capra: The Man and His Films*, ed. Richard Glatzer and John Raeburn (Ann Arbor: Univ. of Michigan Press, 1975); Robert Sklar, *Movie-Made America: A Cultural History of American Films* (New York: Vintage, 1975, rev. 1994); Andrew Bergman, *We're in the Money: Depression America and Its Films* (New York: New York Univ. Press, 1971); and Joseph McBride, *Frank Capra: The Catastrophe of Success* (New York: Simon & Schuster, 1992).

22. Capra, *Name above the Title*, 186.

23. See Susman, *Culture as History*, 196.

24. George L. Mosse, *The Nationalization of the Masses* (New York: H. Fertig, 1974).

25. Susman, *Culture as History*, 264–67.

26. Fine, "Roosevelt's Radio Chatting," compares the voice-over narration of the documentary and this fireside chat, 252–57.

27. The most interesting personality in this respect was Rexford Tugwell, one of the main brain trusters and the "producer," at the Resettlement Administration, of Pare Lorentz's films.

28. Bergman, *We're in the Money*, 141–48.

29. On the relationship between FDR and the press, see Graham J. White, *FDR and the Press* (Chicago: Univ. of Chicago Press, 1979).

30. Almost certainly this was with Warners, for *Meet John Doe* (letter from David Podell to Paul Williams, 7 March 1940, Antitrust Division). This section is the product of an analysis of the Correspondence Files of the Paramount Case 1938–42 at the Antitrust Division of the Department of Justice in Washington, D.C. On the case see also Michael Conant, *Antitrust in the Motion Picture Industry* (Berkeley and Los Angeles: Univ. of California Press, 1960).

31. There seems to be a parallelism between the paralysis of the president—negated by the photographs of the time and sublimated by his traveling, by his extraordinary political dynamism, and by his expressive mobility—and the "paralysis" of the country, which could be overcome by an analogous commitment, a similar engagement of moral strength.

32. "Forty years that could only happen in America; that began with a childhood hate for America." Capra, *Name above the Title*, 236. The first pages of the director's autobiography describe, in melodramatic terms, the American nightmare of a young Capra, from the journey to America, to the work of his mother in an olive grove, to the tragic death of his father, and so forth.

33. Warren Susman, "Personality and the Making of a Twentieth-Century Culture," in *New Directions in American Intellectual History*, ed. John Higham and Paul Conkin (Baltimore: Johns Hopkins Univ. Press, 1979).

34. Lawrence Levine, "Hollywood's Washington: Film Images of National Politics during the Great Depression," *Prospects* 10 (1985): 191; Capra, *Name above the Title*, 240; Levine, "Hollywood's Washington," 189.

35. Some examples: a brand of whiskey used Jackson's portrait with a slogan, "Character marks the leader"; an alcoholic beverages company boasted: "Since

1840—Through 24 Presidential Terms." See *The Democratic National Convention 1936* (Philadelphia: Democratic National Committee, 1936).

36. See William Alexander, *Film on the Left: American Documentary Film from 1931 to 1942* (Princeton, N.J.: Princeton Univ. Press, 1981), and "Native Land: An Interview with Leo Hurwitz," *Cineaste* 6, no. 3 (1974), 2–7.

37. Levine, "American Culture and the Depression," 200–203; quotation from Franklin D. Roosevelt speech, 4 March 1937, as cited in James MacGregor Burns, *Roosevelt: The Lion and the Fox* (New York: Harcourt, Brace, 1956), 299.

38. On economic thought and monopoly, see E. W. Hawley, *The New Deal and the Problem of Monopoly* (Princeton, N.J.: Princeton Univ. Press, 1966).

39. The five different endings that the director tried out for *Meet John Doe* are discussed in Capra, *Name above the Title*, 303–5.

40. Quoted in Bergman, *We're in the Money*, 148.

41. See Giuliana Muscio, "La guerre en celluloid," *Positif* 177 (1976): 40–48, and Clayton R. Koppes and Gregory D. Black, *Hollywood Goes to War: How Politics, Profits, and Propaganda Shaped World War II Movies* (New York: Free Press, 1987).

42. J. F. Carter, *The New Dealers* (New York: Simon & Schuster, 1934), 258.

43. For an analysis of Hollywood's self-censorship and of the battle for the ideological and cultural control of the cinema, see Sklar, *Movie-Made America*. On the Hays Code see also Lea Jacobs, *The Wages of Sin: Censorship and the Fallen Woman Film, 1928–1942* (Madison: Univ. of Wisconsin Press, 1991); *Prima dei Codici 2: Alle porte di Hays/Before the Codes 2: The Gateway to Hays*, ed. Giuliana Muscio (Milan: Fabbri, 1991); and Richard Maltby, "The Production Code and the Hays Office," in Tino Balio, *Grand Design: Hollywood as a Modern Business Enterprise, 1930–1939* (New York: Scribner's, 1993), 37–72.

44. Leonard Quart, "Frank Capra and the Popular Front," *Cineaste* 8, no. 1 (1977), 4–7; Capra, *Name above the Title*, 175–77.

45. Capra, *Name above the Title*, 203.

46. FDR had a favorite conceptualization of "the people": "Frances Perkins noted that he thought of those listening to his Fireside Chats 'individually.' He thought of them in family groups. He thought of them sitting around on a suburban porch after supper on a summer evening . . . He never thought of them as masses." William Stott, *Documentary Expression and Thirties America* (New York: Oxford Univ. Press, 1973), 100. In reference to cinema, the spirit of the Hays Code asserted that cinema was designed to be family entertainment.

7

Mr. Smith Goes to Washington: Democratic Forums and Representational Forms

Charles Wolfe

The Institutional Context

At a rough average, about half a million words of political news and comment are telegraphed out of Washington daily. There is perhaps an equal volume of mailed material—daily and weekly "letters" and "columns," special feature articles, along with an oral flood of speeches, debates, and whatnot poured from local broadcasting stations directly into the Nation's homes. Finally, there is the presentation of political events, personalities, and interviews in the newsreels of at least four national motion-picture producers, and in the "stills" of many press photographers . . . Probably no other city in the world is kept so prominently and continually in the public eye and the public mind.

As a result, most literate inhabitants of the United States are scarcely less familiar with Washington, its policies, personalities, and public buildings, than they are with their own communities; and sooner or later most of them come to the

Reprinted with minor revisions with the permission of the publisher and author from Charles Wolfe, "*Mr. Smith Goes to Washington:* Democratic Forums and Representational Forms," in Peter Lehman, ed., *Close Viewings: An Anthology of New Film Criticism.* Gainesville: University Press of Florida, 1990.

tangible city. They are thoroughly at home here in a historic and political atmosphere which they have breathed vicariously since childhood, and amid surroundings which they have seen pictured countless times.[1]

A 1937 Federal Writers' Project guidebook to Washington, D.C., thus describes political news coverage of the nation's capital in an age of media journalism. Notably absent from this description is any hint that the transmission of information from Washington was anything less than a neutral and natural process, that the system that ostensibly familiarized "literate inhabitants" with the central scene of national politics in America was itself an institutional structure with political force. Yet the passage tacitly acknowledges that what is made possible by the technological media is not simply the dissemination of an image of the "tangible city" of Washington but the forging of a national political identity, an audience's sense of belonging to a historical tradition and of inhabiting a political environment as familiar as home.

It is useful to keep the existence and influence of a mediating network of this kind in mind when attempting to place *Mr. Smith Goes to Washington* historically, for it reminds us that the system responsible for the production and circulation of this particular depiction of Washington—the motion picture industry—operated in relation to other image-making institutions with which it may have simultaneously competed and cooperated at different levels of activity.[2] Hollywood's domain, of course, was that of commercial entertainment. By the late 1930s the very term "Hollywood" had come to stand for both an economic system for the production and delivery of commercial motion pictures to theaters around the world and a particular way of organizing those pictures, a highly conventionalized system for the telling of stories and the display of spectacle and stars. In this sense Hollywood constituted a distinct sphere of activity, yet one bound to the world of media journalism by the industry's need for publicity and promotion and to federal, state, and local governments by the government's power to influence trade practices.

For the moviegoer perhaps the most visible connection between Hollywood's product and the work of media journalism occurred at the exhibition site itself, where the commercial newsreels to which the Federal Writers' Project alludes were shown as part of a package of motion picture entertainment. By way of these newsreels, public officials entered into circulation as political performers—indeed, they could become political stars—and political events were translated into news stories, mininarratives that on occasion included dramatic reenactment. Moreover, the escalation of political conflict in Europe at the close of the decade and the growing popularity of celebrity radio commentators to narrate news about the outbreak of war were met by increased attention to topical news material within the framework of the film exhibitor's program. In some cases the argument for such a move was economic in a local sense: broadcasting news in the theaters might lure the potential filmgoers away from the family radio. But a kind of civic argument—congruent with the long-term economic health of the industry, to be sure—was articulated as well. Three days after the outbreak of war in Europe in September 1939, a columnist in *Variety*, John C. Flinn, proposed that in times of crisis film theaters should be thought of as "places of public assembly, meeting halls of democracy" where the "trend of national thought" was discernible, and that emphasis on this political function of the theater in the social life of the community could bring new prestige to the industry. Here Hollywood's trade press echoed concurrent efforts by the radio industry to promote the "service" it provided citizens by way of its coverage of political events. The chief distinction was the site of political engagement and debate; if radio had transformed domestic space into a new civic space, the commercial film theater, according to Flinn, provided a space for public assembly, a new American "town hall." [3]

The notion that public service was a product to be capitalized on at a time of social stress echoed the formal position articulated during the period by Will H. Hays, head of the Motion Picture Producers and Distributors Association (MPPDA). Well connected in Washington, Hays fended off federal censorship initiatives in the early thirties by overseeing the development of the Production Code Administration (PCA), the industry's self-censoring agency, headed after 1934 by Joseph Breen in Los Angeles. After the passage of the New Deal's National Industrial Recovery Act in the summer of 1933, the Hays Office also assumed primary responsibility for drafting the Motion Picture Code of Fair Competition, which granted tacit approval to the industry's oligopolistic structure and trade practices. But this code remained in effect only until the Supreme Court declared the National Industrial Recovery Act unconstitutional in 1935, and even as one branch of the Roosevelt administration was catering to the demands of the MPPDA, the Justice Department was investigating the film industry for possible violation of antitrust laws. In the summer of 1938 Thurman Arnold, chief of the department's Antitrust Division, filed suit against the industry on these grounds, and efforts by the MPPDA to block this action by drafting a new trade practice code with the Commerce Department were derailed by Arnold in August 1939. Concurrently the U.S. Senate passed the Neely Bill, designed to ban Hollywood's practice of distributing films to theaters in blocks rather than selling them individually; scheduled to be voted on by the House in 1940, it was the object of extensive lobbying at the time of *Mr. Smith*'s release. Events in Europe only exacerbated the MPPDA's economic concerns; with the outbreak of war, foreign markets began to close, an event lobbyists for the industry were quick to note when arguing against both the antitrust and the Neely initiatives, and the threat of federal political censorship was raised anew in Congress.[4]

Hays's public response to these events was to seek high moral ground, projecting an image of the industry as socially responsible and civic-minded. In his March 1939 address to the annual gathering of the MPPDA in New York, Hays argued that producers in Hollywood were increasingly selecting stories that emphasized "Americanism" and "mankind's struggle for freedom" and had discovered that these themes were not incompatible with "the best interest of the box-office." By distributing these films abroad, Hays proposed, the film industry also was countering the efforts of government-controlled media in foreign countries to portray American democracy as a failed political system. As for recent antitrust proceedings, Hays expressed hope that the federal government would recognize the "special significance and peculiarly difficult problems" of the film industry as an international leader in providing "good and necessary recreation at a moderate cost." In short, Hays was formulating precisely the kind of defense of the studio system that would allow the MPPDA to win the government's sanction as an "essential industry" during World War II, with economic profit inextricably linked to public policy at a time of national crisis.[5]

Given a political climate of this kind, it is perhaps not surprising that the Production Code Administration paid close attention to story material submitted to them that depicted the very governmental bodies with which the MPPDA had to deal. Thus, when Lewis R. Foster's "The Gentleman from Montana" was submitted to the PCA for consideration as possible script material by both MGM and Paramount in January 1938, Joseph Breen quickly sent up a red flag, warning that its depiction of corruption in the Senate could be political dynamite both at home and abroad. In late February, when Columbia Pictures expressed interest in the material as well, Geoffrey Shurlock, Breen's assistant, met with three representatives from the studio to discuss the PCA's concerns about the material. Director Rouben Mamoulian visited PCA offices in June to discuss his interest in working on the project for Columbia; Shurlock similarly advised him of the PCA's misgivings.[6]

"The Gentleman from Montana," however, soon came to the attention of Columbia's premier director, Frank Capra, who announced in November that he saw in the story the possibility of making a more overtly political version of his successful 1936 film, *Mr. Deeds Goes to Town*.[7] After spending several weeks in Washington researching the production with writer Sidney Buchman and cinematographer Joe Walker, Capra had a draft of a screenplay ready for PCA inspection in January 1939. Breen's response was considerably milder: he proposed some minor deletions (primarily dialogue written for Smith's cynical secretary, Saunders) that toned down the implication that corruption was pervasive in Washington. But, in deferring to Hays for a "policy" ruling on the material, he advised his boss that the script's emphasis on the recovery of democratic traditions might prove very timely. Hays backed Breen's handling of the case but instructed him to advise Columbia of Hays's personal concern about the project and requested that the studio be especially careful to adhere to Senate protocol in any dramatic reenactments. Passing this message on to studio head Harry Cohn, Breen followed the script closely through its final revision in April. Upon seeing the finished film in September, he declared it a "magnificent picture" and recommended only a single deletion unrelated to political concerns.[8]

Breen's change of heart may have been motivated by alterations to the original material worked by Buchman's script (it is clear he read each version carefully), but it is also logical to assume that he was influenced by Capra's involvement on the project. By 1939 Capra had staked out a unique position as a director in Hollywood. The popular and critical success of his films had given him a platform from which openly to criticize industry practices, including censorship and block booking, and to contemplate independent production.[9] At the same time respect for his work in Hollywood ran deep: he had received Academy Awards for his direction of *It Happened One Night* (1934) and *Mr. Deeds Goes to Town* (1936), and he would win a third for *You Can't Take It with You* (1938) while the PCA's review of *Mr. Smith*'s script was in progress. Moreover, by 1938 Capra had reached celebrity status in the national news media; featured on the cover of *Time* magazine in August and in a photo spread on the making of *You Can't Take It with You* in *Life* in November, he had acquired a reputation both for the control he exercised over his films and his willingness to tackle social themes.[10] His tendency to describe his work as motivated by a desire to both entertain and inspire—if far less gaseous than the pronouncements of Hays—nevertheless conformed to the ideal role the MPPDA chief laid out for the industry. Indeed, Capra's willingness to criticize the moguls of the MPPDA may have given this claim the kind of weight Hays's public statements lacked for many commentators on Hollywood during this period.[11]

Capra's name attached to the project also guaranteed that *Mr. Smith* would attract substantial publicity in advance of its release, and the subject matter of the film only amplified this media interest. Much of the publicity focused on Capra's effort to ensure the accuracy of the film's replication of the Senate chamber and the scripting of a typical Capra plot for this setting. In the popular press this combination of scrupulous documentation and Hollywood dramaturgy was a source of great interest.[12] Behind the scenes, however, the attempt to mix documentation and dramatization of the Washington political scene was not without practical difficulties. James B. Preston, an ex-superintendent of the Senate whose role as technical advisor on the film was much touted in the press, came into conflict with the crew and quit the project at a key moment in the production.[13] Capra also ran up against a Department of the Interior ruling prohibiting the photographing of identifiable figures inside the Lincoln Memorial, thus jeopardizing his effort to dramatize and subjectify the space of the national monument.[14] And the national office of the Boy Scouts, upon reviewing the screenplay, refused permission for the name of their organization to be used in *Mr. Smith* in light of its depiction of the U.S. Senate.[15]

These incidents probably seemed minor at the time, but in retrospect they presaged a controversy that erupted in the nation's capital after the gala premiere of the film at Constitution Hall on 7 October 1939. Sponsored by the National Press Club to honor Preston (the film's consultant on the Senate), the event attracted the Washington political establishment: an estimated four thousand congressmen, press correspondents, and invited guests crowded into the hall, while Capra and his wife shared a special box with the family of Burton K. Wheeler, the Montana senator on whose early career the original story for the film had reportedly been based. But the planned celebration—a promotional event for moviemakers, politicians, and journalists alike—ended up an unhappy affair for all concerned. In his 1971 autobiography Capra describes in detail his memory of the film's cool reception by the audience that evening and the personal attack he endured at the hands of the Washington press corps at a party later that night. In the days to follow, moreover, reporters joined forces with irate senators (led by Majority Leader Alben W. Barkley of Kentucky) to make public their opposition to the film. Several congressmen let it be known that the Neely Bill hearings might be rushed through the House in retaliation. Legal counsel for the association of independent exhibitors (which favored the Neely Bill and was thus not reluctant to fan the flames of the controversy) advised all theaters showing the film to run a trailer disclaiming any intention to discredit Congress or the press. Criticism rapidly spread to the editorial pages of various newspapers around the country. Columbia closely monitored reactions in Washington to gauge the potential effect of the uproar, and industry leaders were rumored to be worried that the domestic release of the film had perhaps been a grave political blunder. Joseph P. Kennedy, U.S. ambassador to England, personally urged Harry Cohn not to release the film overseas.[16]

A general theme of the attacks, as Breen had first warned, was that the film was unpatriotic for suggesting that corruption was deeply rooted in the American political system; more specific critiques from Washington focused on the film's depiction of senators and reporters and the staging of the filibuster. Those assembled at Constitution Hall, Richard L. Strout argued in the *Christian Science Monitor*, had learned how Hollywood viewed (and would have people see) Washington correspondents and politicians: the former were "cynical but lovable drunkards," and the latter "winked their eyes at political corruption." "It is a Senate," Strout went on to complain, "in which galleries freely cheer after speeches and spectators shout down instructions to favorite senators; it is a Senate in which members boo or applaud a colleague or shun him altogether." That the reproduction of the setting was so authentic, he and other critics noted, only made "distortions" of this kind more dangerous. Senator Barkley angrily complained that outside of Washington—in "Queedunk and Podunk and Tracey Corners"—the film might be taken as true to life.[17]

Within a month, however, the furor had died down. Protests against the film had stimulated box-office receipts during its opening run in Washington; further protest from congressmen and reporters thus may have appeared self-defeating. Moreover, harsh criticism from Washington soon engendered a backlash. Most critics in Los Angeles, who had previewed the film two weeks before, were on record as strong supporters; now they were joined by first-string critics for the major New York dailies, who accused the Washington insiders of being exceptionally thin-skinned. Columbia abetted the campaign by circulating a press packet of reviews that emphasized the film's patriotic dimension, and the distribution of a *Photoplay* study guide, endorsed by the National Education Association, to schools around the country probably enhanced the film's reputation as a civic-minded work.[18] In a sense the interpretation of *Mr. Smith* offered by those who had attended the Washington preview came to be supplanted by an alternative one in which the film was understood, in Frank S.

Nugent's phrase, as "a comic celebration of the spirit, rather than the form, of American government."[19] This second assessment, moreover, seems to have laid the groundwork for what has emerged over the years as the dominant cultural reading of the film in which *Mr. Smith* is understood to mark a transition in American popular thought, as doubts raised by the Great Depression at home were superseded by anxieties concerning the outbreak of war overseas, and to respond to those anxieties in a spirit of new nationalism with the invocation of an ideal political inheritance to be reclaimed. On this point Breen had been no less prescient.[20]

But the earlier reaction—shaped by the vested interests of the Washington political community—helps us place this reading in a critical perspective. First, it points to a certain contradiction in that particular American political myth that values the "spirit" of a national government over and against the constraints of its "form," as if the notion of government itself might somehow be detached from those institutional structures and mechanisms by which it is constituted and sustained. Functional systems in this context are seen as a manifestation of a fallen world of real social practices. Second, it illuminates a structural tension produced by the growing power of Hollywood to intervene in the process by which activities in Washington were represented to the public at large. On the one hand, the motion picture industry had the capacity to glamorize these activities, perhaps the very reason the National Press Club sought to celebrate the making of the film in the first place. On the other hand, Hollywood could be considered a threat, a disrupting force with its own procedures for the dissemination of images and ideas from the seat of national politics. Thus, whereas *Mr. Smith* can be logically considered part and parcel of Hollywood's contribution to the renewal of national political sentiment and in this respect to have helped build the kind of bridge between Hollywood and Washington that was to be crucial for wartime consensus, specific groups may have understood that with this interpenetration of systems of national representation they had something to lose—that, by representing Washington on the screen, Hollywood was also modifying the terms by which the nation's capital was to be perceived in the popular imagination.

The Work of the Text

Thus far I have been concerned with the different institutional pressures—both competing and cooperative—that bore upon the making of *Mr. Smith Goes to Washington*, molding it as a social object at a particular historical moment. But it remains to be demonstrated how an understanding of this context helps us grasp *Mr. Smith* as a work of film fiction. To be aware of the varying responses to the project up through the time of its initial release is a step toward clarifying the social relations within which the work was deeply embedded in the late 1930s. But I am also interested here in identifying the work of this filmic text, the particular forms of coherence it mobilizes in constructing a fiction out of images, events, and political discourses drawn from the social field of which it is itself a part—in short, in specifying how the film transforms the social material it engages.

Mr. Smith Goes to Washington, like the passage from the Federal Writers guidebook quoted previously, offers a model for the relationship of national political institutions to a diffuse public as mediated by a news network. But where the guidebook describes a circular communication process operating in a state of perfect equilibrium, with the information transmitted out of Washington wholly commensurate with the "reality" of the city experienced by the visitor, *Mr. Smith* dramatizes imbalances and deceptions in a system that functions smoothly only to the extent that genuine political motives and machination are masked. Under the terms of the guidebook's model, "informed" visitors, having absorbed in advance a stream of words and images flowing out of the city, are as at home in Washington as they would be in their local community; presumably they can either return to that community with the reality of Washington reconfirmed by lived experience or stay to serve the ongoing reproduction of the image of that city in the "public mind." In *Mr. Smith*, however, the journey of the protagonist to Washington results in a divided conception of the capital city. For Smith, standing in front of the visitor's information counter at Union Station, his eye caught by a view of the distant Capitol dome, it is the repository of a set of political ideals. For politicians and the press, however, it is a scene of compromise, chicanery, even corruption. The trajectory of the central character opens up the city to incompatible "readings"; Washington emerges as an unstable symbolic site.

Here we can isolate one aspect of the work of the text: its narrative construction, its plotting of a story. In simplest form this narrative is signaled by the film's title, itself an allusion (as the scoring of "Yankee Doodle [Went to Town]" under the credit sequence suggests) to a familiar narrative motif in American popular culture: the journey of an innocent protagonist from the country to the city, where he or she is subject to mockery or exploitation. The premise of *Mr. Smith* thus can be said to activate a narrative founded on a binary motif that is at once culturally deep-rooted and topically charged. The spectator, fresh from a credit sequence printed on colonial signboards and overlaid with a colonial folk tune, is plunged at the outset into a world of contemporary political brokering, an inside view of the operation of a powerful political machine, set in motion (and at risk) by the death of a front man in the U.S. Senate. Deferred during the course of the opening passages is the debut of the film's title character, whose absence from and ignorance of any such scene of political intrigue are central to his value to Boss Taylor's machine, as well as to the fictional plotting of the film itself, which will exploit the gap between Smith's knowledge and that of the professional politicians to generate dramatic tension and irony.

Our introduction to Smith in the banquet sequence, however, inaugurates a countermovement in the narrative, one of retrospection, a power grounded in knowledge of and sentiment for the past. Thus, against the machine's manufactured ballyhoo that opens the passage, Smith invokes the memory of his socially committed father, and at the close of the sequence he exchanges tearful glances with his Boy Rangers as "Auld Lang Syne" swells up on the sound track. Then, his back to the forward motion of the train that propels him to a senatorial post in Washington at the behest of the political machine, Smith elicits from Joseph Paine a recollection of the senior senator's early crusades with Smith's father. Loss pervades the scene—a cause lost by a slain father, a father lost to his son, ideals lost by the partner who survives—but planted here by the plot (under the guise of a recollection of early story material) is a model for political action (even if self-destructive) and a bond between two characters (established by their exchange of looks and the articulated memory they share) that will inform the film's climactic scene on the Senate floor. With Smith's arrival in Washington, this retrospective view then broadens to encompass a national political mythology. Smith's tour of the monuments and memorials of Washington weaves fragments of political icons, documents, and folk tunes into a kind of mythic reverie—Smith's reverie, the film suggests, but also a collective myth presumably shared by other visitors: an old man who assists his young companion in reciting the Gettysburg Address, for example, or a solitary black man who stands reverently before the statue of the Great Emancipator.

A path through these conflicting views of federal politics is plotted by way of a narrative pattern of double exposure. Gradually exposed to the system he serves, Smith comes of age as an agent in the center of national political activity and (in a subordinate but interwoven story line) as romantic partner to Saunders, his secretary and tutor. Members of the political establishment in turn are exposed to Smith and to those "lost" values with which he is associated. In a series of metaphorical moves by the fiction, Smith is figured as a contemporary Jefferson or Lincoln, and the "gaze" of the commemorative statue of Lincoln is explicitly interpreted by Saunders as a summons to Smith to accept the role of contemporary political hero. Arresting Taylor's machine just at the moment when its graft scheme is about to be unwittingly enacted by the Senate and sustaining that arrest through recourse to a filibuster, Smith brings to a halt the scripted proceedings of the Senate and substitutes for them a renewal of national political covenants within a Senate chamber where only a handful of representatives of a public constituency are licensed to speak and to act. Imagery first evoked during the young visitor's historical reverie—a montage designed by Slavko Vorkapich in which spatial and temporal limits seem temporarily suspended[21]—now finds expression within a democratic forum for official political discourse and rule-governed public debate.

Here we can isolate a second way in which the film transforms social material: through performance. Performance figures, first of all, *within* narrative. The maturation of the hero and the conversion of cynics both hinge on a series of vocal performances by

Smith, occasions for the protagonist to test his capacity to speak persuasively before skeptical auditors in contexts of increasing dramatic import.[22] "Character" becomes the locus point for the condensation of narrative tensions; having learned of his betrayal by Paine, Smith is forced to cope with those conflicting conceptions of the capital city that the film has dramatized. Silenced, on the verge of fleeing this scene of betrayal, he is then redirected by Saunders toward his heroic performance on the Senate floor. The central political question the film raises—what *is* Washington, a repository of political ideals or the scene of their inevitable compromise?—thus closes down around the question of character psychology and behavior. Smith fights back against disillusionment while Paine wrestles with guilt until public confession by the latter vindicates the former.

Performance, moreover, figures at the level of the production of this fiction. The very notion of a "Jefferson Smith" performing a heroic act depends on the real work of a film actor whose body and voice—recorded and synchronized by the machinery of cinema—provide a site of coherence for character construction. Through the vocalization and comportment of James Stewart, Smith's activity acquires a particular rhythm, tonality, and emotional investment. To transcribe the speeches Smith delivers would be to undo precisely the work Stewart performs, together with his companion actors (Claude Rains as Paine, Jean Arthur as Saunders, Edward Arnold as Taylor, et al.), who collectively provide a resonant backdrop of gestures and vocal inflections against which Stewart's idiosyncrasy as an actor—a simultaneous suggestion of eagerness and hesitancy—gains dramatic color.[23]

From this perspective the filibuster in *Mr. Smith* functions in part as theatrical tour de force, at times a one-man show. But Stewart's performance never ruptures the fiction it serves; rather it doubles and deepens it. Its willful, searching aspect is interpreted within the fiction as a politically significant event, in the words of renowned radio news commentator H. V. Kaltenborn, as "the American privilege of free speech in its most dramatic form." Exploited here is a drama inherent in the Senate filibuster as a political tactic: the deliberations of a body of elected representatives operating under principles of majority rule are temporarily suspended so as to allow a single individual to hold the floor indefinitely and speak his piece without interruption. A loophole in the formal procedures of the Senate, the right to filibuster accommodates an eccentric act, the duration of which seems governed not by social limits but rather by the physical capacity to sustain a performance. The legal text Smith seeks to enact is replaced as an item of narrative interest by his defense of his motives or, to be more precise, by the *performance* of that defense. For all the earlier emphasis placed on legislative procedure—with Saunders tutoring Smith in the encumbered process by which a bill is written and passes into law—focus shifts here to spectacle itself as a bearer of political meaning. The filibuster, Kaltenborn observes, is "democracy's finest show."

Yet if Stewart-as-Smith performs center stage through much of this passage, it is the particular conceit of this fiction that the character is persuasive precisely to the extent that he appears politically inadequate. As portrayed by Stewart, ordinary Mr. Smith is the kind of performer Roland Barthes has labeled the "imperfect orator," the speaker whose vocal patterns question his own authority and resist the restrictive discourse of any legal text. "Correcting, adding, wavering," notes Barthes, "the speaker . . . superimposes on the simple message that everyone expects of him a new message that ruins the very idea of a message and, through the shifting reflection of the blemishes and excesses with which he accompanies the line of discourse, asks us to believe with him that language is not to be reduced to communication."[24] In this instance the "blemishes" and "excesses" of Smith's performance point toward an ideal truth, irreducible to oratory, never to be fully "said" if it is to remain equal to the enormity of the sentiment to be conveyed.[25] Thus, paradoxically, Smith exercises greatest influence over his colleagues as his control of his performance erodes; it is the dissipation of his vocal and physical mastery that seems to rivet the attention of those who had turned their backs on him when he performed at full strength, and it is his physical collapse, center stage, that elicits a confession from Paine, which in turn motivates a dizzying reversal from melodramatic violence to comic celebration at the close.[26]

Reenacted here is a spectacle of martyrdom, a central component of the mythology of political heroism in America from Abraham Lincoln to Martin Luther King, Jr. What is perhaps most remarkable about Smith as a heroic figure of this kind, however, is the limits placed on the range of his knowledge at his moment of triumph, his lack of any sense of destiny (or premonition of personal doom), a mystical motif that runs through the legends of Lincoln and King. In contrast to the depiction of Lincoln in historical fictions of the late 1930s, for example, Smith never embodies History itself as a narrational force; he may know the past and may finally catch a glimpse of his present predicament, but he never has privileged access to the future.[27] The height of his powers perhaps comes at that moment when he springs the idea of a filibuster on his colleagues (and to a certain extent on us), but what is underscored as the final drama unfolds is his remoteness from the true scene of battle and his ignorance of the full implications of his action, including a triumph born of defeat.

Behind his odd victory, then, we might discern an unresolved conflict between those ideals the film gives voice to through the figure of Smith and the institutional structures within which his vocal performance functions. Smith's original motive in staging the filibuster, it is important to keep in mind, is to use the Senate as a platform from which to speak to the people back home and so reclaim his political legitimacy and personal honor. But the very notion of a federal deliberative body—with diverse geographic regions represented at a national congress—denies the possibility of any immediate relationship between an elected spokesperson and his or her constituency. Free speech, a central tenet of democratic idealism, requires an open field of transmission, a free press, or, in light of the technological changes in the dissemination of political information since the days of Thomas Jefferson, free media, that neutral, natural system implied by the Federal Writers' guide to Washington.

From the very outset of *Mr. Smith Goes to Washington*, however, the news media have been presented as a parallel and to a certain extent rival social force to the political institutions they cover. In the opening expository move of the narrative, a Washington reporter phones his editor with news of Smith's predecessor's death, offering us the first glimpse of a media network with which the political machine must deal. As if in direct counterpoint to the public relations ballyhoo of the Taylor machine, moreover, an exploitative Washington press corps works to alter the image of

Smith from small-town folk hero to rural buffoon upon his arrival in the city. That it is Smith's knowledge of native American hand signals and animal calls that initially makes him an easy target for the journalists only serves to underscore the fact that—with his homing pigeons, his fumbling with the telephone—Smith is a technological primitive transplanted to the center of a vast media world. Radiating out from Washington to various regional constituencies, that network is heavily dependent on the technology of transcribing, amplifying, and transmitting the human voice.

The Senate chamber, however, is a theatrical preserve within this electronic environment. News service reporters "cover" proceedings, but as gallery stenographers who must exit to an adjacent room to relay their reports to distant locations. In the conference room where the Committee on Privileges and Elections hears testimony that has been rigged against Smith by Taylor's machine, microphones are prominently displayed (as they were at Smith's send-off banquet early on) and voices reverberate tinnily. No such devices, however, are to be found on the Senate floor. Prompted by Saunders's hand signals, Smith speaks to the only audience he has: a gallery audience with a penchant for impulsive outbursts and a Senate president whose reign over the proceedings gradually loosens until, in the final moments, he sets gavel aside and the chamber is transformed into an arena for spontaneous cheering and dancing.

Between this public drama and a *national* audience, however, is a media system over which neither Smith nor the president has control. After the filibuster is launched, Taylor swings into action, effectively controlling all channels of communication back to Smith's home state. When Saunders, newly converted to partisan journalism, attempts to establish an alternative network by way of a telephone link to the Boy Rangers back home, the film dramatizes, in a series of blow-by-blow counterthrusts, how Smith's defenders are brutally silenced by their technologically superior counterparts. Paine then gains permission to import into the hermetic space of the Senate chamber for Smith's inspection thousands of hostile telegrams "wired" from constituents whose opinion has been made by the Taylor machine. In the end, then, the media seem either complicit with Taylor or ineffectual in opposing him.

In the two brief scenes in which H. V. Kaltenborn appears, however, the news media function thematically and textually in a different way. The film's inclusion of this famous radio news analyst—and the broadcasting equipment of the CBS and NBC radio networks—seems a gesture toward topical referentiality, in effect suspending the postcredit disclaimer that "the names, characters and incidents used herein are fictitious."[28] Kaltenborn's appearance in the fiction suggests that the filibuster the film plots is no less newsworthy an event than, say, the Munich conference of August 1938, the coverage of which had vaulted him to national fame and helped to expand the market for network radio news, or the Senate neutrality debates, on which Kaltenborn reported in September and October 1939.[29] Concomitantly, a sequence such as this is a mechanism by which the film seems to address external events: social reality not only penetrates the fiction, but the fiction is directed outward in relation to the daily news. The commentary scripted for Kaltenborn exploits this when he notes that envoys of two dictatorial powers in the galleries have come to witness "democracy in action." The viewer of 1939 is thus instructed in how to relate events in the fiction to political events overseas.

Yet having been interpolated into the text in this fashion, Kaltenborn also is transformed. His status as celebrity journalist outside the fiction may grant him a certain interpretive authority, but the framing of his performance by the fiction limits that authority as well. For "Kaltenborn" (the newscaster in the film whose role the real-life Kaltenborn plays), the meaning of the filibuster may be unambiguous, but events that transpire outside his purview may well lead the film spectator to question the notion that this "show" unequivocally signifies the power of free speech or that Kaltenborn fully speaks the truth of this scene for the text. After the film has contrasted the scene in the Senate with violent acts of repression perpetrated by Taylor's thugs, "Kaltenborn" in his second appearance simply calls attention to the heroic dimension of Smith's doomed performance before a packed house that has gathered "to be in on the kill." Placing Smith's martyrdom in the foreground, this interpretation also neatly sidesteps the matter of institutional conflict and repression powerfully evoked by the intercutting of distant but related events.[30]

The inadequacy of Kaltenborn's radio commentary to account for the full panorama of events we witness is in part a matter of the plotted distribution of narrative information, the discrepancy between what this character tells us and what we have come to know. But we might also gauge its inadequacy in terms of a discrepancy in the stylistic richness of contrasting means of narration. Mise-en-scène in the two scenes in which Kaltenborn appears is relatively static and constricted. In shadow in the foreground right are radio equipment, an operator, and two NBC mikes; Kaltenborn stands in profile midground, facing his CBS mike to the left; beyond is a door to the Senate chamber. As if to punch up the scenes visually, the camera cuts in closer during his monologues—four times in the first instance, three in the second—ending on extreme, telephoto close-ups of his face in profile at the mike. But these close-ups only serve to emphasize what is most distinctive about the passage to begin with: the isolation and immobility of the newscaster, reading his script and cut off from the scene he intermittently describes, and a planar, uncontoured perspective on him.[31]

Contrast this with almost any other sequence in the film: the dynamic economy with which a series of phone calls links key political figures across the breadth of the country in the opening sequence, exemplifying the motor force of the political machine that

7.1. Radio news commentator H. V. Kaltenborn in *Mr. Smith Goes to Washington* (1939).

7.2, 7.3., 7.4. Scenes of the U.S. Senate chamber in *Mr. Smith Goes to Washington* (1939).

the passage introduces; the graphic counterpoint of the political and musical scoring of Vorkapich's montage tour of Washington; the carefully timed exchange of looks between Smith and Saunders in his office as the eager senator, in search of the proper words for his boys' camp bill, moves back and forth between two framed images: a Western landscape painting and the lighted Capitol

dome outside his window; the frontal reaction shots of Smith—wounded and silent—when Paine betrays him at the Senate hearing and again when he returns to the Lincoln Memorial to gaze up at his hero one last time. Above all, contrast the space of Kaltenborn's side room with the filmic construction of the Senate chamber itself. However faithful the decor to the original design of that chamber, the power of the drama played out in this space is less a matter of replicated ornamentation and statuary than of shot-by-shot articulation of a plastic space: aerial views of the amphitheater floor framed by tiered galleries (fig. 7.2); wide-angle shots of the senators' desks, alternately occupied and empty, defining a curvilinear arena (figs. 7.3 and 7.4), and of the collapsing body of Smith in its inner ring; low-angle shots of Smith backed snugly by the converging diagonal lines of the cornice or angled over Paine, with the Senate clock, press gallery, and paneled skylight beyond (figs. 7.5 and 7.6). Perhaps most important, the film draws on a point-of-view editing structure through which classical film style subjectifies a fictional space, fixing Smith's performance within a network of facial and vocal reactions, most crucially those of Saunders, the Senate president, and Paine.[32]

Here, then, we might identify a third way in which *Mr. Smith Goes to Washington* transforms social material: by way of the "performance" of the film itself as an unfolding series of shifting views

7.5. Jefferson Smith (James Stewart) addressing the Senate in *Mr. Smith Goes to Washington* (1939).

7.6. Smith appealing to Senator Joseph Paine (Claude Rains) in *Mr. Smith Goes to Washington* (1939).

7.7. Smith points to the Capitol dome in *Mr. Smith Goes to Washington* (1939).

and modulating sounds. To conceptualize the film thusly is to approach the foundations of the text, to consider the range of filmic processes through which the fiction is made available to the spectator. From this perspective the problems of articulation that are explicitly raised by Smith in his late-night office session with Saunders—how does one put a lighted dome into a legislative text?—implicitly redound to the benefit of cinema, a medium of images and sound in time. If Smith's words are insufficient, the film has recourse to the image of the body of the actor; to a soft-focus lighting effect that seems to bathe Saunders, his auditor, in the very illumination (at the "end of the tunnel") that he describes; and to a subtle orchestration of familiar melodies on the sound track that carry with them connotations of the sentimental folk culture that he would revive. The film draws on a variety of cinematic effects, not the least of which is the optical trick by which a two-dimensional, painted image of the Capitol dome on the film set appears as an illuminated monument against a night sky on the screen (fig. 7.7). With this in mind, we might recast the notion of the Senate chamber as a *theatrical* space—in which the expressive hesitations and shifts in emotion of the performer and the spontaneous responses of his auditors transform a "staged" event into a seemingly "authentic" one—so as to account for the work of the host medium. The placement of characters within a particular mise-en-scène, the fragmentation and recombination of performances within a network of reaction shots and vocal over-lays, and the restriction and revelation of narrative information are all part of the text's regulation, its government, of its own component parts.

We might say that *Mr. Smith*, as a text, *absorbs for cinema* a variety of means for addressing an audience: architecture and sculpture that guide a tourist's eye, the typographical and pictorial allure of a newspaper's front page or a billboard, theatrical performance within a politically charged arena, and the electronic amplification and transmission of the human voice. Whatever problems the fiction raises concerning the possibility of genuine political discourse in an age of technologically mediated relationships, it never calls into question this ground. If Taylor's exploitation of American folk culture for private profit and political gain is debunked within the fiction, the opening moment of this filmic text, in which the logo of Columbia Pictures is underscored with a musical phrase from "Columbia, the Gem of the Ocean," aligns patriotic folk culture with corporate self-promotion, seemingly without irony. The cinema of Hollywood emerges as an ideal medium for the revivification, authentication, and dissemination of political and cultural ideals; it is a guarantor of a compelling experience (a Capra film) yet itself is not subject to the critique of machination and mediation the fiction otherwise provides.

Effaced in the Federal Writers' Project guidebook description of coverage of Washington is any notion of historical change in the representation of the nation's capital; before or after halftone printing, radio, or motion pictures, Washington remains the same imaginary place. The controversy in Washington after *Mr. Smith*'s premiere, in contrast, raised questions about the representation of Washington in the form of film fiction and Hollywood's economic and political stake within a changing media environment. When Richard L. Strout worried that an "easy-going" viewer might find the film "pleasant and heart-warming in Mr. Capra's well-known manner," or when Nelson Bell of the *Washington Post* complained that Capra's sense of drama, humor, and melodramatic punch made a fraudulent filibuster appear rational and patriotic, they voiced concern about the manipulation of political material in the hands of a talented Hollywood director.[33] Similarly, Senator Alben Barkley's condescending complaint about the wide-eyed acceptance of the film not as fiction but fact in cultural backwaters seems an anxious assessment of both the representational power of film and the systemic power of Hollywood to reach and consolidate a vast national audience. From this perspective, congressional saber rattling about the passage of an antiblock-booking bill does not seem quite as arbitrary a response to the controversy as one might first think.

In the fall of 1940, however, congressional sabers were stilled (and antitrust action was temporarily suspended) as the major studios signed consent decrees with the Justice Department limiting blocks of films to five and placing a moratorium on the purchase of new theaters. Senate hearings on pro-Allied propaganda from Hollywood were undertaken by Wheeler and Gerald P. Nye (R-N.D.) in the fall of 1941 but then were quietly abandoned in December as America went to war. The following February Hollywood was declared an "essential industry"; the popular media soon would be saturated with film stars making a pitch on behalf of the war effort, and theaters would become increasingly open to the circulation of government films.[34] The trajectory of Capra's career is no less instructive. Two months after Pearl Harbor, he was in Washington organizing a military film unit of Hollywood personnel to produce propaganda films for recruits.[35] Four of these films were eventually distributed nationwide in the first-run theaters of the major studios.

But this wartime alignment of institutions itself was short-lived. The consent decrees with the Justice Department never took hold, and renewed antitrust action culminated in a 1948 Supreme Court ruling that forced the major studios to divorce themselves of theater chains. Hollywood's vulnerability to congressional action was demonstrated in its capitulation to the Red Scare tactics of the House Un-American Activities Committee beginning in 1947.[36] Furthermore, the notion that the motion picture theater might be considered in some sense a "meeting hall of democracy," a spatial extension of the sphere of representational government in a media age, held sway only briefly. In the long run commercial broadcasting, not Hollywood, would cash in on the claim of public service to national governance by way of the televised network news.

Hollywood's relation to Washington and the news media during this period thus might best be thought of as one of ongoing negotiations among powerful institutions with overlapping but varied interests, marked by compacts and conflicts that were layered and shifting. Moments of disturbance and readjustment serve to illuminate the history of Hollywood's relation to a broader spectrum of social and political institutions, a history that today—when the collapse of entertainment, information, and politics (and the interchangeability of actors, anchormen, and politicians) has itself become a media cliche—holds particular interest. The writing of this history, moreover, has much to gain from attention to specific films. If as a social object *Mr. Smith* occasioned public debate and private discussion, the record of which is partially available to us through existing documents, as a filmic text it translated cultural and political material of both a topical and mythic kind into the formal systems of the Hollywood cinema: narrational, specular, auditory. Offering a fictional model for social relations, *Mr. Smith* as a text addresses that fiction to a film spectator, and in the process it negotiates social relations of another order. A task of historical criticism is to make this work evident as well.

Notes

1. *The WPA Guide to Washington, D.C.* (New York: Random House, 1938), 7. Revised and condensed from *Washington: City and Capital* (Washington: Government Printing Office, 1937), first commercially published as *Washington, D.C.: A Guide to the Nation's Capital* (New York: Hastings House, 1942).

2. In contrast to the institutional analysis I am proposing here, historical assessments of *Mr. Smith Goes to Washington* have tended toward broad speculation concerning the possible relation of the film to American social values in the late 1930s. To the extent that questions concerning the production and reception of the film have been factored into these accounts, they have tended to be circumscribed by a sole concern with the capacity of director Frank Capra to articulate a social vision for his audience. Analyses of the film based on this model can be traced back to Richard Griffith's 1939 review, in which he proposed that Capra was so attuned to his audience that *Mr. Smith* should be evaluated as "an index to the temper of the popular mind." *New Movies: The National Board of Review*, November 1939, 13–15; reprinted in *From Quasimodo to Scarlett O'Hara: A National Board of Review Anthology, 1920–1940* (New York: Frederick Ungar, 1982), 319–22. Acknowledging the methodological pitfalls in proposing a relationship of this kind between artworks and society, Robert Sklar in a 1975 essay on Capra raises

provocative questions concerning Hollywood's status as social institution, although the director's capacity to communicate institutionalized values and beliefs remains Sklar's central concern. "The Imagination of Stability: The Depression Films of Frank Capra," in *Frank Capra: The Man and His Films*, ed. Richard Glatzer and John Raeburn (Ann Arbor: Univ. of Michigan Press, 1975), 121–38. Nick Browne, "The Politics of Narrative Form: Capra's *Mr. Smith Goes to Washington*," *Wide Angle* 3, no. 4 (1979), 4–11, likewise calls attention to Hollywood as a locus of media power but primarily as a way of defining Capra's role as ritual storyteller and democratic martyr. The history of Hollywood's relationship to media institutions, however, is addressed in a particularly forceful way by Browne in "System of Production/System of Representation: Industry Context and Ideological Form in Capra's *Meet John Doe*," in *Meet John Doe*, ed. Charles Wolfe (New Brunswick, N.J.: Rutgers Univ. Press, 1989), 269–88.

3. For the growth of radio news, see David Holbrook Culbert, *News for Everyman: Radio and Foreign Affairs in Thirties America* (Westport, Conn.: Greenwood Press, 1976), 4–6; Robert W. Desmond, *Tides of War: World News Reporting, 1931–1945* (Iowa City: Univ. of Iowa Press, 1984), 73–84. For radio broadcasts in film theaters, see *Variety*, 30 August 1939, 1, 18; 13 September 1939, 8; 8 November 1939, 2; John C. Flinn, "Film Showmanship," *Variety*, 6 September 1939, 8. For an example of radio publicity, see RCA's *Listen*, no. 15, a five-page advertisement published in *Life*, 3 October 1938, 35–39.

4. For the role of the Hays Office, see Garth Jowett, *Film: The Democratic Art* (Boston: Little, Brown, 1976), 164–259; J. Douglas Gomery, "Hollywood, the National Recovery Administration, and the Question of Monopoly Power," *Journal of the University Film Association* (spring 1979): 47–52; and Richard Maltby, "The Production Code and the Hays Office," in Tino Balio, *Grand Design: Hollywood as Modern Business Practice, 1930–1939* (New York: Scribner's, 1993), 37–72. Activity by the Justice and Commerce Departments was reported on in the *New York Times*, 8 June 1939, 30; 13 June 1939, 5; 16 August 1939, 12; and 18 August 1939, 17. The progress of the Neely Bill was covered in the *New York Times*, 15 July 1939, 8, and 18 July 1939, 14, and in *Variety*, 13 December 1939, 3, and 20 December 1939, 4. For the effect of events of Europe, see *Variety*, 13 September 1939, 3; 4 October 1939, 4; and 27 December 1939, 5; and the *New York Times*, 10 September 1939, sect. 9, 3, and 17 September 1939, sect. 10, 3. Senator Elmer Thomas (D-Okla.), for example, called for a complete prohibition on all war films, newsreels, and radio broadcasts on the grounds that spreading too much news of the conflict might endanger American neutrality. The press was to be exempt. *Variety*, 4 October 1939, 2.

5. Hays quoted in the *New York Times*, 28 March 1939, 25. Noting a shift in policy from previous reports in which Hays had emphasized entertainment over and against social comment, Frank S. Nugent interpreted the 1939 report as evidence that the "Americanism campaign" in recent Hollywood films was a planned development. "Will Hays, Movie Fan," *New York Times*, 2 April 1939, sect. 10, 5.

6. Breen letters to Louis B. Mayer (MGM) and John Hammell (Paramount), 19 January 1939; Breen report to Hays, 31 January 1938; Shurlock memos to Breen, 26 February 1938 and 10 June 1938; Production Code Administration case file for *Mr. Smith*, Academy of Motion Picture Arts and Sciences Library, Beverly Hills, Calif. (hereafter cited as PCA case file, Academy Library). Foster's story

reportedly was based on the early career of Burton K. Wheeler, who as a freshman senator in 1924 attacked corruption in the Harding administration, was indicted on trumped up charges, and was then exonerated as the Teapot Dome scandal unraveled. Postmaster General in the Harding administration before his acceptance of the MPPDA post in 1922, Hays was never tainted by the scandal but may have had personal reservations about a project focusing on Wheeler. Capra indicates in his autobiography that Wheeler was not amused by *Mr. Smith* at the premiere, but when Wheeler wrote his autobiography years later his collaborator proudly noted that the senator's life was "the stuff of which melodramas [such as *Mr. Smith*] are made." See Frank Capra, *The Name above the Title* (New York: Macmillan, 1971), 282; Burton K. Wheeler and Paul F. Healy, *Yankee from the West* (Garden City, N.Y.: Doubleday, 1962), ix.

7. Capra interviewed by Frank Daugherty, *Christian Science Monitor Weekly Magazine*, 9 November 1938, 5. Joe Sistrom, one of Columbia's representatives at the February meeting with Shurlock, seems to have been the conduit to Capra (*Name above the Title*, 254). According to Joseph McBride in his 1992 biography of Capra, Mamoulian claimed responsibility for convincing Cohn to buy the controversial story, then swapped it with Capra in exchange for Clifford Odets's play, *Golden Boy. Frank Capra: The Catastrophe of Success* (New York: Simon & Schuster, 1992), 401–2.

8. Breen to Cohn, 30 January 1939; Breen to Hays, 31 January 1939; Francis Harmon memo (for Hays) to Breen, 7 March 1939; Breen to Cohn, 8 March 1939, 24 March 1939, 17 April 1939, and 21 April 1939; Breen to Hays, 20 September 1939; all in the PCA case file for *Mr. Smith*, Academy Library. Substantial revisions to the script were made after principal photography began, including the addition of the scene between Paine and Smith on the train (handwritten by Capra on his copy of the script), scenes between Smith and Saunders before the filibuster, and Vorkapich's montage of Taylor versus the Boy Rangers. Capra's revised final script, 1 April 1939, Frank Capra Collection, Wesleyan Cinema Archive, Middletown, Conn. (hereafter cited as Wesleyan Cinema Archive). Breen made no comments concerning these changes.

9. See, for example, Capra's "A Sick Dog Tells Where It Hurts," *Esquire* 5, no. 1 (1936): 87, 130. That *Mr. Smith* quickened interest in the Neely Bill is ironic in that all of Capra's films at Columbia from 1936 to 1939, including *Mr. Smith*, were sold individually rather than in blocks. Columbia sales manager report in *Mr. Smith* correspondence file no. 4, Wesleyan Cinema Archive. While *Mr. Smith* was in production, there also was much discussion in the industry about efforts by Capra to establish his own production company. He announced its formation (with screenwriter Robert Riskin) three weeks before the film was released. *Variety*, 26 July 1939, 3; 2 August 1939, 2; and 18 October 1939, 4; *New York Times*, 4 October 1939, 31.

10. In 1938, for example, Capra was the subject of a *Time* cover story ("Columbia's Gem," 8 August 1938, 35–38), a *Life* photoessay on the making of *You Can't Take It with You* (19 September 1938, 42–47), and profiles in the *Saturday Evening Post* (Alvah Johnston, "Capra Shoots as He Pleases," 4 May 1938) and the *Christian Science Monitor Weekly Magazine* (Frank Daugherty, "He Has the Common Touch," 9 November 1938, 5).

11. Frank S. Nugent, for example, ridiculed Hays's 1939 MPPDA report (see note 5 above) but praised Capra in several articles on *Mr. Smith* (see note 18 below). For a more detailed discussion of the way in which Capra's public profile served as a cultural signpost marking the social circulation of his films, see Charles Wolfe, *Frank Capra: A Guide to References and Resources* (Boston: G.K. Hall, 1987), 10–35.

12. In the introduction to an eight-page photospread on *Mr. Smith*, *Life* magazine noted that Capra had "joined melodrama and background, Hollywood and Washington, fiction and fact, with spectacular success." The layout to follow was divided into two parts: one recounted the plot by way of a series of production stills; the other illustrated how the Senate chamber had been faithfully reconstructed. "Movie of the Week: *Mr. Smith Goes to Washington*," 16 October 1939, 67–74.

13. Capra's retrospective commentary in his autobiography suggests that Preston's contribution was rightly celebrated at the time, but his correspondence from the period indicates that he was disenchanted with Preston's condescending attitude on the set and angered by the fact that Preston quit the film just before the shooting of the scene in the Senate press room. *Name above the Title*, 276–80; Capra to John Stuart, 20 July 1939, in *Mr. Smith* correspondence file, Wesleyan Cinema Archive.

14. The restrictions on shooting an identifiable figure with the statue may explain why Smith and the statue appear together only in extreme long shot from behind interior columns. Closer shots (some of which were filmed at Columbia's studio) were later intercut so as to create a sense of spatial proximity. According to John Stuart, who handled the negotiations with Secretary of the Interior Harold Ickes (and arranged for some pick-up shots with James Stewart and Assistant Director Art Black in July), the local branch of the MPPDA in Washington registered concern about the sequence, and there was a good deal of suspense about whether the final version would be approved. Stuart to Capra, 12 July 1930; Capra to Stuart, 20 July 1939; *Mr. Smith* correspondence file, Wesleyan Cinema Archive. For an account of the problems this photographic regulation caused during shooting, see James Stewart's interview with Leonard Maltin in Jeanine Basinger, *The It's a Wonderful Life Book* (New York: Knopf, 1986), 81–82.

15. Correspondence between Capra and James W. West, chief executive of the Boy Scouts, suggests that West may also have been miffed that scout officials were not hired as consultants. In response to West's political critique of the script, Capra offered a spirited defense of the project, a warm-up for later debates. West letter to Capra, 29 March 1939; Capra telegram to West, 1 April 1939; West to Capra, 3 April 1939; *Mr. Smith* correspondence file, Wesleyan Cinema Archive.

16. Capra, *Name above the Title*, 253–93; *New York Times*, 24 October 1939, 19; 25 October 1939, 1, 54; and 1 November 1939, 4; *Time*, 30 October 1939; Richard L. Strout, *Christian Science Monitor*, 10 and 27 October 1939; Harlan Kennedy, *Washington Post*, 20 October 1939; Nelson S. Bell, *Washington Post*, 21 October 1939, 16. Also see Capra letter to William Wilkerson, 20 October 1939; Nate Spingold to Capra, 30–31 October 1939; and Joseph P. Kennedy to Cohn, 17 November 1939; all in the *Mr. Smith* correspondence file, Wesleyan Cinema Archive. A report by James P. Cunningham in *Motion Picture Herald*,

28 October 1939, 13, suggested that the campaign against the film was inaugurated by the Chicago Tribune Press Service rather than the Senate itself. Hollywood columnist Jimmie Fiedler also reported that other studios had made plans to buy *Mr. Smith* from Columbia and withdraw it from circulation so as to stave off federal action, but the MPPDA quickly squelched this rumor. *Motion Picture Herald*, 4 November 1939, 8.

17. Strout, *Christian Science Monitor*, 19 October 1939, 1. Barkley quoted in *Variety*, 25 October 1939, 54. Protests of this kind were bipartisan and, although it might have been possible to infer from Taylor's deceptive use of a deficiency bill an oblique critique of New Deal relief measures, such an interpretation of the film did not figure into congressional complaints. A topical political link Capra and Riskin could not have foreseen, however, was forged when, in the very week that *Mr. Smith* went into national release, a filibuster to block passage of Roosevelt's arms-embargo repeal was led by Rush Holt of West Virginia, a thirty-four-year-old Democrat who had broken with the party leadership in the 1936 election and was an arch foe of New Deal programs, especially the Works Progress Administration (WPA). Two weeks after their photospread on Hollywood's "amazing reproduction of the Senate," *Life* magazine delighted in this coincidence, proposing that life imitated movies—and perhaps *Life*. "The U.S. Senate Winds Up Its 'Great Debate' on American Neutrality," 30 October 1939, 18–19.

A shifting ground for political interpretation is also suggested by reports that *Mr. Smith* roused audiences to their feet as an antifascist work in Marseilles and Toulouse, France, just before the Vichy ban on American films in 1942, but also was received as an attack on American politics when shown (perhaps with an altered ending) in Moscow in 1950. Georges Sadoul, "Capra ou la renovation des mythes," *Lettres Françaises*, 24 November 1945, 7; *Hollywood Reporter*, 20 December 1950, 2; *Variety*, 20 December 1950, 3, 19.

18. *Daily Variety*, 4 October 1939; *Film Daily*, 6 October 1939, 8; *Variety*, 11 October 1939, 13; *Box Office*, 14 October 1939, 65; William R. Weaver, *Motion Picture Herald*, 7 October 1939; James P. Cunningham, *Motion Picture Herald*, 28 October 1939, 13; Edwin Schallert, *Los Angeles Times*, 4 October 1939, sect. 2, 32, and 25 October 1939, sect. 2, 15; Howard Barnes, *New York Herald Tribune*, 20 October 1939, 14; 22 October 1939; and 29 October 1939; William Boehnel, *New York World-Telegram*, 20 October 1939 and 28 October 1939; Frank S. Nugent, *New York Times*, 20 October 1939, 27; 22 October 1939, sect. 9, 5; and 29 October 1939, sect. 9, 5; Max J. Herzburg, ed., *Photoplay Studies* 5, no. 21 (1939). A copy of Columbia's press packet of favorable reviews is held in the *Mr. Smith* correspondence file, Wesleyan Cinema Archive.

19. Nugent, *New York Times*, 29 October 1939, sect. 9, 5.

20. At the next meeting of the MPPDA in New York, Hays was reported to be concerned about the controversy, but no official action was proposed (*Variety*, 1 November 1939, 4). The question of the film's politics seems to have faded quickly; of the four letters of complaint retained in the PCA file, three are from journalists protesting the depiction of reporters in the film (one incredulous that the film had escaped "the tentative agreement" he understood to have been in effect against the misrepresentation of reporters on the screen). The fourth is a complaint from the Legion of Decency about intoxication scenes in this and other recent Hollywood films. PCA case file for *Mr. Smith*, Academy Library.

21. From one perspective, of course, this passage might be seen simply as one of economical temporal *compression*, after the fashion of the conventional Hollywood montage sequence, covering in three minutes and twenty-five seconds what the plot tells us is a five-hour period. But this tour is also something of a *de*tour from the main narrative up this point, and the dense layering of images is only broadly chronological. A historical past is evoked through the animation of static icons, and a traveling shot past the Lincoln Memorial is edited so that the middle section of a spatially continuous, frontal shot of the columns is removed and placed after symmetrical, angled views from the left and right. The sequence is also graphically complicated by the superimposition of the waving lines of stripes on an American flag. The passage was greatly praised by critics at the time.

22. This aspect of the film has attracted a good deal of critical attention in recent years. For close analyses, see Browne, "Politics of Narrative Form"; Brian Gallagher, "Speech Identity and Ideology in *Mr. Smith Goes to Washington*," *Film Criticism* 5, no. 3 (1981), 12–22; and Charles Affron, *Cinema and Sentiment* (Chicago: Univ. of Chicago Press, 1982), 118–31.

23. For critics in 1939 this performance was considered the one in which Stewart matured as an actor, displaying a capacity to render psychologically plausible wide swings in emotion—from comic embarrassment to fury, from youthful passion to bitterness. The New York Film Critics honored him for his labors with its annual best actor award.

24. Roland Barthes, "Writers, Intellectuals, Teachers," in *Image-Music-Text*, ed. and trans. Stephen Heath (New York: Hill & Wang, 1977), 191–92. Barthes places great stress on the fact that such a performance, no matter the degree to which it seeks to undermine its own authority, cannot escape a legality grounded in the very act of speech making and the social premises that make oration possible.

25. See Raymond Carney, *American Vision: The Films of Frank Capra* (Cambridge: Cambridge Univ. Press, 1986), 299–344, for a provocative discussion of this dimension to Stewart's performance in terms of Capra's exploration of an American aesthetic of acting.

26. The first draft submitted to the PCA in January 1939 ends with Paine committing suicide but leaving behind a note that exonerates Smith. Smith then returns home with Saunders to be elected to serve a full term as senator. In the revised April script, Paine's suicide attempt is blocked and his confession is voiced on the Senate floor. This script also called for a coda in which the windows of the *Jackson City Press* are smashed, Governor Hopper takes credit for Smith's appointment, and Smith and Saunders, while being treated to a hometown parade, discover Paine watching from the sidewalk and bring him home to Jeff's mother. In June 1939 Buchman scripted a slightly different ending in which Jeff arrives home to find that Paine has sent the Boy Rangers "a new press for new lost causes" and announces that he is married to Saunders. Production stills indicate that a scene in which Smith, Saunders, Paine, and Mrs. Smith ride together in a hometown parade was shot, but it did not appear in the released version. PCA case file for *Mr. Smith*, Academy Library; Capra's revised final script, Wesleyan Cinema Archive.

27. See, for example, the endings to *Young Mr. Lincoln* (Ford, 1939) and *Abe Lincoln in Illinois* (Cromwell, 1940) or the Warner Bros. Vitaphone short, *Lincoln in the White House* (1939). The locus classicus of recent critical attention to this question is "John Ford's *Young Mr. Lincoln*," collectively authored by the editors

of *Cahiers du cinéma*, no. 223 (August 1970); translated by Helen Lackner and Diana Matias, *Screen* 13, no. 3 (1972), 5–44. Also see Nick Browne, "The Spectator of American Symbolic Forms: Rereading John Ford's *Young Mr. Lincoln*," *Film Reader*, no. 4 (Evanston, Ill.: Northwestern Univ., 1979), 180–88; and Marsha Kinder, "The Image of Patriarchal Power in *Young Mr. Lincoln* (1939) and *Ivan the Terrible, Part 1* (1945)," *Film Quarterly*, Winter 1985–86, 29–49.

28. By the fall of 1939, Kaltenborn was heard nightly in a fifteen-minute broadcast sponsored by Pure Oil and reportedly earned an income of $2,000 a week. War in Europe, an economic boon to the business of radio news in America, may also have whetted the appetite of movie audiences for behind-the-scenes glimpses of radio news personalities such as Kaltenborn. To satisfy the curiosity of tourists about radio reports on events in Europe, for example, NBC began allowing visitors to the RCA building in New York to observe news broadcasts through a window (*Variety*, 6 September 1939, 23; 13 September 1939, 1; 25 October 1939, 1, 54). One reviewer of *Mr. Smith* observed that Kaltenborn's name was "almost as lively box-office as a film star's" and that his appearance, like the film's realistic settings, brought "the whole matter of government as it is achieved in the nation's capital smack into the audience's lap, unvarnished and unlibeled" (William R. Weaver, *Motion Picture Herald*, 7 October 1939, 35, 38). The radio broadcast was topical in another sense as well; radio correspondents first obtained access to Senate gallery facilities in 1939. Edward W. Chester, *Radio, Television, and American Politics* (New York: Sheed & Ward, 1969), 62.

29. In his coverage of the neutrality debates, Kaltenborn offered an interpretation of the congressional filibuster that contradicts the one scripted for "Kaltenborn" in the film. On 21 September Kaltenborn quoted the warning of Senator Arthur Vandenberg (R-Calif.) that "to filibuster on this issue would justify those who say that the democratic process will not work," and on 10 October he observed that isolationists in the Senate were agreed "there's little joy in talking for a lost cause." Kaltenborn radio scripts, 1939, H. V. Kaltenborn Collection, Wisconsin Center for Film and Theater Research, Madison, Wis.

30. Kaltenborn's commentary thus functions in a fashion similar to what Pierre Machery has described as a "detachable utterance," a statement that seems to have been taken directly from ideology and inserted into the texture of a novel but that is also transformed by the new fictional context. "Detachable utterances are not detached utterances," Machery argues. "They are in the work not as real objects but as fictional objects . . . They are in the text not as intruders, but effects." *A Theory of Literary Production* (London: Routledge & Kegan Paul, 1978), 297.

31. Thomas Elsaesser has proposed that what is often taken as the "ponderous" style of the Warner Bros. biopic cycle directed by William Dieterle in the late 1930s may be a function of the historically vanished intertext of live radio broadcasting and Roosevelt's fireside chats, with the film spectator positioned to identify with an audience as well as a protagonist. See "Film History as Social History: The Dieterle/Warner Bros. Biopic," *Wide Angle* 8, no. 2 (1986): 15–31. A similar stylistic logic may be at work in *Mr. Smith* but in such a fashion as to emphasize a split between the radio commentary of Kaltenborn, with whom identification is never cued by the text, and the filibuster by Smith, who functions as both performer and optical relay in a dynamically edited sequence. That Capra's film

served as an intertext for radio programming is suggested by the remark of a re-viewer that the 1939 radio program "We the People" conveyed "a hint of brim-ming over with surprise. The tempo has to pick-up Capra-like, to convey the im-pression" (*Variety*, 20 December 1939, 28).

32. Capra shot the filibuster with multiple cameras and microphones placed at various vantage points around the set so that he could record performances simul-taneously, thus anticipating the techniques of "live" television coverage of politi-cal events today. But contrast the flexible, volumetric space of this filmically con-structed Senate chamber with the flat, constricted space defined by the telephoto lenses of immobile television cameras that have recently been allowed to enter the Senate chamber. The image of Kaltenborn poised outside the side-room door now seems to presage the transformation of the chamber into a media space, but as a televisual backdrop for the speech making of legislators from whose oratory sound-bites are extracted for the evening news.

33. Richard L. Strout, *Christian Science Monitor*, 19 October 1939, 1; Nelson Bell, *Washington Post*, 20 October 1939, 16. Over the years, Capra often suggested that *Mr. Smith* was singled out for attack because it was a film rather than a novel or a play and that the Washington press corps envied and feared the power of the culturally disreputable visitors from Hollywood. See, for example, his first public response to the controversy in the *Christian Science Monitor*, 27 October 1939, 3, as well as his 1971 account in *Name above the Title*, 289–92. In his autobiography Capra finesses the question of the support the film received from established crit-ics and commentators within the news media by subsuming this response under the general category of vox populi, but clearly these were voices—as Columbia's publicity department understood well—of a particularly potent kind in countering opposition to the film, and their verdict is an index of the degree to which Holly-wood by the late 1930s could command a base of support within a civic and cul-tural sector.

34. See Jowett, *Film: The Democratic Art*, 277–78, 297–320.

35. Capra, *Name above the Title*, 315–22.

36. For a subtle institutional analysis of the Supreme Court ruling, see Lea Jacobs, "The Paramount Case and the Role of the Distributor," *Journal of the Uni-versity Film and Video Association* 35, no. 1 (1983), 44–49. On the House Un-American Acitivities Committee hearings, see Larry Ceplair and Stephen Englund, *The Inquisition in Hollywood: Politics in the Film Community, 1930–1960* (Garden City, N.Y.: Anchor Press/Doubleday, 1980).

8

Studio Metamorphosis: Columbia's Emergence from Poverty Row

Brian Taves

Columbia Pictures was unique among the principal Hollywood studios of the 1930s. As a result, most references to Columbia Pictures highlight a historiographical problem in the studies tracing this era. Standard conceptions link Columbia to a director, Frank Capra, and a genre, screwball comedy. These correlations have too often become generalized equations for historical surveys. Although Capra's films and certain screwball comedies are, from any aesthetic standpoint, the best of Columbia's output, they were decidedly not representative of the studio's product.[1] By contrast, similar basic parallels, such as that typically made for the centrality of horror films at Universal during the same decade, hold considerably more true. The Capra films and screwball comedies, indeed big budget films generally, were exceptions for Columbia, in terms of both content and production. The exhibition and profit from such major pictures were not typical of the program material that made Columbia a viable business enterprise.

Instead, Columbia must be placed not simply in terms of achievements and textual highlights, but also within an industrial context that takes into account its lowly position within the Hollywood hierarchy. Most of the studio's other product has been dismissed, and unlike such studios as MGM, Paramount, RKO, Warner Bros., Fox, or even Universal, dwelling on a few Columbia A films provides an even more than usually skewed perspective.[2] Columbia's A output was extraordinarily limited; over 80 percent of Columbia's films were unquestionably B product by the most flattering estimate. Whereas other studios in the top eight provide a sufficient quantity of A product for the canonical selection to be somewhat accurate, such an approach to Columbia is entirely unbalanced. To isolate the Columbia A film and ignore the remainder is to elide the basis of production that distinguished the studio, the underlying commercial and artistic means by which Columbia survived—as well as the vast quantity and range of B films offered to 1930s spectators. Not until well into the 1940s did Columbia become recognized as an important, consistent force within the industry, and meanwhile the enormous base of B filmmaking allowed the studio to survive until its A films reached a sufficient plateau of success.[3]

Strategies for Success

At the beginning of the 1930s, Columbia was barely regarded as one of the eight principal producing concerns. Its films, talent, and generic conventions were still planted in Poverty Row. Much of its product was so firmly aimed at rural markets that it was rarely reviewed by such civic publications as the *New York Times*. Even *Variety* and *Film Daily* reviews are far from complete in their coverage of Columbia's output. Throughout the 1930s many Columbia pictures received only one review from the various industry journals. A number of films were not reviewed until well after release; for instance, Tim McCoy's Western *The Prescott Kid* (1934) was ignored for nearly two years after it was placed on the market. Harry Cohn had a running feud with the editor of the *Hollywood Reporter*, who delighted in providing advance criticism of the studio's product.[4] *Daily Variety* almost ignored Columbia films while simultaneously reviewing nearly every Universal picture. The trade press regarded Columbia as far below Universal; Columbia was seen primarily as a source of filler material for double bills, especially B Westerns, comedy shorts, and, later, serials. Not until 1935 was Columbia recognized as an independent that was likely to endure.

Columbia began in 1922 in one room with six employees as the

C.B.C. Film Sales Company, a firm specializing in states-rights product.[5] The founders, the brothers Jack and Harry Cohn, and their associate Joe Brandt—hence the initials C.B.C.—had learned the movie trade at Universal. Soon they took the majestic name Columbia Pictures Corporation, which had been used by an unrelated firm that expired in 1917. Other than a loan of $100,000 from A. P. Giannini of the Bank of Italy, Columbia relied on weekly profits from its pictures to finance each new production; only modest financing came from private resources.[6]

The first Columbia films were shorts, Westerns, and cheap action "stunt pictures"; features were added to the program to boost profitability. Although none of these films could become major financial successes, they were nearly invariably modestly profitable, as long as costs were strictly contained. Budgets were usually under $20,000, and Columbia became one of the first studios to have its own lab. The planning of annual programs began with a list of catchy titles, with stories devised later that often bore little or no relation to the title. For example, a 1933 Tim McCoy Western, *Rusty Rides Alone*, includes no character named Rusty.

In the 1920s, outdoor shooting was common to avoid the cost of sets, and streets were photographed rapidly without city permits. Leading players provided their own makeup, and the crew usually consisted of a director, often doubling as producer, and cameraman, with an assistant for each. Winning the nickname "the germ of the ocean," Columbia and the Cohns instituted a policy of frugality that would have put the brothers Warner to shame. The Cohns refused to print more than one take of a scene or hire stand-ins for major stars and recycled prison footage from *The Criminal Code* (1931) in nearly every prison picture through the 1940s.[7]

Since the company's founding, the two brothers Cohn had been in constant conflict, Jack believing Harry an extravagant filmmaker and poor businessman. In 1932, with the retirement of partner Joe Brandt, Harry avoided Jack's attempt to oust him and instead bought out Brandt's share to assume preeminent control of the West Coast branch. Harry Cohn became company president and chief of production, the only individual among the principal Hollywood studios to hold both positions. Cohn's was the longest continuous regime in movie studio history, lasting until his death in 1958. He personally owned about one fourth of the stock, and most of the remainder was owned by employees and directors of the company, minimizing potential volatility. By remaining largely in private hands, Columbia managed to retain greater independence and avoid the labor troubles and major entanglements with Wall Street faced by other studios. Although Cohn did not know how to spell the name of his own studio (he preferred "Colombia"), throughout his lifetime Columbia never showed a deficit and produced an average of forty or more films annually.[8]

At first Columbia, along with several dozen similar companies on Poverty Row, rented studio facilities from others. Four years after its founding, Columbia acquired eight acres for a studio on Gower Street in Hollywood, where it remained until the early 1970s. Facilities in adjoining buildings were added through the next decade, and the B unit was segregated to Sunset Boulevard. In March 1935, a forty-acre Burbank ranch, which eventually grew to eighty acres, was bought for outdoor locations, enhancing the practicality of producing Westerns.[9]

From the outset Columbia avoided theater ownership, and perhaps as a result did not experience the near-brushes with bankruptcy faced by most of the other vertically integrated studios during the Depression, when only Columbia and Loew's remained in the black. The studio began by distributing through the states-rights system and then opened its own exchanges in 1926. The next year a Columbia production, *The Blood Ship*, starring Hobart Bosworth, became the studio's first picture accepted for exhibition at the prestigious Roxy Theater in New York. In 1929, with the assistance of Wall Street brokerages and the public sale of securities, Columbia bought and consolidated studio facilities and exchanges. A national distribution organization was formed, which became international two years later.

To minimize risk, Columbia was reluctant to spend on what Harry Cohn perceived as luxuries. Columbia was slow to take advantage of such novelties as Technicolor, waiting until 1943 to make its first color film. Even in the 1950s, Cohn avoided the lure of wide-screen, preferring controversial material, often shot in black and white.[10] However, the studio made the transition to sound easily, adopting the Western Electric sound-on-film process.

Frank Capra directed the studio's first part-talkie, *The Younger Generation*, as well as its first all-talking movie, *The Donovan Affair*, both in 1929. The coming of sound made Columbia, like other studios, partial to stage adaptations. As late as 1931, seven of the year's top releases originated in the theater: *The Criminal Code*, *The Guilty Generation*, *Meet the Wife*, *Men Are Like That/Arizona*, *The Miracle Woman*, *The Pagan Lady*, and *Subway Express*. The studio continued to look toward the theater as often as literature for potential properties. In 1937 Columbia even announced its intention to produce plays in New York as a testing ground for new material.[11]

Generally, Columbia is described as a studio that suddenly burst into important status with *It Happened One Night* in 1934.[12] This is not the case; Columbia's rise to prestige both had begun earlier and was to last longer. Actually, Columbia began the 1930s trying to move into predominantly high-grade product, only to fall back and, as the decade wore on, promise only a few such offerings. Columbia's output steadily grew in quantity from its inception to reach a high of thirty-two films in 1928 and then fell back with the arrival of sound to twenty-two in 1929.[13] Output by 1930 was back to around thirty films annually, and that year Columbia reported for the first time profits of over one million dollars. The success of some of the studio's early big budget enterprises, including *Submarine* (1928) and *Flight* (1929), encouraged concentration on fewer but higher-quality films. Expansion took place during the early years of the 1930s, as Columbia tried to leap into the majors with a single jump.

This policy was reflected in the advertisements Columbia placed in *Film Daily Yearbook*. The 1930–31 season promised a "superior twenty," a Barbara Stanwyck special attraction, and eight Westerns with Buck Jones—along with 104 shorts, including travelogues, newsreels, sing-alongs, screen snapshots, and comedies, many of them animated. By comparison, in 1930 Paramount was the most prolific studio, with 64 features, while among other important small companies Tiffany offered 27, Sono-Art 20, and Pathe, 14. Adjoining advertisements feature Columbia directors Roy William Neill, Western specialist Louis King, and shorts creator Eddie Buzzell, along with writer Jo Swerling, who became one of the studio's most prolific contributors.[14]

For the next two years, Columbia's records reveal that, outside of placing Westerns in a special category, the studio did not, as a matter of internal policy, distinguish between A and B films, big and lower budget projects; nearly all films were listed together as prestige items.[15] For instance, Columbia's top hit of 1932, the Barbara Stanwyck melodrama *Shopworn*, was made in less than twenty days. Very few pictures, including A films, ran longer than seven reels (seventy minutes), and many were only six reels (sixty minutes). The results of increased outlays, with overhead averaging $175,000 a picture, were not commercially, or even artistically, impressive.[16] The combination of the Depression's effect on the box office and the comparative failure of many ambitious films caused profits to drop, although output remained stable through 1933. The overall expansion was a failure, and budgetary contraction set in as Columbia executives realized that the move to major status would be slow.

By 1933, Columbia's advertised specials were down by half, to ten features; later there were a half-dozen, and by 1936, a mere three. Only in 1934 did Frank Capra's name become a major advertised selling point.[17] Although the studio remained profitable, dividends were suspended for three years until mid-1934, and salaries were cut the previous year. Instead of boosting the program's entire level, Columbia resumed its old position of producing nearly all B product, filling the growing exhibitor demand for double-feature material. Rather than trying to rival the majors, Columbia cut back on prestige efforts in favor of abundant inexpensive product.

Only a few specials per season were produced, along with several more modest A films. Specials were different from A films; there were no more than several specials annually, marked by a significant investment, while there were likely to be more than a half-dozen A movies. The A pictures featured secondary but recognizable stars and schedules and running times only a bit longer than B films. Expenses on A productions were limited to the amount of revenue attainable through second-run houses. Although the As received occasional first-run showings, the budgetary constraint avoided the risk of more than a few annual high-cost films. This minimized the danger encountered in the previous escalation of the entire program, while still guaranteeing the likelihood of several specials a year that would qualify for awards, first-run releases, and higher returns. Columbia's few annual top specials were often distinguished by borrowed directors, stars, and other imported talent and almost always had little in common with the general run of product turned out by the studio's contract personnel. Although many of the specials and A films were critical and commercial failures, today only a few of the successful specials, and hardly any of the As, tend to be remembered.

The success of this policy was confirmed in 1934 when Columbia matched its million dollar profit of 1930, largely because of the phenomenal success of *It Happened One Night* and of *One Night of Love* with Grace Moore, two of the top box-office hits of the mid-1930s. However, the Academy Award sweep of 1934 for *It Happened One Night* and the equal commercial success of *One Night of Love* did not suddenly catapult Columbia into the top ranks of the industry. Although Columbia's gross revenues grew from a quarter million in 1926 to $11 million in the 1933–34 season to $20 million in 1937, these accounted for only about 5 percent of the industry's total volume of business, a percentage that remained constant.[18] Instead, the success of *It Happened One Night* and *One Night of Love* indicated that Columbia was more than a Poverty Row outfit, a studio of occasional possibilities.

Forgotten Failures

Because of the success of *It Happened One Night*, Frank Capra was regarded as a unique and desirable talent, the man behind much of Columbia's rising prestige, and other studios were quick to bid for his talents. However, Capra's growing penchant for lengthy shooting schedules and high-cost stars soon made his Columbia films so costly—from $1.5 to 2 million—that they could not become profitable, despite achieving some of the highest box-office grosses of the time. As a result, Capra's departure from Columbia at the end of the decade was not mourned; other, nearly as successful pictures, like *The Awful Truth* (1937), cost $600,000 and stayed on schedule.[19]

Similarly, Grace Moore's operetta vehicles, with their integrated musical numbers, went downhill from her initial two offerings, *One Night of Love* and *Love Me Forever* (1935), which had benefited from the able guidance of Victor Schertzinger as director and co-songwriter. Her subsequent films, *The King Steps Out* (1936), *When You're in Love* (1937), and *I'll Take Romance* (1937), became less musical and more comedic. The series was typical of the problems Columbia encountered moving toward major status and continuing high quality. The Moore vehicles proved ever more inappropriate for her talents, less centered on her musical appeal, and with steadily weaker romantic subplots. For instance, *Love Me Forever* offers plausible narrative and characterizations, with Moore opposite an effective Leo Carillo as a gangster with a sensitive, artistic side, with whom she forms an unusual platonic alliance. On the other hand, *When You're in Love*, Robert Riskin's sole directorial effort, featured endless and incredibly wordy, cliche-spouting speeches for Cary Grant, who is favored over Moore in shots, dialogue, and story. The cost of the Moore films and their steadily declining income soon made them net losers at the box office, and the series ended.

Although 1930s Columbia is associated with such popular screwball comedies as *Twentieth Century* (1934), *She Married Her Boss* (1935), *The Awful Truth*, and *Holiday* (1938), for every comedy success there were many more commercial and critical disasters. The latter included *So This Is Africa* (1933), *The Lady Is Willing* (1934), *Adventure in Manhattan* (1936), *And So They Were Married* (1936), *It's All Yours* (1937) (featuring a dreadfully mismatched Madeleine Carroll and Francis Lederer), *She Couldn't Take It* (1935) (a failed straight mix of comedy and gangster), and *If You Could Only Cook* (1935) (a slow, lethargic comedy to which Columbia attempted to attach Frank Capra's name as a selling point). Other comedies, like *She Married an Artist* (1937), *More Than a Secretary* (1936), and *Start Cheering* (1938), more farce than screwball, were moderately successful. Many notable films that have been mistakenly lumped with comedy, like *Platinum Blonde* (1931), *Lady for a Day* (1933), *Lady by Choice* (1934), and *The Whole Town's Talking* (1935), actually have only some amusing plot devices and are essentially poignant, melodramatic stories.

Several other tentative bids to increase Columbia's importance began and ended with failure during the middle to late 1930s.

Although net profits nearly doubled between 1934 and 1935, they quickly plummeted again until World War II; in 1939 the company barely avoided a loss when it declared no net profits at all. During the late 1930s, while income nearly doubled to $20 million by 1938, profits declined from close to $2 million until they vanished altogether. Occasionally, there was misleading publicity to the contrary, such as Columbia's amusing statement inaugurating 1937, announcing a bid to join the ranks of "pretentious" producers, promising "to adopt a policy of striving for ten above average films a year."[20] In fact, the prospects of big budget films were always variable, and Columbia's specials and A films of the late 1930s were simply not popular enough to boost corporate profitability until the wartime prosperity of the 1940s.

Columbia Bs

Instead, the studio followed the old maxim of "popular films at comparable costs." Generic emphases shifted from melodramas in the early 1930s toward action films from the middle to end of the decade. By 1936, output had nearly doubled to over fifty films annually, with all of the growth occurring in the B division. From the mid-1930s into the 1950s, the B section was among the studio's most profitable and prolific divisions. It accounted for 70 percent of Columbia's output and was recognized as a leading supplier of program staples. Near-quickie production schedules of two weeks and less were standard and remained common through the end of the decade, and Columbia features averaged a cost of less than $200,000 to produce. By 1938, running times were typically sixty-six minutes, eighth among the studios; by comparison, MGM averaged ninety minutes.

The decision to emphasize a prolific schedule of largely program pictures proved wise. With the Great Depression casting a shadow over box-office receipts, many exhibitors tried a strategy of double bills. While seeming to offer two films for the price of one, the practice usually meant, at best, an A and a B, two in-between pictures, or even two B films. Numerous small, underfinanced companies attempted to supply the growing demand for double-bill pictures, but the majors quickly displaced them and filled the temporary slack. By 1937–38, the many small indepen-

dent concerns that proliferated from 1934 to 1936 were beginning to vanish as Republic and Monogram took over a field that
had formerly been occupied by numerous other small companies
of nearly equal size. While the output of low-budget productions
declined and concentrated in fewer hands, Columbia took advantage of the relatively stable demand to have a nearly guaranteed
double-bill market it could readily fill. This was particularly oppor-
tune, since Columbia did not have an exhibition chain of its own.

In 1935, Columbia reached Harry Cohn's long-time goal of
releasing a film a week, a threshold maintained for fifteen years.
His philosophy was that to make one good picture a year he had
to keep the plant continuously operating with B material and exhibitors had to accept his other ordinary films. As Cohn remarked,
"Every Friday the front door opens and I spit a movie out into
Gower Street."[21] Cohn's approach toward production would remain largely unchanged over the years, and B material remained
an enormous part of Columbia's output through the late 1950s,
when it was one of the last companies to discontinue such prolific
offerings. Even re-releases reflected this B proclivity; the summer
reissues for 1938 included not only *Man's Castle* (1933), *Mr. Deeds
Goes to Town* (1936), and *She Married Her Boss*, but also *The Man
Trailer* (1934) and *The Riding Tornado* (1932), with Buck Jones
and Tim McCoy, respectively.

By 1935, a unit system at the studio began to receive press no-
tice, although several producer units had been operating without
publicity since 1931. For a year Bryan Foy headed a virtually autonomous B unit, which produced such quality B films as *The Un-
welcome Stranger* (1935). Then Columbia replaced Foy with the
talented Larry Darmour, a skilled low-budget independent producer who arranged to have a separate group. The Darmour unit
soon included such stars as Ken Maynard and, most significantly,
Jack Holt, the Columbia veteran who was now back after a brief
hiatus at Universal; Holt became the principal luminary of Columbia's best B offerings. Generally speaking, Darmour's Holt
series developed well, producing high-class second features that
continued Holt's star status well into the 1940s. In Darmour's
B unit, which continued until the producer's death in 1942, there
was an effort to find other reliable action formulas for B pictures
outside of the sagebrush and a greater willingness to increase the

budgets. Various contract directors worked for Darmour, with Lewis D. Collins handling the bulk of the productions.

Maynard became Columbia's second-string Western star, appearing in pictures produced in two weeks or less. He replaced Tim McCoy, whose career had declined until he was working at such Poverty Row companies as Puritan. However, Maynard's popularity dropped precipitously shortly after he was signed, and he made a mere six films for Columbia. Jack Luden, followed by Bob Allen, in a series of "Ranger" Westerns, were unsuccessfully offered as potential successors; nearly all of these vehicles were written by Nate Gatzert and directed by Spencer Gordon Bennet. Finally settling into McCoy's former position on the lot was Charles Starrett, usually featured with musical interludes by the Sons of the Pioneers. The initial Starrett films were made in as little as eight days; though hardly memorable, they are generally polished and slick within the formulaic limitations of the B Western. Typified at best by *Two-Fisted Sheriff* (1937) and most conventionally and traditionally by *Rio Grande* (1938), Starrett quickly became an established Western star, continuing his series at Columbia into the 1950s. When Buck Jones left the studio in 1938, Starrett moved into his position as Columbia's top Western star. William "Wild Bill" Elliott, after a successful appearance in the studio's third serial, *The Great Adventures of Wild Bill Hickok* (1938), took the position Starrett had graduated from as the lead in the secondary Western series.

Despite their B flavor, Columbia's Westerns do offer a few distinguishing features. During the first half of the decade, Tim McCoy and Charles "Buck" Jones were the premier contract stars in the form at Columbia. Tim McCoy's Columbia Westerns tended to be aimed at more general audiences, with the films and attendant publicity portraying him as a romantic matinee idol, appealing to women as well as juvenile spectators. Jones's films were more male-oriented, as in the attenuated, elliptical historical drama of the Pony Express, *The Overland Express* (1938). However, McCoy was always secondary competition; Jones and his horse Silver were the premier figures in the genre. Jones was the cowboy phenomenon, the top Western star of his time; he was making $7,500 weekly from radio, magazines, and movies. The Buck

Jones Rangers was one of the country's largest youth groups, with 3.5 million members.[22]

Jones applied his popularity to improving the quality of his product, and some of his films offer rich subtexts. Whereas McCoy, Starrett, and other secondary Columbia Western stars had to be satisfied with brief shooting schedules, Jones spent three weeks or more for his own hour-long, six-reel films, a schedule allotted more prestigious seven reelers. In the mid-1930s, he tried directing himself during a period at Universal, and he returned to Columbia with his own separate production unit, Coronet Pictures.

Jones experimented with the Western formula more than any other such star of the time, with a large proportion of his films deviating from the cowboy versus rustlers theme in ways that presage the changes of the late 1940s. For instance, the anticlerical *Unknown Valley* (1933), similar to Sir Arthur Conan Doyle's novel *A Study in Scarlet*, tells of a bizarre religious cult clearly modeled on the early days of the Mormon church. *California Frontier* (1938) explicitly details, through style and a manner of social consciousness, the cruelty shown the Mexicans by the new settlers from the United States immediately after California joined the union. The relentless oppression toward the Mexicans is grimly highlighted, with a portrayal of the violence and neurotic behavior similar to that of the later psychological Western. Other Jones films also embody a revisionist view of the old West. In *White Eagle* (1932), he plays an Indian, in love with a white girl, who encounters the persistent racism of the whites; Jones treated the theme again in a serial remake of the story. Critics were divided; *Variety* panned the original *White Eagle* mercilessly, but other reviews lauded the picture, saying it was an unusual Western that would revive the genre's popularity.[23]

Among Jones's later starring vehicles was *Hollywood Round-up* (1937), a remake of a Richard Dix picture of the previous year, *It Happened in Hollywood*. Although disliked by critics for its divergence from formula, *Hollywood Round-up* was a clever satire, rare in the genre for its reflexivity. The film told of Jones's own rise from stuntman to take the place of another Western star, and the cast was filled with performers whose careers were in decline, including Helen Twelvetrees, Grant Withers, and Jones himself.

Mysteries and Westerns were most common in the B unit during the 1930s, together with domestic melodramas. Unique to Columbia, however, were numerous pictures focusing on the difficulties of primarily male occupations, from construction workers to factory foremen. The types of jobs portrayed included engineers (*Shakedown*, 1936), race car drivers (*Speed Demon* and *High Street*, 1932; *Straightaway*, 1934; *In Spite of Danger*, 1935; *Speed to Spare*, 1937), lumbermen (*Roaring Timber*, 1937), oil men (*The Woman I Stole*, 1933; *Outlaws of the Orient*, 1937), seal hunters (*North of Nome*, 1936), and *Coast Guard* (1939), as well as numerous films about airplane pilots, reporters, newsreel men, sportsmen, and boxers. Such heroes had assignments to get dams finished and factories back to work (*A Dangerous Adventure*, 1937; *Dangerous Intrigue*, 1936), build roads (*Too Tough to Kill*, 1935), demolish buildings (*The Wrecker*, 1933), run railroads (*Lightning Flyer*, 1931; *Dangerous Crossroads*, *When Strangers Marry*, 1937), and win motor boat races (*Speed Demon*, *Superspeed*, 1935; *Motor Madness*, 1937). In such work the heroes encounter troubles with sabotage or interfering female proprietors or nature, but they overcome obstacles with a ruthless resolve to finish the task. The counterpart of these male films were *Child of Manhattan* (1933), *Paid to Dance* (1937), *Ten Cents a Dance* (1931), *The Devil's Playground* (1937), and *Missing Daughters* (1939), dealing with the dance hall milieu, a favorite occupation for Columbia women's films.

Films that might legitimately be called crime or adventure have not been included here, leaving what might be called an occupational genre, those films emphasizing a certain occupation, its locale, and the specific challenges that went with it.[24] They all shared a concentration on stereotyped models of brawny masculinity, with practicality, determination, and physical strength prized. Despite the variety of jobs depicted, the films emphasized that these were "man-size" positions, for tough blue collar he-men types. They followed a gritty formula for "getting the job done," subordinating romance and relying on male friendship.

Such actors as Victor Jory, Paul Kelly, Charles Quigley, and Don Terry played these bare-knuckled, sleeves-rolled-up hard hats. *Variety* commented of *A Dangerous Adventure* (1936), a tale of the steel mills, that Don Terry was becoming Columbia's "bonebreaker," bidding to take on the "iron-muscle" material the studio had usually handed the older Jack Holt. Indeed, in *"B" Movies*, Don Miller notes that in 1937, with Richard Dix, George Bancroft, Victor Jory, and Jack Holt, Columbia stars "possessed the strongest jaws in the industry."[25]

Perhaps the best of these Columbia occupational films is *Roaring Timber*, directed by Phil Rosen and casting Jack Holt as the head of a lumber camp. The camp is owned by a young woman whose father was killed on the job; he is replaced by Holt. The expected romance is even more perfunctory than that usually found in B Westerns. Yet *Roaring Timber*, shot over six weeks in New York state, contains some spectacular exterior lumber scenes with a feeling for the outdoors, and its craft and pace help to make the unlikely narrative seem probable. The *New York Times* review served to summarize not only *Roaring Timber*, but also many other Columbia occupational films:

> An inventory of the obstacles and disasters which lie between Jack Holt, the hard-driving, square-shooting woods boss, and delivery of the eighty million feet of timber in sixty days, as per schedule, is enough to convince us that anybody except Jack would have been crushed, confused, or at least discouraged, by it all. But such handicaps as the owner's death, the pretty daughter's taking charge, the plotting general manager, the sabotaging engineer, and the following items, to wit: 1 broken dam, 1 collapsed trestle, 1 dynamited trestle, 1 log train wreck, 1 forest fire, 1 general walkout and 1 free-for-all, only slightly less violent than the Battle of the Marne, are so many arboreal hors d'oeuvres for Jack . . .
>
> What we principally like about the picture is the fact that there isn't any silly stuff like kissing or holding hands in it, and though we are doubtless meant to infer that Jack gets the boss's daughter (Grace Bradley) as a reward for sending the timber crashing down to the mills on contract time, no mention of anything as sissy as love ever passes between them. You know how Jack feels from the beginning ("No society dame is gonna tell me how to run this camp"), but after all Grace is a regular fellow.[26]

A factor leading to the development of this genre was a 1932–34 cycle that attempted to expand the roles Western stars could portray beyond the standard cowboy persona in which they had been typecast. During these years, Tim McCoy, besides playing cowboys, also portrayed a fire fighter, race track driver, airplane pilot, telephone repairman, policeman, reporter, and state trooper, while Buck Jones was cast as race car drivers and stunt men. By exploring possible hybrid variations on action genres, Columbia hoped to increase the popularity of Jones and McCoy beyond Western devotees. The most interesting variation was *The Thrill Seeker* (1933), in which Jones plays an impractical daredevil whose only skill is telling tall stories of his own deeds. This places him in perilous situations for which he has no aptitude whatever, since his claims to be an expert rider, pilot, or driver are false. *Variety* applauded *The Thrill Seeker* as a generic conglomeration, labeling it a "a Munchausen type of farce."[27]

However, occupational films could also offer a social side. They suggest that in this genre Columbia has at least as credible a claim to having created a working man's cinema as the simultaneous Warners efforts of the 1930s. A useful example comes from Columbia's "taxi" films, *They Met in a Taxi* (1936), *A Fight to the Finish* (1937), and *Two in a Taxi* (1941).

They Met in a Taxi, starring Chester Morris as the cabbie, portrayed how he makes an unlikely connection with the New York aristocracy through one of his fares, Fay Wray. Their romance follows lightly comedic lines, while on the more serious side Morris and another cabbie, an ex-con played by Lionel Stander, prove that Wray was innocent of having stolen a valuable string of pearls. Morris's cabbie is shown as bourgeois, and his occupation is an unusual way to set the remainder of the plot in motion. This was one use of the genre, simply to give the protagonist an occupation that justified his actions. The scriptwriter was Howard J. Green, who would also collaborate on the script of *Two in a Taxi*.

The occupational genre could also be much more serious in intent; both *A Fight to the Finish* and *Two in a Taxi* deal with taxi wars. They portray the independent driver's struggle against entrenched corporate or municipal power, offering wider industrial and ecomomic implications. In *A Fight to the Finish*, hard-slugging Don Terry offers a hero who battles his opponents with his fists, whereas Russell Hayden in *Two in a Taxi* tries to escape his hopeless situation by marrying his sweetheart and acquiring a gas station. Both find the odds virtually overwhelming; *A Fight to the Finish* climaxes with the murder of Terry's friend in a deliberate frame-up. Terry's opponents are personified villains and are comparatively easy to overcome; in *Two in a Taxi*, however, the forces keeping the protagonists in their lowly niche are omnipresent, part of the capitalist system. Although the chronically "short-of-cash" cabbies support Terry, buying him a new taxi so he can resume his former work, the cabbies in *Two in a Taxi* offer no encouragement to Hayden; they are envious, resentful, and competitive. Even the hotel doormen in *Two in a Taxi* treat the independent driver shabbily, and dialogue compares the position of the independent driver to recently invaded Finland. *Two in a Taxi* also offers a curious character among the drivers, the "professor," who reads a pamphlet with a star on it, entitled "The New Social Order." He suggests avoiding the police as one more social enemy and notes that, as long as the present system continues, drivers will always be racing each other for fares.

The conflict in *A Fight to the Finish* centers around a struggle of the cabbies, who initiate violence, to regain their position after they have been replaced by tough ex-cons when new management takes over the hack bureau. *Two in a Taxi*, although filmed on an even tighter schedule, has less reliance on action for its plot, showing the relative complexity that this occupational genre could reach without ever extending beyond the B category. The milieu in *Two in a Taxi* is the same as that of its predecessors, but the tone is far more serious, clearly expressing the liberal viewpoint of its original screenwriters, Malvin Wald and Morton Thompson, who regarded their story as an "urban *Grapes of Wrath* for the cab drivers."[28] The socialist overtones are evident from the outset; workers of different occupations have the same interests, and all have a common enemy in management no matter what field, a concept conveyed in theatrical-style dialogue. The situation is no different for women than men; when Hayden's sweetheart, played by Anita Louise, obtains a modeling job, it is only through accepting another man's offer, who then believes that she owes him her future and favors.

The characters are in no way idealized; they are realistic and flawed, with Hayden, for instance, jealous of his girlfriend because of his own lack of self-confidence. Although both *A Fight to the Finish* and *Two in a Taxi* are elegies of suffering, the latter is considerably more somber, avoiding the conventions of action films utilized in *A Fight to the Finish*. While the charmless tough-guy Don Terry is more apt casting for a cabbie than is cheerful Russell Hayden, Terry's persona makes his ultimate success more predictable. The supporting casts in both films emphasize the character's proletarian background.

Two in a Taxi exposes the daily difficulties faced by the drivers and the near-impossibility of breaking out of a dead-end cycle of borderline financial stability, in which everyone is chronically short of money, in need, and trying to get ahead. As Hayden's character remarks, he is crowded in with all the other little guys, and hacking is like a one-way street, with nothing at the end; indeed, *One Way Street* was the working title. No matter how hard Hayden's driver works, with overtime and penny-pinching, it is impossible for him to accumulate the $300 needed to buy the gas station. Trying to raise money on his cab, the driver learns that what he thought was an asset is only another sinkhole of debt—conveyed by photographing the cabbies through the prison-like bars that guard a banker. Working for racketeers seems to offer easy money, but when another driver accepts the work he is killed—leaving his starving family more desperate than ever, with the stigma of shame added to their privation. Just as Hayden's driver gains $100 through a reward, he accidentally yet ironically turns the wrong way down a one-way street, and the hack bureau fines and suspends him, in what seems the final straw to end his hopes. Only through the deus ex machina of a soft-hearted seller accepting a lower price for the service station is an upbeat conclusion reached.

Topicality and Ideological Contradictions

These films are typical of the studio's response to the Depression and prevailing social conditions. There was no consistent bias for or against the New Deal, and no standard political slant emerges from the totality of Columbia product. The Capra films, distinguished by an autonomy that was rarely—and never regularly—allowed other filmmakers at the studio, remain distinct when placed in the context of the studio's other product. For instance, in 1933, Columbia turned out *Mussolini Speaks*, an adulatory feature documentary inspired by Harry Cohn's admiration for the dictator. While Cohn was slow to realize the dangers posed by Mussolini's militarism, his company also produced the pacific *Lost Horizon* (1937), the antithesis of such a glorification of fascism. Yet, as a percentage of cost, *Lost Horizon* grossed far less than *Mussolini Speaks*.[29]

Such political contradictions were not unusual among Columbia films of the 1930s. Just as Capra in *Mr. Deeds Goes to Town* exalted small-town virtues in the Depression, two other unsentimental, acutely observed Columbia films of the same time, *Theodora Goes Wild* (1936) and *Party Wire* (1936), denounced small-town life. *Party Wire*, a Jean Arthur vehicle directed in Capra fashion by Erle Kenton, is a bitter exposé of how malicious gossip can ruin a reputation and nearly cause a suicide. Beneath its screwball surface, *Theodora Goes Wild* is a strong denunciation of the civic and religious constraints imposed on life and art in a small country village. Even more opposed to the Capra viewpoint is *The Party's Over*, a satirical 1934 stage adaptation recounting how a young artist is nearly stifled by a clutch of freeloading relatives he must support. Unlike Capra's pixilated eccentrics, the family in *The Party's Over* bleeds the artist dry emotionally and financially, imposing on his generous spirit until his fiancee finally convinces him to repudiate them.

Presaging *Mr. Smith Goes to Washington* (1939), *The Night Mayor* and *Washington Merry-Go-Round*, two 1932 films with Lee Tracy as politicians, create a pattern Capra would later follow. *The Night Mayor* and *Washington Merry-Go-Round* exalt the hero who bucks the system, fighting to the point of defeat. Such a politician is distinguished *not* by his viewpoint, but by the *way* he fights, courageously and loudly opposing big, entrenched interests for the "little guy," the average voter. However, what will benefit that "little guy" never goes beyond such safe generalities as an end to corruption and an appreciation of veterans. Lee Tracy in *Washington Merry-Go-Round* could be equally modeled on FDR, Huey Long, or the legacy of insurgent, progressive Republicanism. The film is introduced in typically vague manner with a quotation from

James Truslow Adams's *The Epic of America*: "If the American dream is to come true and to abide with us, it will, at bottom, *depend on the people themselves*."

The appearance of topical material was almost unavoidable given Columbia's avoidance of any period pictures outside of Westerns. The studio's art direction was distinctive only for its continual evocation of contemporary, daily settings—experience that would be useful when the studio later produced such postwar social consciousness films as *All the King's Men* (1949) and *On the Waterfront* (1954).[30] Political content was found in other genres, and Columbia was responsible for some of the most unrelievedly downbeat portraits of the Depression. These included *Man's Castle*, *One Way Ticket* (1935), and even the Bing Crosby musical *Pennies from Heaven* (1936). *Pennies from Heaven* was also typical of the bleak vehicles prepared for Edith Fellows, Columbia's answer to Shirley Temple, in which Fellows was usually cast as an unfortunate orphan. Political topics were not limited to the A ranks; before the 1936 release of Warners' famous *Black Legion*, Columbia had distributed a similar expose of the Ku Klux Klan among its better programmers, entitled *Legion of Terror*. *Smashing the Spy Ring* warned of German espionage as early as 1938.

Columbia produced two of the most absurd racket-busting pictures in 1938 with *Crime Takes a Holiday* and *I Am the Law* (a B and an A, respectively), wherein law enforcers happily violate the very legal system they are supposed to enforce. In *I Am the Law*, disaffected law professor Edward G. Robinson uses his sabbatical to hire his students to extort money from merchants. He then manipulates the media to capture the criminals who control the community. Both these films were acknowledged in advertising, publicity, and reviews to be based upon the growing fame of New York District Attorney Thomas Dewey, despite his avowed protests against the use of his reputation. As *Variety* noted, *I Am the Law* would "make Dewey hold his head" and "make intellectuals groan."[31]

Yet a certain moderately progressive vein does run through a number of Columbia films, including the standard social diagnosis of crime in *Juvenile Court* (1938), *One Way Ticket*, *Parole Racket* (1937), *Penitentiary* (1938), *Crime and Punishment* (1935), or even some of the revisionist strains evident in the Buck Jones

Westerns. Both of the studio's premier detective series, Lone Wolf and Boston Blackie, commencing in earnest at the end of the decade, concerned reformed thieves who have gone straight, although the police remain forever skeptical. The B Western formula contained a wide opening for a key social theme of the time, the loss of farms to foreclosure during economic hard times. This situation was seen in a straight good and evil format, with greedy bankers against the cowboys, as in the 1932 Tim McCoy vehicles *Two-Fisted Law* and *The Fighting Code*. Columbia clearly recognized contemporary economic realities and occasionally exalted heroes who fight the representatives of big business, but no specific party or ideological view was endorsed.

The invocation of such themes seems to have been based more on their potential box-office draw than any particular partisan bias. The studio's philosophy was simply to exploit topical material. The Capra films are endemic of this willingness, and his own references to contemporary issues go back long before the *Mr. Deeds-Mr. Smith-John Doe* trilogy. *The Miracle Woman* was an exposé of crooked evangelism drawn from the career of Aimee Semple McPherson and was echoed a few years later in a separate Columbia B film, *Racketeers in Exile* (1937). Capra's *American Madness* (1932) depicted selfish bankers, and *Flight* (1929) dealt with American intervention in Nicaragua.

Studio Talent and Contractual Methods

The roster of Columbia's contract stars, talent, and technicians was limited and seldom changed throughout the 1930s. Specials were different, drawing their aura from imported directors and stars. For big name talent, Columbia relied on loans or freelances, who signed to short-term or single-picture deals. This practice allowed a wide range of choice and contractual flexibility, as well as saving on payroll overhead. The best-remembered filmmakers at Columbia, outside of Frank Capra, were those who passed briefly through the studio, engaged on a one- or two-film basis to handle one of the year's top films, as in the case of Dorothy Arzner (*Craig's Wife*, 1936), Richard Boleslawski (*Theodora Goes Wild*), George Cukor (*Holiday*), John Ford (*The Whole Town's Talking*), Tay Garnett (*She Couldn't Take It*), Howard Hawks (*The Criminal Code*,

Twentieth Century, Only Angels Have Wings, 1939, *His Girl Friday,* 1940), Gregory La Cava (*She Married Her Boss*), Leo Mc-Carey (*The Awful Truth*), and Norman McLeod (*Pennies from Heaven*).[32] Individuals signed to brief deals did not remain with the studio; they were borrowed to increase prestige and salability. Only occasionally did such directors contribute to the weekly output of B product, where lesser known but still notable directors had brief stints. For example, Dudley Murphy, who had made a significant reputation in black films, directed one Columbia outing, the programmer *Don't Gamble with Love* (1936), which included an unusual visit to a black nightclub. In 1939–40 Nick Grinde directed a series of Boris Karloff films at Columbia.

Not all of these brief associations with Columbia were successful. Some stints quickly turned sour and lowered their prestige, as in 1937 with Ernest Schoedsack's *Outlaws of the Orient* and *Trouble in Morocco,* in 1934 with Frank Borzage's *Man's Castle* and *No Greater Glory* and Josef von Sternberg's *Crime and Punishment* and *The King Steps Out.* In 1934, Lewis Milestone first took over, without receiving credit, *The Lady Is Willing.* He then began his own production of *The Captain Hates the Sea,* which took twice its allotted shooting schedule and reportedly garnered meager profits. Similarly, Wesley Ruggles's production of *Arizona* (1940) became a titanic fiasco, costing well over one million dollars.

Harry Cohn's clashes with stars, writers, and directors made many reluctant to work for him, including those under contract.[33] Cohn generally found talent before it was noticed elsewhere, between jobs, or after it had fallen into disfavor. For instance, after director Marion Gering had been expelled from Paramount, Cohn hired him for *Lady of Secrets* (1936) and *Thunder in the City* (1937), a Robert Sherwood satire of American hucksterism. When Columbia sought new contract directorial talent, it generally promoted from within the ranks of assistant directors, as with C. C. "Buddy" Coleman, Sam Nelson, and David Selman, whereas Eddie Buzzell emerged from the production of short films. Directors signed from other studios had often been associated with smaller Poverty Row concerns. Lesser Columbia directors, occasionally handed major assignments, included D. Ross Lederman, Louis King, Otto Brower, Spencer Gordon Bennett, Elliott Nugent, Gordon Wiles, and Lewis D. Collins.

Nonetheless, Columbia did have an assortment of capable contract directors, other than Capra, who were routinely given A assignments, among them Victor Schertzinger, Albert Rogell, Alexander Hall, Lambert Hillyer, Erle C. Kenton, Harry Lachman, John Brahm, and Roy William Neill. Although few of these have received scholarly attention, nearly all deserve reexamination. Leon Barsha, for instance, skillfully enhanced the dramatic value of some of the weakest Columbia B scripts, especially Westerns, such as *Two-Fisted Sheriff*. In their time Victor Schertzinger, Alexander Hall, and Roy William Neill were the most highly respected directors at Columbia besides Capra. Hall was noted for such comedies as *There's Always a Woman* (1938), and Schertzinger won a reputation for his musicals.

Roy William Neill did the most consistently arresting work at Columbia during the first part of the decade; his direction was marked by a distinctly continental flair, with skillful pacing, expert performances, and a clever use of the camera to reflect the tone of the surroundings and genre. This was especially notable in *The Ninth Guest* (1933), in which all visual elements are integrated toward the presentation of a bizarre mystery with high gloss. An ultramodern yet subliminally distorted set design was used to expressionistic effect, and the stylization was reflected in the cinematography and acting. Neill's *Whirlpool* (1934) was a small gem in which Jack Holt, unjustly accused of a crime, commits suicide rather than allow the reputations of his wife and daughter (with whom he has developed a nearly incestuous relationship) to be ruined; such a familial sacrifice is rarely found outside the woman's film. A specialist in thrillers, Neill continued after leaving Columbia in 1935; he is best remembered for directing nearly all the Sherlock Holmes series with Basil Rathbone at Universal in the 1940s.

Of equal caliber in thrillers, although less closely identified with Columbia, was Harry Lachman, particularly in *The Man Who Lived Twice* (1936), which succeeds in involving the spectator in the psychological uncertainty over whether the title character's reformation is genuine. Lambert Hillyer moved with equal facility between B and A films, displaying skill at either level in whatever genre. Hillyer was equally at home with an action-dominated B or an A melodrama like *The Most Precious Thing in Life* (1934).

Indeed, Hillyer functioned at Columbia in the same way that Michael Curtiz did at Warner Bros. in the early 1930s, in the range of projects to which he was assigned and the quality he derived from them. Hillyer also wrote as well as directed and was especially prolific in B Westerns, a form that only occasionally utilized the full potential of his talent.

Cohn's approach to hiring directors was repeated in the choice of talent in front of the cameras. Columbia kept few stars under contract, and its roster of character actors was smaller than at studios comparably prolific in output. Long-term arrangements with players were avoided on the supposition that their continuing appeal was uncertain. This reduced the large overhead involved in maintaining a stable of stars and permitted greater choice in story properties, since material did not have to be purchased simply to keep stars busy.[34] Grace Moore was an example of the wisdom of this policy. Previously unsuccessful in Hollywood, she was hired on an experiment and became Columbia's queen of operetta, but her vogue was brief and after only five films she was released.[35]

In 1933, the only name male leads were Donald Cook, Jack Holt, and Richard Cromwell, and that year Columbia gave up on its effort to make Cromwell an all-around leading young star. Elderly Walter Connolly mostly played supporting roles, although the studio tried to make him an Emil Jannings-type star, the disillusioned old man buffeted by fate, in the old-fashioned but surprisingly popular *Whom the Gods Destroy* (1934). Although Columbia tried Western star Tim McCoy in a variety of noncowboy roles, only Holt had a distinct box-office following across the genre spectrum. Within his range, Holt brought a consistent quality to his fifty-four films at Columbia from 1928 through 1942, exhibiting a sense of gallantry and gentlemanly toughness.

Leading ladies were few; outside of actresses for the Westerns, Columbia kept only Jean Arthur and Ann Sothern under contract. Barbara Stanwyck and Carole Lombard were associated with the studio at the beginning of the decade but did not stay long enough to be strongly identified with Columbia, although they helped some films to success at the box office. Lombard performed at Columbia in some of her most effective dramatic vehicles—*No More Orchids* (1932), *Brief Moment* (1933), and *Lady by Choice* (1934). Later in the 1930s, Columbia could boast, among actresses, only

Fay Wray, Edith Fellows, and Grace Moore. Although attempts were made to create romantic stars in Marian Marsh, Florence Rice, Rosalind Keith, Jean Parker, and Wyn Cahoon, only in 1938 with the addition of Rita Hayworth did the studio acquire a name that would last.

Through the decade, Columbia added few players to its roster. When outside stars passed through the studio, their services were used in only one or two pictures before they rejoined a major company. Only Melvyn Douglas, brought in for comedy pictures, was a lasting male success; there were dismal attempts to salvage the careers of players such as James Dunn, Lew Ayres, and William Gargan, while hopefuls Robert Allen, Victor Jory, Charles Quigley, and Don Terry never found the popularity the studio hoped for. By the mid-1930s Ralph Bellamy had become the most active Columbia player, an all-around bland leading man for any Columbia role, from musical to action, regardless of his suitability for the part.[36] Richard Dix and Leo Carillo were added for a time, but they made little impression. Dix was brought in for a year during 1936–37 and cast in some of the studio's best A films, most of them with the word *devil* in the title: *The Devil's Playground*, *Devil's Squadron*, *The Devil Is Driving*, *It Happened in Hollywood*.[37] The studio also marketed four comedies with Joe E. Brown: *The Gladiator*, *Wide Open Faces* (both 1938), *Beware Spooks!* (1939), and *So You Want to Talk?* (1940).

Columbia management's increasing belief in its own product by 1936 is indicated by the slow expansion of film credits, allowing the names of such individuals as executive producers William Perlberg and B. P. Schulberg to appear on screen. A similar status was also achieved by the longtime but often routine contributions of such department contract talent as Stephen Goosson (art direction), Babs Johnstone (interior decoration), Kalloch (gowns), and Morris Stoloff (musical direction). Previously, only directors, cameramen, editors, and writers were noted on the screen, along with assistant directors and sound engineers in publicity. Columbia had a wide range of writers, including some of the best in the industry, and writing seems to have been one of the few professions for which Harry Cohn admitted some respect. The scenarists included not only Robert Riskin, but also such notables as Sidney Buchman, Jo Swerling, and Dorothy Howell; others were

Harold Buchman, Fred Niblo, Jr., Lambert Hillyer, Lee Loeb, Ethel Hill, Grace Neville, Bruce Manning, and Harold Shumate. The studio boasted some of the top cinematographers in the industry, a group who combined artistry with speed and whose lighting and camerawork graced nearly every Columbia picture, regardless of the budget or genre, down to quickie Westerns and shorts: Joseph August, Lucien Ballard, Benjamin Kline, Henry Freulich, Teddy Tetzlaff, Joseph Walker, and Franz Planer.[38] During the mid-1930s, elaborate and lengthy montages were popular in Columbia films of all type and budget, including *Jealousy* (1934), *One Night of Love*, *Whom the Gods Destroy*, *One Way Ticket*, *The Final Hour* (1936), and *The Man Who Lived Twice*.

Imports, Series, and Program-fillers

Throughout the decade of the 1930s, Columbia often responded differently from nearly all of its competitors to business pressures. The studio demonstrated a propensity for picking up for release various independently made productions, most of which had little to recommend them, even from a box-office vantage point. In this way, for instance, Columbia acquired the infamous midget Western *The Terror of Tiny Town* (1938). Many of these pickups were tentative at best, receiving minimal distribution under Columbia's aegis. Under similar circumstances, Columbia also acquired the laudable Sunset production *Heroes of the Alamo* (1938), a near documentary-style film which, despite mediocre talent and an extremely low budget, was a considerably more balanced and accurate historical treatment of this event than many later, bigger-budget versions. Columbia also distributed Pare Lorentz's government documentary, *Fight for Life* (1940). Less commendable, but more important commercially, were Sol Lesser and Principal Productions's two Richard Arlen vehicles from Harold Bell Wright novels, *The Calling of Dan Matthews* (1935) and the lethargic *The Mine with the Iron Door* (1936).

British quota regulations prompted Columbia to join English independent ventures, only a few of which were imported to the United States—*The Lady Is Willing*, *The Song You Gave Me* (1934), *Abdul the Damned* (1935), *The Beloved Vagabond* (1937), and *Thunder in the City*. With the approach of war, an increasing number of independent European productions dealing with the conflict were released by Columbia in the United States. These included the Irving Asher productions, *Behind the Maginot Line* and *Clouds over Europe/Q Planes*, both directed by Tim Whelan; the Harefield production directed by Michael Powell, *U-Boat 29/The Spy in Black* (all 1939), and the Aldych production, *Mad Men of Europe* (1940).

Unlike any other studio, Columbia not only set up a corporate unit within England but took advantage of a brief loophole in the quota laws to sponsor production in the dominions, investing in Canadian and Australian production. *Rangle River*, one of the half-dozen feature films produced in Australia during 1936, was made possible when Columbia provided financing and sent director Clarence Badger to film the Western-style Zane Grey frontier story. Badger was so impressed with Australia that he remained and made only one more film.

In Canada, Columbia backed the hitherto struggling efforts of maverick producer Kenneth J. Bishop, who had tried for several years to turn Victoria, British Columbia, into a rival for Hollywood with elaborate studios and scenic locations. After sending the Buck Jones company to British Columbia to make one feature in the area in 1932, *McKenna of the Mounted*, Columbia returned in 1936 to bankroll over a dozen features that became nearly the only viable feature productions in Canada during the entire decade. There were not only additional Westerns, most with Charles Starrett in some of his early Columbia pictures, but also a variety of whodunits and other pictures on a par with Columbia's backlot B films, with performers such as Rita Hayworth and Charles Starrett and directors like David Selman, Leon Barsha, and Nick Grinde.[39] These efforts did not became a simple case of Hollywood imperialism, but often reflected their milieu and backgrounds. *Tugboat Princess*, a 1936 vehicle for Edith Fellows, was specifically grounded in local laws governing orphans and adoption and utilized both subjects in the narrative, shot amid the ships and harbor at Victoria. The picture proved sufficiently affecting for press notices to remind viewers that the film's tearful plot was indeed fictional.

Shorts, from the first a significant studio offering, remained a vital part of Columbia's program through 1959. Animation had been important at the beginning of the decade, when Disney signed with Columbia for distribution from 1929 to 1932, followed by Charles Mintz's Krazy Kat and Scrappy series. Slapstick, out of fashion elsewhere, remained a principal source of humor in Columbia shorts. In the mid-1930s, Jules White and Hugh McCollum took over and reorganized the unit, which featured such players as Andy Clyde, Leon Errol, and the newly added Three Stooges. Columbia became the mecca for experienced creators of comedy who could not find work elsewhere, including Del Lord, Clyde Bruckman, Buster Keaton, Charley Chase, and Harry Edwards. Shot in one to five days at less than $35,000 apiece, the Columbia two-reelers were popular, whatever their virtues when seen today. Exhibitor eagerness for access to the shorts, especially those of the Three Stooges, often led them reluctantly to accept Columbia's B features. As one exhibitor wrote of a short in 1936, "Play this with some of the weak pictures Columbia has been putting out this season and it might make them forget the feature."[40]

Unlike Universal, in the early 1930s Columbia could not offer exhibitors a complete package including serials and newsreels. However, with the demise of such independent serial producers as Mascot and smaller companies, Columbia decided in 1937 to enter the serial field with *The Jungle Menace*, competing primarily with Universal and Republic. Columbia was already a mainstay of the Saturday afternoon audience through its Westerns, and the steady profitability of these productions may have convinced the studio to expand its participation in this market to include serials. To produce these initial ventures, Columbia again contracted with an independent, in this case Louis Weiss, one of the longest-lasting but lowest-budgeted inhabitants of Poverty Row. For their first serial offering, Columbia bought the services of *Bring 'em Back Alive* animal documentarist Frank Buck for his first foray into a dramatic starring role. *The Jungle Menace* proved highly popular, attracting more than the typical number of juvenile patrons for its weekly chapters. Exhibitors were immediately convinced that Columbia was a viable entry into the serial field, where it would remain active through the mid-1950s and the death of the form. Seven more serials of all types followed in the next three years, from 1937 to 1939: *The Mysterious Pilot, The Great Adven-*

tures of Wild Bill Hickok, *The Secret of Treasure Island*, *The Spider's Web*, *Flying G-Men*, *Mandrake the Magician*, and *Overland with Kit Carson*. During these years, features were often assembled from Columbia's serials and distributed separately. Nonetheless, Columbia serials were always regarded as a notch below those of Universal or even Republic, without the story values or production quality those studios attained.

Columbia's series in the 1930s were few and largely unsuccessful. Among short-lived series were Bob Allen's failed half-dozen Ranger Westerns and the even less durable Five Little Peppers, with Edith Fellows. Finally, near the end of the decade the studio did create some successful series, first with the initial *Blondie* in 1938. The Lone Wolf only became popular with Warren William in 1939 after unsuccessful attempts to find a star appropriate to the role. These performers had included Melvyn Douglas in *The Lone Wolf Returns* (1936) and Francis Lederer in *The Lone Wolf in Paris* (1938), a virtual remake of the previous year's version of *The Prisoner of Zenda*. More durable series like Jungle Jim, Rusty, Boston Blackie, Crime Doctor, Ellery Queen, and The Whistler were all to emerge from Columbia in the 1940s.

Columbia detective series in the 1930s included two literary offerings: an expensive and unsuccessful pair of Rex Stout's Nero Wolfe mysteries—*Meet Nero Wolfe* (1936) and *The League of Frightened Men* (1937)—and a duet of Adolphe Menjou detective thrillers based on Anthony Abbott's Thatcher Colt novels, *The Night Club Lady* (1932) and *The Circus Queen Murders* (1933). The longest-lasting Columbia series of the decade was Ralph Bellamy's four 1934 mystery vehicles as Inspector Trent, a detective with no distinguishing features other than Bellamy's standard performance: *Before Midnight*, *The Crime of Helen Stanley*, *The Girl in Danger*, *One Is Guilty*. Probably the most memorable of the Trents is *The Crime of Helen Stanley*, one of the decade's "in-studio" murder mysteries, with an effective utilization of the background of standing sets and its milieu of filmmakers and the studio atmosphere.

Although earlier Columbia mystery comedies, like *Murder in Greenwich Village* (1936), were dreadful, the two imitation Thin Man films in the 1938 Bill and Sally Reardon Private Detectives series achieved a standard worthy of their progenitor. *There's*

Always a Woman and *There's That Woman Again*, both directed by Alexander Hall, offered a husband-and-wife team of bumbling, fallible investigators with little ratiocinative skill, who were far more laugh-inducing than the Thin Man team. The series promised success until the sequel replaced Joan Blondell, a near one-woman show at her most scatterbrained in *There's Always a Woman*, with Virginia Bruce, while Melvyn Douglas remained as the sidekick spouse.

With the consolidation of several independent concerns into Republic in 1935, Columbia ascended in industry perception, moving up a notch as Republic assumed Columbia's former position as the lowest distinct entity. A slow transition would, during World War II, see Columbia enjoy more growth than any other production company and in the dozen years after the war become among the most successful studios. When its competitors gave up their exhibition units in the consent decrees that ended the Paramount antitrust case, Columbia received the final break necessary to move into major status during the 1950s.

By making a gradual climb toward status and prestige while continuing to support itself with a steady output of cheap but reliably popular programmers, Columbia followed a course different from Warner Bros.'s quick ascent into the majors with the coming of sound. Most aspiring film companies have followed the Warners pattern, striving for vast expansion and a quick move into major status, as indeed Columbia tried unsuccessfully in 1930–32. Although equally successful, the more patient path Columbia eventually adopted has been rarely imitated, and no other studio has accomplished a comparable transformation.

By most standards of aesthetic quality, Columbia's product of the 1930s is, for the most part, negligible at best. With a few exceptions, I have not tried to indicate that Columbia is deserving of a reexamination of product; the worthy films have been well picked over through the years, with only a few minor gems neglected. Nonetheless, Columbia's prolific output must be understood and recognized within the overall endeavor of accounting for classical cinema and Hollywood in the 1930s. Columbia in the 1930s challenges us as a unique business enterprise, unlike the other studios, setting a stable groundwork for a slow but definite expansion into a major status, rising from Poverty Row to international survivor of the 1990s, a one-of-a-kind achievement in Hollywood history.

Notes

1. Textual observations are based on personal viewing from 1988 to 1990 of nearly half of the studio's 1930s features, most of the Columbia films that survive today in viewable form. Nitrate prints, negatives, and master positives of most of the other films exist in archives but are unavailable at this writing for study, although information concerning these works has been gathered from press materials and reviews.

2. Columbia itself, as opposed to Capra and screwball comedy, has been the subject of little published scholarship. There are individual chapters on Columbia in Douglas Gomery, *The Hollywood Studio System* (New York: St. Martin's, 1986), 161–72; Gene Fernett, *American Film Studios* (Jefferson, N.C.: McFarland, 1988), 41–47; and Beverly Heisner, *Hollywood Art* (Jefferson, N.C.: McFarland, 1990), 255–73. The most meticulous coverage is in Joel Finler's *The Hollywood Story* (New York: Crown, 1988), 68–87, 265, 276, 281–86. Other treatments by David Shipman, *The Story of Cinema* (New York: St. Martin's, 1982), 476–81, and Ethan Mordden, *The Hollywood Studios* (New York: Knopf, 1988), 179–90, are decidedly impressionistic and confined to the celebrated canon of texts. These take their cue from Rochelle Larkin, *Hail, Columbia* (New Rochelle, N.Y.: Arlington House, 1975), a survey book richer in illustrations than insight, and Bob Thomas, *King Cohn* (New York: Putnam's, 1967), an anecdotal and sensationalized biography of the studio boss. Despite these drawbacks, *King Cohn* remains the most thorough history of Columbia and the source of most subsequent commentary on the studio. Only in 1989 did Columbia become the last of the major studios to receive film-by-film treatment in the Crown series with Clive Hirschhorn's *The Columbia Story* (New York: Crown, 1989), a book that is not only methodologically but also factually flawed. The book suffers from bizarre organizational devices that only serve to highlight and perpetuate misperceptions of the studio; much of the product of the B unit and foreign co-productions are shunted off from the chronological sections into various appendices for Westerns, series and serial films, and British productions. Contemporary sources on Columbia are even more elusive; industry trade papers nearly always avoided any detailed analysis of Columbia, unlike other studios of comparable size, and information is largely found in brief news items and columnists' bits.

3. Perhaps the only other studio that presents a similar gulf dividing its A and B product is Republic. In the decade after World War II, Republic developed a prestige program while remaining committed to the foundation of programmers and Westerns that provided its base of income. However, unlike Columbia, Republic ultimately failed in its bid to reach major status, although it also tried for

two decades. For a detailed analysis of the B film in the 1930s, see Brian Taves, "The 'B' Film: Hollywood's Other Half," in Tino Balio, *Grand Design: Hollywood as a Modern Business Enterprise, 1930–1939* (New York: Scribner's, 1993), 313–50, 431–33.

4. Thomas, *King Cohn*, 212.

5. "Cinema Success Story," *New York Times*, 14 April 1935. "State rights" films were sold and distributed on a state-by-state or regional system, with flat fees paid for these limited "rights" to exhibit in a particular area. State-rights films tended to have a limited but predictable market, especially in rural areas, allowing small but regular profits to, for example, the producers of extremely low-budget Westerns or ethnic films.

6. Thomas, *King Cohn*, 16–29, 30, 34.

7. Ibid., 112.

8. On Cohn's longevity, see ibid., 40–41, 77–81; on stock ownership, see "A Unique Motion Picture Enterprise," *Barron's*, no. 106 (25 March 1935): 14; on Columbia's output, see Thomas, *King Cohn*, 197–206, 86.

9. Thomas, *King Cohn*, 163.

10. Heisner, *Hollywood Art*, 270.

11. Douglas W. Churchill, "Hollywood Re-enters the Broadway Market," *New York Times*, 10 January 1937.

12. Larkin, *Hail, Columbia*, 62–63.

13. Definitive figures for the studio's output are difficult to obtain, since the total number of pictures distributed by Columbia is different from the total it produced. The studio picked up films produced by others, and not all of its own films, especially the British dominions productions, were distributed by Columbia in the United States.

14. *Film Daily Yearbook, 1931* (New York: Film Daily, 1931), 257–62.

15. There is little surviving documentation on Columbia; the most valuable material are the charts showing seasonal programs and production dates, in the Columbia collection, Yale Film Study Center, Yale University, New Haven, Conn.

16. "Cinema Success Story," *New York Times*.

17. *Film Daily Yearbook, 1932* (New York: Film Daily, 1932), 477; *Film Daily Yearbook, 1933* (New York: Film Daily, 1933), 98; *Film Daily Yearbook, 1934* (New York: Film Daily, 1934), 162; *Film Daily Yearbook, 1935* (New York: Film Daily, 1935), 136; *Film Daily Yearbook, 1936* (New York: Film Daily, 1936), 452.

18. "Unique Motion Picture Enterprise," *Barron's*, 14. By 1940, Columbia spent $8.8 million annually to achieve gross film rentals of $13.2 million, a 6.5 percent share of the market.

19. Thomas, *King Cohn*, 121–30, 148–52.

20. On profits, see ibid., 123, 148. Quotation from Churchill, "Hollywood Re-enters the Broadway Market."

21. Finler, *The Hollywood Story*, 71.

22. John T. McManus, "The Life of a Ranger," *New York Times*, 4 April 1937.

23. For reviews of *White Eagle*, see *Film Daily*, 24 September 1932, 6; *Motion Picture Herald*, 1 October 1932, 54; *New York Times*, 24 September 1932, 18; *Variety*, 27 September 1932, 21.

24. By the end of the 1930s, Columbia began to claim a position as a producer

of adventure films; this position lasted into the 1950s, with an increasing emphasis during the 1940s on swashbucklers. Such productions had been occasional since the Jack Holt-Ralph Graves pictures *Submarine*, *Flight*, *Hell's Island* (1930), *Dirigible* (1931), and *War Correspondent* (1932). Ever since *Submarine*, the studio had been partial to underwater films, with two remakes, *Fifty Fathoms Deep* (1931) and *The Devil's Playground* (1937), and such similar pictures as *Below the Sea* (1933) and *The Best Man Wins* (1935). Columbia favored contemporary adventure in the Holt-Graves films and *The Last Man* (1932), *Escape from Devil's Island* (1935), *Eight Bells* (1935), and *Hell Ship Morgan* (1936); Chinese settings appeared in *Prince of Diamonds* (1930), *War Correspondent*, *Roaming Lady* (1936), and *North of Shanghai* (1938). Columbia's first real formula adventure films emerged in 1937 from the Darmour unit with *Outlaws of the Orient* and *Trouble in Morocco*, both with Jack Holt under Ernest Schoedsack's direction. The next year saw *Flight into Nowhere* and *Adventure in Sahara*, a virtual remake of *Mutiny on the Bounty* (1935), with the setting of the French Foreign Legion substituting for the British Navy.

25. *Variety*, 15 September 1937, 13; Don Miller, *"B" Movies* (New York: Curtis, 1973), 52.

26. B.R.C., "At the Rialto," *New York Times*, 19 August 1937, 23.

27. *Variety*, 17 October 1933, 27.

28. Malvin Wald, interview by author, Los Angeles, 27 June 1985.

29. *Mussolini Speaks* is a seven-reel documentary edited and compiled by Jack Cohn in 1933, with narration by Lowell Thomas. The early years of Mussolini are described, showing his birthplace and scenes of his youth, climaxing in his march on Rome. Then, to mark his tenth anniversary in power, Mussolini addresses an enthusiastic crowd in Milan, as cutaways indicate the deeds of his administration and its promises for the future. Reviewers acknowledged that the film was propaganda, but also claimed it was interesting. *Motion Picture Herald* recommended it for community groups and schools, while *Variety* believed the film's prime appeal would be to Italians. *Mussolini Speaks* was developed from two reels of edited footage of his address before a throng in Naples in summer 1931, recorded by newsreel cameras. The footage was shipped to America and bought by Columbia for $10,000 and a percentage of profits. Harry Foster, of the New York office, suggested illustrating the address with footage of the dictator's accomplishments. Editing had added and deleted material, including photographs and travelogue bits, with a commentary appended. The resulting film grossed one million dollars. Cohn made a trip to Italy to be decorated by the dictator, who much appreciated the value of Columbia's supportive theatrical documentary. On his return, Harry Cohn remodeled his headquarters to imitate Mussolini's style, with outer and inner offices before his own. The visitor had to pass through a long chamber that left him brightly lit, while Cohn's high-perched desk at the end was in semidarkness. See Thomas, *King Cohn*, 102–4; for reviews of *Mussolini Speaks*, see *Film Daily*, 11 March 1933, 4; *Motion Picture Herald*, 18 March 1933, 34; *New York Times*, 13 March 1933, 18; *Variety*, 14 March 1933.

30. Heisner, *Hollywood Art*, 273.

31. Douglas W. Churchill, "Hollywood and Its Little Women," *New York Times*, 15 May 1938; *Variety*, 31 August 1938, 18.

32. Dorothy Arzner was the only woman director to work at the studio in the 1930s; other women in creative positions were such screenwriters as Dorothy Howell, who worked on numerous early 1930s scripts, and Tess Slessinger, who adapted her own short story into the film *Girl's School* (1938).

33. The "opportunities" Columbia offered filmmakers have, I believe, been overestimated by many scholars, who have not given sufficient attention to the various dictatorial demands and budgetary constraints Harry Cohn placed on talent. For instance, Robert Florey, director of *Two in a Taxi*, was a typical example of the talented directors who preferred to leave the studio rather than be around Cohn's abrasive, offensive personality. Florey worked at Columbia at two different times in his career, on each occasion making some of his finest films, *The Romantic Age* (1927) and *The Face behind the Mask* and *Meet Boston Blackie* (both 1941). The purported directorial freedom Cohn granted was, for Florey, less desirable than an escape from the studio chief's personal crudeness. After completing his fourth Columbia film, *Two in a Taxi*, Florey departed Columbia in 1941 for Warner Bros. Jack Warner's production interference was equally overt, although less crass, but Warners offered more substantial budgets and shooting schedules.

34. "Unique Motion Picture Enterprise," *Barron's*.

35. Thomas, *King Cohn*, 94–99.

36. Ibid., 112–13.

37. B. R. Crisler, "Gossip of the Films," *New York Times*, 15 November 1936.

38. "A Paradox, a Paradox," *New York Times*, 10 March 1935; Finler, *The Hollywood Story*, 84–85, 265.

39. The other films produced under Bishop auspices were: 1936—*Lucky Corrigan/Fury and the Woman, Lucky Fugitives/Stop, Look and Love*; 1937—*Secret Patrol, Stampede, Vengeance/What Price Vengeance*; 1938—*Convicted, Murder Is News, Special Inspector/Across the Border, Woman against the World*; 1939—*Death Goes North, Manhattan Shakedown/Manhattan Whirligig*. Columbia also picked up one Canadian film for distribution, *Lest We Forget*, a World War I documentary directed by Frank C. Badgley.

40. H. M. Gerber, *Motion Picture Herald*, quoted in Ted Okuda with Edward Watz, *The Columbia Comedy Shorts* (Jefferson, N.C.: McFarland, 1986), 11; see also Leonard Maltin, *The Great Movie Shorts* (New York: Crown, 1972), 6–9, and B. R. Crisler, "Random Notes on Picture Personalities," *New York Times*, 26 June 1938.

9

Notes on Columbia Pictures Corporation, 1926–1941, with a New Afterword

Edward Buscombe

Conceptualizing the Film Industry

he film industry: the cinema—how are these terms related in film criticism? *The film industry* describes an economic system, a way (or ways) of organizing the structure of production, distribution, and consumption. Historically, such organization has, in Britain and America, conformed to the usual pattern of capitalist activity; film can be seen as an industry like any other. It has passed from the primitive stage of small-scale entrepreneurial activity to the formation of large-scale monopolies, securing their position by vertical integration spreading from production into distribution and exhibition. Since World War II the industry has, like other forms of business, developed toward diversification and the formation of multinational corporations. In other respects, too, film has developed like other industries. Production, in particular, has been based on a division of labor of a fairly extreme kind. From early days the industry has employed the techniques of mass advertising, and it has required the injection of huge sums of capital, resulting in the passing of

Reprinted by permission of the author from Edward Buscombe, "Notes on Columbia Pictures Corporation 1926–1941." *Screen* 16:3.

control of the industry from its original owners and from the primary producers.

In film criticism, the term *film industry* implies a way of looking at film that minimizes its differences from other forms of economic activity, a way that is of course predominantly that of those who actually own the industry. Its characteristic descriptions are sufficiently indicative of a perspective: "the trade," "marketing," "exploitation," a "package," "product."

The cinema suggests something else. While the term might, notionally, encompass the industry, the pull is surely in a different direction. *The cinema* implies film as art. As Raymond Williams has shown with convincing detail in *Culture and Society*, the opposition between art and industry has a long history in our culture. The division between the two is experienced everywhere as deep, but nowhere deeper than in film. On the one hand, we are given to understand, is the industry, churning out product for financial gain. On the other are artists, creating enduring works of personal expression or comment on life and society. Such an opposition has taken different forms at different times. Sometimes it has been geographic. In America there was Hollywood, the industrial system par excellence. In Europe (usually excluding Britain, apart from its documentaries), there were artists: Renoir, Dreyer, Bergman, Antonioni, and so forth. Later the auteur theory, as applied to American cinema, changed the emphasis. Though Hollywood was still an industry, through diligent critical work some artists could be winnowed from the chaff, artists who, against the odds, managed by luck, cunning, or sheer genius to overcome the system, the industry. The auteur theory, whatever its "theory" may have been, did not in practice abolish the distinction between art and industry; it merely shifted the line of demarcation.

One might suppose that a little common sense would tell us that such a distinction is nonsense, that all film is both industry *and* art, in some sense. Even the lowest, most despised products (choose your own examples) are made with some kind of art. Do they not share the same language as the acknowledged masterpieces; do they not tell a story, try to affect the spectator's emotions? They may do it more or less effectively, but isn't this a difference of degree, not of kind? Conversely, in the making of the most spiritual and sublime films, grubby bank notes change hands.

The film stock on which the masterpiece is recorded may come from the same batch used to shoot the potboiler on the adjoining stage.

Yet proof that the mutual exclusion of art and industry operates at a level too deep to be affected by mere common sense can be found not only in the dominant critical attitudes but in the organization of social institutions. To give an example close to home: the British Film Institute (BFI) was set up, as its Memorandum of Association states, "to encourage the development of the art of the film." At the same time it is stated that the BFI is not permitted "to control nor attempt to interfere with purely trade matters." Art not only can but must be divorced from industry. And the split is preserved even in the structure of government. Whereas the BFI is administered by the Department of Education and Science, the film industry comes under the Department of Trade and Industry. Thus, the opposition art/industry has to be seen not merely as a "mistake" in film criticism that can be easily rectified by a more careful look at the facts, but as the result of a whole practice of thinking, talking, writing, and disseminating inscribed in institutions like the BFI, those parts of the education system that handle film, and exhibition/viewing practices—the art-house circuit and its audiences—the "immaterial" thought both reflecting and being part of this apparatus; in short, as part of an ideology.

The main concern here, however, is not with the origins of such opposition but with its consequence for film criticism. This may be baldly stated: there has been scarcely any serious attempt to think about the relationship between art and industry with regard to films produced in what have historically been for us the two most important filmmaking countries, namely Great Britain and the United States. Criticism has been devoted not to relating them but to separating them out, and in practice this has meant that critics have concentrated on the beauties and mysteries of art and left the industry, presumably a tougher plant, to take care of itself. Study of the industry might require knowledge of, say, economics or of how films are actually made, knowledge that critics have not been expected to acquire. The main effort of criticism, therefore, has gone into the study of film texts viewed as autonomous, self-sufficient entities or, occasionally, as reflections of society, but certainly not as reflections of the industry that produced them, unless they are being dismissed as rubbish. Even recent work deriving from structuralism and concerned to open up the text, to "deconstruct" it, has tended to take the film as given and has ignored questions of how the organization of a film text might relate to the organization of an industry or to specific working practices.

It is in respect to Hollywood, the largest field of activity in both filmmaking and criticism, that the lack of a history of the industry is most glaring. Of course, there is a certain amount of information around. Statistics have occasionally been assembled (government and trade reports on Hollywood in the 1930s are listed in the notes of Leo C. Rosten's *Hollywood: The Movie Colony, the Movie Makers*, a book that has some useful material on this period). There are one or two books, again on the 1930s, that assemble some facts about the economics of the industry (e.g., F. D. Klingender and Stuart Legg, *The Money behind the Screen*, and Mae D. Huettig, *Economic Control of the Motion Picture Industry*). But, of course, they do not attempt to make any connections between the economics and the actual films produced. There is also the ragbag of publicity releases, inaccurate box-office returns, and general gossip that makes up the trade press (*Film Daily, Motion Picture Herald, Variety, Hollywood Reporter*, etc.). To this may be added a host of "biographies" (or ghosted autobiographies) of prominent industry figures, of which *Hollywood Rajah* by Bosley Crowther (on Louis B. Mayer) and *King Cohn* by Bob Thomas (on Harry Cohn) are representative examples. Little that is useful can be gleamed from such works, which mostly string together collections of anecdotes about the "great men." On such questions as the financial structures within which they were obliged to operate or the actual working methods of their studios, they are for the most part silent. Of studio histories, properly speaking, there are none, with the possible exception of Richard Schickel's book *The Disney Version*, which is hampered by his failure to get any cooperation from the Disney studio itself—a fact, of course, that is not without its significance, since it indicates the difficulties of this kind of work.

Indeed, the neglect of industry history is not only a consequence of critical attitudes and priorities that have abandoned the field to those whose interest does not go beyond personalities. It is also the result of very real practical problems. The fact is that the history of the American film industry is extremely difficult to write because many of the basic materials that would be needed are simply not available. The statistics are incomplete and unreliable. The trade press presents only the acceptable face of the business, even when one can get access to it (the BFI Library, virtually the only collection of such periodicals in Britain, has no run of *Variety*, although there are plans to acquire one [It has, since this essay first appeared, done so.]). The biographies and studio histories, where they exist at all (e.g., Bosley Crowther's *The Lion's Share* on MGM), are largely based on reminiscences. Concrete documented evidence in the form, say, of studio memoranda, accounts, and other records is almost totally lacking. If such records still exist, they are mostly locked away in studio vaults. And the history of technological development in Hollywood has still to be written. Last, the films themselves—such prints as have been preserved are often impossible to see. The situation is little different from that which exists in relation to the history of the Elizabethan stage, with this exception: infinitely less method and application has gone into researching it.

The result is that, when Hollywood has been written about, its industrial dimension has been ignored. Much of the writing has been based on an idea of history as one damned thing after another. Even such a prestigious work as Lewis Jacobs's *The Rise of the American Film* scarcely rises above this, most sections being simply annotated film lists. The only principle to compete has been auteurism, which leaves film history at the stage reached by history proper in the nineteenth century, when Carlyle defined it as the lives of great men. Deliberate attempts to get away from auteurism, such as Colin McArthur's *Underworld USA* (on the crime film) and Jim Kitses's *Horizons West* (on the Western) are ultimately broken-backed books. Genres may be related to aspects of American history, but in the end it is the auteurs who dominate the account.

Some recent, more promising directions have been pursued. Patrick Ogle's work on deep focus (*Screen* 13, no. 1) or that of John Ellis and Charles Barr on Ealing Studios (*Screen* 15, nos. 1–2, and 16, no. 1) have from different perspectives tried to make connections between films and the nature of the industry that produced them. *The Velvet Light Trap* has brought to light valuable material on the studio system, though the use that has been made of it has often been disappointing. But the gaps in our knowledge are still enormous.

The Question of Determination

One consequence of the existence of such gaps has been that attempts to relate Hollywood films to the society that produced them have simply by-passed the industry altogether. The result has been a series of short circuits. Hollywood films are seen as merely "reflecting" society. On the one hand is society, seen as a collection of facts, attitudes, psychological patterns, or whatever. On the other are the films, where one sees such facts and attitudes mirrored. Though it may be conceded that the mirror sometimes distorts, insofar as there is a theory behind such a view it is a naively realist one; indeed, how could it be otherwise? If there is no conception of Hollywood as an industry with its own history, specific practices, economic relationships, and technological and other material constraints, if film is seen as something that somehow mysteriously appears and having appeared is simply there, fixed and given, then how is one to understand the nature of any mediation? To confine ourselves again to the period of the 1930s, a book such as Andrew Bergman's *We're in the Money* devotes a mere four pages to "A Note on the Movie Industry and the Depression," which ends thus: "The preliminaries completed, we proceed to the black and white footage itself." And in the black and white footage the social comment can simply be read off as if the films were so many sociologists' reports. Here is an admittedly rather extreme example: "Tod Browning's 1932 MGM film, *Freaks*, had a cast made up of pinheads, human torsos, midgets, and dwarfs, like nothing ever in the movies. And what more stunted a year than 1932 for such a film?" (p. 168).

One might expect that more specifically Marxist attempts to relate Hollywood to American society would display a little more rigor and subtlety. Bourgeois cultural theories, with their assumptions about the values of artistic freedom and personal expression, are obviously ill equipped to deal with a medium so conditioned by money, technology, and organizational structures. Books such as Bergman's, which dispense with most of that theory (though never completely—some auteurs, such as Capra and Vidor, make an appearance) seem to have no theory at all to replace it. Marxism, on the other hand, proposes a sophisticated understanding of the relations between society, a system of production, and the actual product. Yet such Marxist models as have been put forward for understanding Hollywood have suffered from a crudity that has had the effect of deadening further thought. The crudest model of all is that encapsulated in Godard's phrase "Nixon-Paramount." The model implied in such a phrase has had obvious attractions for the political avant-garde and indeed contains some truth. But the truth contained in such vulgar Marxism is so vague and general as to have scarcely any use at all. Ideological products such as films are seen as directly caused by the nature of the economic base of society. A capitalist system produces capitalist films, and that is all there is to it. Alternatively (but the slight sophistication is scarcely a modification), the products of Hollywood are bourgeois and capitalist because the particular industry that produces them is capitalist. And the more specific the model becomes, the more its crudity is exposed. Thus, in the first section of the *Cahiers du cinéma* text on *Young Mr. Lincoln* (translated in *Screen* 13, no. 3), we are told that, since Hollywood is involved with big business, its ideology is not just a generally capitalist one. It supports the more reactionary wing of the political spectrum represented by the Republican Party.

The *Cahiers* text is only one example of a desire to show not only that Hollywood is a part of bourgeois ideology in general but also that some Hollywood films are intended to carry a specific and reactionary message that has a direct reference to a particular political situation. Another example of such overpoliticization comes in a recent issue of *Jump Cut* (no. 4, November-December 1974), which contains an interpretation of *King Kong* as an anti-Roosevelt tract. The article conveniently states its premises in a footnote:

> This article is built round two suppositions. First, that all huge business corporations (such as RKO) are conservative Republican unless demonstrated otherwise, and that their

products (like *King Kong*) will reinforce their interests instead of betraying them. Second, that the auteur theory in its standard application is not a germane approach when dealing with a political film, especially under the tight studio control of the 1930's. A political film would only be allowed release if its philosophy was in line with that of the studio which made it. Therefore, RKO studio will be regarded as the true "auteur" of *King Kong*, despite the innumerable personal touches of its artistic crew.

Although the phrase "unless demonstrated otherwise" indicates that the author, Gerald Peary, is aware of the dangers of over-simple generalizations, his assumptions still seem open to two major objections. First, is it not possible that even in Hollywood (not noted perhaps for its political sophistication) there were in the 1930s people who could see that the survival of capitalism (and hence of their "huge corporations") was not necessarily synonymous with the victory of the Republican Party, especially a Republican Party so discredited as the one that had been led to electoral disaster and intellectual bankruptcy by Herbert Hoover? Second, what exactly *are* the interests of such corporations? In the long term, obviously, the survival of a system that allowed them to make profits. But in the short term, surely it was those profits themselves. Is it to be assumed that studio executives saw the possibility of profits in attacking a leader who had so recently demonstrated his popularity at the polls (especially among the cinema-going section of the public)? Or should we assume that the political commitment of the studio executives overcame their dedication to profits?

It seems unlikely, but our ignorance about Hollywood generally and about the particular organization of RKO is such that we cannot answer these questions. Precisely for this reason we ought to beware of assuming any answers. Even if we do assume, with the authors in *Cahiers* and *Jump Cut*, that a studio is owned by big business and that one of its products promotes the political and hence economic interests of the company (I say *apparently* because the actual interpretation of the films seems open to question), it does not necessarily follow that the political meaning is the direct result of who owns the studio. *Post hoc* is not *propter hoc*.

The lack of any detailed knowledge of industry history, then, suggests caution on the question of the political orientation of Hollywood in the 1930s. First, is it true that the film industry was controlled by big business? And is this the same as the Republican Party? (There was business influence among the Democrats, too.) Second, if it is true, can one assume a direct effect on the ideology of Hollywood films? Even the term *ideology* seems to pose a problem here. It is one thing to argue that, using the term in its classical Marxist sense (or as refined by Althusser) to mean a general world view or structure of thought situated primarily below the conscious level, Hollywood films are ideological expressions of bourgeois society. It is quite another to argue that they support a specific set of political attitudes. Bourgeois society is more than simply the Republican Party. And in any case Marxist theory only claims that ideological products are determined *in the last instance* by the economic relations existing at the base of society. The arguments about *Young Mr. Lincoln* and *King Kong* seem to assume that facts about who controls the film industry can provide a sufficient explanation of a film's ideology, ignoring the dimension of the institutional structures that may intervene between the economic base and the final product. Without a knowledge of these structures, one cannot say that these films are *not* propaganda, but, if they were intended as such, as the *Cahiers* and *Jump Cut* articles imply, it is a strange sort of propaganda that requires an ingenious interpretation thirty or forty years later to make its point. Surely it would have to be demonstrated that such a reading was available to an audience at the time.

The Case of Columbia

These problems were thrown into relief by a viewing some time ago of *American Madness*, directed for Columbia in 1932 by Frank Capra. The story of the film concerns Dickson, the manager of a small-town bank (played by Walter Huston). The directors of the bank are financiers of the old school (pre-Keynesians), dedicated to tight money policies that they pursue ruthlessly and selfishly. Dickson, however, has a different view of what the function of a bank should be. He believes that money should be put to work to create jobs and opportunities. His policy is to lend to small businessmen, trusting in his own assessment of their good intentions rather than in the security they can offer. His beliefs are put to the test when a run on the bank occurs; the run is stopped and his faith in his clients vindicated when the little people he has helped rally round to deposit money and so restore confidence in the bank.

The program note that accompanied the screening of the film at the National Film Theatre suggested that the character of Dickson might have been based on A. H. Giannini, a California banker who was influential in Columbia's affairs in the 1930s. Such a suggestion raises one immediate difficulty, in that it seems to assume that the apparent, or manifest, meaning of the film is the only one and ignores the possibility that the latent meaning may be quite different. The film might be about other things besides banking. The suggestion excludes, that is, the possibility of analyzing the film along the lines of the *Young Mr. Lincoln* text, which finds that, despite the film's apparent project of supporting the Republican cause in the 1940 presidential election, the "real" meaning of the film undermines this. (The problem of such readings, despite their obvious attractions, is that it is never explained how in practice the subversive meaning of the film becomes available to the people to whom it might be of some use, i.e., the working class.) Nevertheless, the suggestion seemed worth following up because of the possibility that it might throw some light on the question of Hollywood's relation to politics in the 1930s and on the nature of the production system generally. And this might, in turn, tell us something about Capra's films.

Robert Mundy, in a review of Capra's autobiography in the American *Cinema* (7, no. 1 (1971): 56), speculates on how it was that Capra was able to make films that so closely embodied his personal ideas. He suggests two reasons: first, that Capra was working for a small studio where freedom was greater, and second, that Capra's vision "was unusually consonant with the vision of America which Hollywood purveyed with such commercial success in the 1930's. Ideologically his films were rarely at odds with the image of life which the studios believed the public wanted to see." Mundy avoids the facile assumption that Capra was "in touch" with America and that his films arise out of some special relationship to the people and the mood of the time. Instead, he suggests that Capra's work is an expression of the point of view of his *studio*. He concludes, however, that we need to know more: "A persuasive history of Columbia in the 1930's [is] needed before an informed critical account of Capra's work can be written." Quite. The problem is to know where to start, given the problems of such research outlined above. Mr. Giannini seemed to offer a way in.

He is referred to in some books about Hollywood, but as far as I know never more than in passing, as a prominent California banker who was involved in movie financing. In several of the references, there is a curious uncertainty about his initials. Sometimes he is called A. P. Giannini, sometimes A. H. Thus, Philip French, in his "informal" history of the Hollywood tycoons *The Movie Moguls*, mentions him on page 25: "In fact the first banker to take the cinema seriously was the Californian A. P. Giannini, the son of an Italian immigrant, whose Bank of Italy (later renamed the Bank of America) has played an important part in movie finance since before the first world war." On page 79 we read: "A. H. Giannini, the influential movie financier whose Bank of Italy had a special claim on Hollywood consciences of whatever religious denomination."

The mystery of A. H. or A. P. was cleared up only when I looked up Giannini in the *National Cyclopaedia of American Biography*. It seems that there were two of them. (Obviously, I am not the first person since Mr. Giannini père to be aware of this fact, but it seems as though Philip French was not when he wrote his book. Of such confusions is film history made.) It's worth giving some details of their careers, since they are relevant to Capra's film. A. H. and A. P. (or, to give them their full names, Attilio Henry and Amadeo Peter) were brothers. Both their parents were natives of Italy; their father had been a hotel keeper but had come to California to try farming. Amadeo was born in 1870 and his brother four years later. The older brother had gone to work at the age of twelve in his stepfather's firm of wholesale commission agents in San Francisco, and while still in his twenties he formed the Columbus Savings and Loan Society. In 1904 he founded the Bank of Italy. Giannini's bank was of a novel kind. Branches were set up in small towns across the country to attract the savings of the man in the street, and Giannini even started savings schemes in schools. His bank specialized in making loans to small businesses with minimal collateral and introduced the practice of lending money for house purchase repayable in monthly installments. He seems to have been a man of some determination and imagination; during the great San Francisco earthquake and fire of 1906, Giannini was the first to reopen his bank, setting up his desk on the waterfront while the fire still raged. By 1930 he had built up his banking interests to the point where the holding company, the Transamerica Corporation, was the largest of its kind in the world, with assets of one billion dollars. Giannini's unorthodox methods did not endear him to more conservative financiers on Wall Street; particularly deplorable were his policies of encouraging wide public ownership of his corporation and of assisting his employees to become stockholders through profit-sharing schemes.

His brother Attilio (sometimes called Dr. Giannini, though he abandoned medicine when made vice president of his brother's Bank of Italy) was involved in various movie companies between the world wars. In 1920 he lent Chaplin half a million dollars to make *The Kid*. In 1936 he became president and chairman of the board of United Artists and, though he resigned from this position in 1938, he retained an influential position in the film industry by virtue of his place on the voting trust that controlled Universal Pictures. He was also involved with several so-called independent production companies, such as Selznick International Pictures and Lesser-Lubitsch. None of these organizations possessed large chains of movie theaters. It was the tangible assets of real estate that tempted the Wall Street banks into movie finance in the 1920s. Giannini does at least seem to have been more interested in making pictures.

Giannini's main importance for present purposes is his role in Columbia. The company was originally formed in 1920 as CBC, the letters standing for the names of the three men who set it up: Harry Cohn, Joe Brandt, and Harry's brother Jack. All of them had previously worked for Carl Laemmle at Universal. Attilio Giannini lent them $100,000 to get started. In 1924 the company changed its name to Columbia Pictures Corporation (possibly an echo of the Columbus Savings and Loan Society?). Giannini continued to be closely involved. In 1929 the studio decided to

9.1. Harry Cohn in an undated early photograph, inscribed to friends. (Museum of Modern Art/Film Stills Archive)

establish their stock on the New York exchange, but 96 percent of the voting stock was concentrated in the hands of a voting trust. In 1932 Joe Brandt was bought out by Harry Cohn (after Jack Cohn had attempted to enlist Giannini's support in a coup against his brother), and thereafter the voting trust that controlled the company consisted of the two Cohns and Giannini. Unlike most studios at this time, Columbia had no debts to the New York investment banks and instead was run as a family business.

Giannini's position was therefore a powerful one. Unfortunately, no one has actual knowledge of how he used it. All that can be done is to suggest what his influence might have been, given the kind of background from which he and his brother came. The

Gianninis were quite separate from the New York banking establishment. Not only was theirs a different kind of business (deposit
as opposed to investment banking), involving them with different
kinds of clients; they were Catholics (unlike the Rockefellers and
Morgans), they were second-generation immigrants, they came
from the other side of the country, and their social attitudes were,
as far as one can tell, less patrician. A. P.'s entry in the *National
Cyclopaedia* says that he "has ever been known as a friend of the
poor and struggling" and, if ever a banker could be so described,
it seems likely that he was. Not surprisingly, therefore, he supported the Banking Act introduced by Roosevelt in 1935 because,
he said, he preferred a measure of government control to domination of the banks by the Wall Street establishment. In 1936
he actively supported Roosevelt's campaign for a second term, at
a time when Wall Street considered FDR as no better than a Communist. It seems reasonable to assume that his brother shared
A. P.'s liberal views.

The Gianninis might, then, be seen as a kind of contradiction
in terms: populist bankers. The populists of the nineteenth century had regarded bankers as the physical embodiment of all that
was evil and believed that the agricultural problems of the Midwest were largely caused by a conspiracy of monopolists on Wall
Street keeping interest rates up and farm prices down. (Amadeo
Giannini was, we are told, greatly interested in agricultural progress.) The little man, the populists contended, stood no chance
against those who commanded such resources and used them for
selfish purposes. But the Gianninis believed in deliberately aiding
such small businessmen and farmers, who got no help from Wall
Street. In this respect they were in line with the policies of the
New Deal, which attempted to get big business under some kind
of government control while at the same time trying to raise farm
prices and help small firms and individuals by encouraging banks
to make loans, by refinancing mortgages, and so on.

This, too, is Dickson's policy in *American Madness*, and it
seems plausible that the character is indeed based on Dr. Giannini.
The question then is: What do we make of it? A simple and tempt-
ing theory might be constructed: Capra's film doesn't so much
capture what "people" were thinking at the time as represent the
thinking of a New Dealer on the voting trust controlling Colum-

bia. Such a theory certainly has its attractions. First, it provides a corrective to the crude assumption that Hollywood = big business = the Republican Party. Second, other Capra films, such as *Mr. Deeds Goes to Town*, *Mr. Smith Goes to Washington*, and *You Can't Take It with You* also embody the populism that was a powerful element in the New Deal. Third, the situation of Columbia itself, quite apart from the beliefs of those in control, might well be seen as impelling it toward the New Deal coalition of anti-establishment forces. Despite the Academy Awards Capra collected for the studio in the 1930s, it never entirely freed itself from its Poverty Row origins. Although the company bought its own studio in 1926 and in 1929 set up a national distribution organization,

9.2. Depositors demand their money in *American Madness* (1932). (Museum of Modern Art/Film Stills Archive)

at the beginning of the 1930s Columbia was still producing fewer than thirty features a year (to MGM's forty-three), and most of these were destined for the lower half of a double bill. Output increased steadily during the decade, but the studio was never in the same league as the majors. In 1935, for example, the total volume of business of Loew's, the parent company of MGM, was $85 million; Columbia's was $16 million. Thus, Loew's had nearly 22 percent of the total volume of business of the industry, and Columbia had only 4 percent. And despite the characteristically violent swings in the film industry each year from profit to loss and back again, these relative percentages did not change for the rest of the decade. Columbia was unable to increase its share of business because, unlike the major studios, it owned no chain of theaters to serve as a secure outlet for its product. All the money it made came from the sale of its own pictures to theaters owned by other studios. MGM and the other majors could, and frequently did, recoup losses on their own films by profits on the exhibition of other companies' output.

A potential advantage of this relative weakness was that Columbia preserved its financial independence. It had not had to borrow heavily from the banks to finance the acquisition of theater chains, and as a result the studio was still in the control of the men who had founded it, the two Cohns and Giannini. Its independence of Wall Street meant that it might well become the focus of anti-establishment forces and that, if it did, it had the freedom to make films which reflected that, always providing, of course, that it could sell them to the theaters.

But caution is necessary even before trying to test out such a thesis. Capra, in his autobiography, devotes several pages to recording how charmed he was by Roosevelt's personality; yet, he says, this only made him "almost a Democrat." One might suppose that Capra, a first-generation immigrant, an Italian Catholic born in Sicily, was a natural Democrat. But the political content of his films, while embodying support for the underdog, does not attach itself to any party. His belief in the people goes hand in hand with a classically populist distrust of *all* their leaders. And other tendencies in his films, such as a pervasive anti-intellectualism and a hostility to central government, are certainly not characteristic of the New Deal.

Nevertheless, there is a kind of radicalism in his films that would certainly not have commended itself to the fiercely Republican Louis B. Mayer, for example, and it therefore seems worth pursuing the thesis that Columbia might have been a focus for Roosevelt sympathizers. Harry Cohn, who controlled the production side of the company throughout the period, seems to have had no interest in politics at all. It is true that he visited Mussolini in 1933 after Columbia had released a complimentary documentary entitled *Mussolini Speaks*. But Cohn seems to have been more impressed with the intimidating layout of the dictator's office than with his politics. When Cohn returned to Hollywood, he rearranged his own office in imitation. Capra remarked, in an interview at the National Film theater, that Cohn did not care about the politics of his studio's films. His concern was with their money-making potential, which he estimated with a "foolproof device . . . If my fanny squirms it's bad. If my fanny doesn't squirm it's good. It's as simple as that" (quoted in *King Cohn*, page 142). If Giannini had wanted the studio to take a pro–New Deal stance, then it seems as though Cohn would have had no particular objections.

The only way of testing whether there was such a policy in default of any access to whatever records of the company may still exist is to look at the films that Columbia made during the period and to find out what one can about the people who made them. It's at this point that the sheer physical difficulties of this kind of work intrude. Taking the period 1926–41, from just before the introduction of sound to a year or so after Capra left Columbia (an arbitrary choice, but less arbitrary than some and one that corresponds very roughly to the period of the Depression and the consequent New Deal as far as World War II), Columbia, despite being one of the smaller studios, made (by my calculations) 627 feature films. (The figure may not be exact because the *Film Daily Year Book*, from which the calculation is made, lists the films of each year twice, once under each studio and once in alphabetical order for the whole industry. Titles appearing in one list do not always appear in the other.) To make those films the company employed 67 different producers, 171 directors, and 269 writers. (The figure for writers is from 1928; they are not credited in the *Year Book* before that date.) By *writers* is meant those credited with a screenplay. Authors of the original stories from which the films were made might amount to another two or three hundred people. There are also fifteen people whose names appear at one time or another as directors of the company, Columbia Pictures Corporation.

These are the people within the organization whose position would have allowed them to influence the political content of the films. One might wish to argue that everyone (actors, cameramen, designers, right down to the studio policemen) had some kind of influence, however small. Melvyn Douglas, for example, who acted in many films for Columbia during the 1930s, was active in liberal causes. I have excluded these workers from consideration mainly because, given the nature of the production process as far as one understands it and the rigid division of labor, their control over the political content (if any) of a film would have been less. Actors did not make up their own lines. In any case one has to stop somewhere, and it's not too easy to find out who the studio policemen were.

One is thus faced with a preliminary list of 522 people; to be precise, the number is slightly fewer because the division of labor was not absolute and some writers directed or vice versa. But there is not much overlapping, and the total must be around 500 (this for one small studio during a mere fifteen years of its fifty-year existence). The BFI Library has a card index system that allows one to check whether the library has entries on individuals in books, in periodicals, or on microfiche. I accordingly looked up everyone who worked on more than the occasional film. Very few of these names appear in the index; when they do it is often merely a reference to a tiny cutting in *Variety* recording the person's death and giving a short list of the films they worked on. (This is a criticism not of the state of the library but of the state of film history.)

A few things do emerge. Columbia seems to have been, in the higher echelons, a tight-knit community (one precondition perhaps of a consistent policy). One of the producers was Ralph Cohn, the son of Jack. Everett Riskin, another producer, was the older brother of Robert, who wrote several of Capra's screenplays. Sam Briskin, general manager of the studio in the early 1930s and executive in charge of production from 1938 to 1942, was the brother-in-law of Abe Schneider, treasurer of the company during most of this period. Briskin's brother, Irving, was another producer at Columbia. Yet this doesn't tell us much about an industry where the pull of family relationships was always strong and where "the son-in-law also rises" was a standard joke.

On the political affiliations of the vast majority, I found no information at all, nor even any information on their lives that would permit a guess. Some very few wrote books or had books written about them but, with the exception of Cohn and Capra, their careers were peripheral to Columbia. A few more have been the subject of articles in film magazines, and from these one can glean scraps of information. Richard Maibaum, who wrote a few scripts for the studio, was the author of some antilynching and anti-Nazi plays before coming to Hollywood. Dore Schary, whose Democratic sympathies were well known, was also a writer at Columbia in the 1930s. So, very occasionally, were Donald Ogden Stewart, associated with left-wing causes at the time, and Edward Chodorov, involved with committees for refugees from Spain and Germany and later more or less blacklisted. But this scarcely amounts to much. Stewart, after all, wrote a lot of scripts for MGM.

More significant, at first sight, than the presence of "liberals" is the fact that exactly half of the Hollywood Ten were actually employed at Columbia during the 1930s, namely, Edward Dmytryk, Dalton Trumbo, Herbert Biberman, John Howard Lawson, and Lester Cole. But a concerted Communist effort at the studio is hardly likely. Only Dmytryk worked there more than occasionally, and he during his time as a contract director was making routine B-feature films (musicals, horror pictures, thrillers) that, one must assume, offered little scope for the kind of social comment Dmytryk put into *Crossfire*. One or two other Communists who worked at Columbia testified before the House Un-American Activities Committee four years after the 1947 hearings that sent the Ten to jail. Paul Jarrico, who wrote for Columbia the screenplays of *No Time to Marry* (1938) and *The Face behind the Mask* (1941), was called before the committee in 1951 but refused to testify and pleaded the Fifth Amendment. Another called before the committee in 1951 was Sidney Buchman. One of Harry Cohn's favorite writers, Buchman specialized in comedy. Among his credits for Columbia are *Whom the Gods Destroy* (1934); *I'll Love You Always*, *Love Me Forever*, *She Married Her Boss* (1935), *The King Steps Out*, *Theodora Goes Wild*, *Adventure in Manhattan*, *The Music*

Goes Round (1936), *Holiday* (1938), *Mr. Smith Goes to Washing-ton* (1939), *The Howards of Virginia* (1940), and *Here Comes Mr. Jordan* (1941). Buchman admitted that he had been in the Communist Party from 1938 to 1945 but refused to supply the committee with the list of names of other members they required and was cited for contempt. He was found guilty and given a one-year suspended sentence and a $150 fine.

Buchman clearly occupied an influential position at Columbia. He was a producer as well as a writer and was associated with some of Columbia's greatest successes in the late 1930s and early 1940s. But if *Mr. Smith* is satirical about Washington life, it retains an unswerving, even touching, faith in American political institu-tions, and it is difficult to see that Buchman's membership in the Communist Party had any great effect on what he wrote. Indeed, many of his associates seem to have been surprised to learn that he was a Communist.

It may be that a more detailed search through such records as are available would turn up some decisive evidence. But, on what has been presented thus far, it seems unlikely that, Dr. Giannini notwithstanding, there was any deliberate policy of favoritism to the New Deal or left-wing causes. The same conclusion seems likely to follow from the films. Here again, one is attempting gen-eralizations based on woefully inadequate knowledge because, apart from those directed by Capra, I have seen very few of the films Columbia made during the period. Nevertheless, some im-pressions can be gained from looking at the records. In the late 1920s and early 1930s, the staples of the studio's output were ad-venture and action films, comedies, often mildly risqué, and the occasional exposé (one of Jack Cohn's first successes at Universal was to convince Carl Laemmle of the box-office potential of *Traffic in Souls*, a sensationalist feature on the white slave trade). Westerns and thrillers made up the rest of the production schedule. Of course, titles can be misleading, but a list of the films produced in 1928 probably gives a fair indication of at least the type of films being made: *That Certain Thing, The Wife's Relations, Lady Raffles, So This Is Love, Woman's Way, Sporting Age, The Matinee Idol, Desert Bride, Broadway Daddies, After the Storm, Golf Wid-ows, Modern Mothers, Name the Woman, Ransom, The Way of the Strong, Beware of Blondes, Say It with Sables, Virgin Lips, Scarlet*

Lady, *Court Martial*, *Runaway Girls*, *Streets of Illusion*, *Sinners'
Parade*, *Driftwood*, *Stool Pigeon*, *The Power of the Press*, *Nothing to
Wear*, *Submarine*, *The Apache*, *The Lone Wolf's Daughter*, *Restless
Youth*, *The Sideshow*.

Besides Capra, directors working regularly for Columbia at this
time included the veteran director of serials George B. Seitz (*The
Perils of Pauline*) and Erle Kenton, another veteran who had been
in pictures since 1914. The policy, one guesses, was one of efficient professionalism dedicated to getting the most out of Columbia's meager resources. Not only did Columbia make fewer
films; they also spent less on each production than the major studios. (Few of their films at this time ran more than seventy minutes.) This would seem to leave little room for the carefully considered personal statements of the kind Capra aspired to later in the
1930s. This is not to say that there was no possibility of social or
political comment, however, as the history of Warners at the same
time shows.

After Capra's astonishing success with *It Happened One Night*
in 1934, which won Columbia its first Oscars and enormously increased the studio's prestige, pictures of the earlier type were sup-
plemented by the occasional more expensive production. Though
Columbia had contract players of its own (e.g., Jack Holt, Ralph
Bellamy, or, in Westerns, Buck Jones and Charles Starrett), they
could not compare in box-office appeal with the stars of bigger
studios. Columbia could not afford the budgets that having bigger stars would have entailed. On the other hand, it could never
break into the big time without them. Harry Cohn's solution to
this vicious circle was to invite successful directors from other studios to make occasional pictures for Columbia, pictures that
would be given larger than usual budgets and that would have
stars borrowed from other studios. Careful planning permitted
short production schedules and kept costs down to what Columbia could afford. Capra, too, was given increasingly larger budgets
and outside stars. Thus, some big-name directors came to work at
Columbia during the later 1930s, often tempted by the offer of
being allowed to produce their own films. Among the titles produced at Columbia during the period after *It Happened One
Night* were:

1934: *20th Century* (dir. Howard Hawks, with John Barrymore and Carole Lombard), *The Captain Hates the Sea* (dir. Lewis Milestone, with Victor McLaglen and John Gilbert); 1935: *The Whole Town's Talking* (dir. John Ford, with Edward G. Robinson), *She Married Her Boss* (dir. Gregory La Cava, with Claudette Colbert), *She Couldn't Take It* (dir. Tay Garnett, with George Raft and Joan Bennett), *Crime and Punishment* (dir. Josef von Sternberg, with Peter Lorre); 1936: *Theodora Goes Wild* (dir. Richard Boleslawski, with Irene Dunne); 1937: *The Awful Truth* (dir. Leo McCarey, with Cary Grant and Irene Dunne); 1938: *Holiday* (dir. George Cukor, with Cary Grant and Katharine Hepburn); 1939: *Let Us Live* (dir. John Brahm, with Maureen O'Sullivan and Henry Fonda), *Only Angels Have Wings* (dir. Howard Hawks, with Cary Grant, Thomas Mitchell, and Richard Barthelmess), *Golden Boy* (dir. Rouben Mamoulian, with Barbara Stanwyck and Adolphe Menjou); 1940: *His Girl Friday* (dir. Howard Hawks, with Cary Grant and Rosalind Russell), *The Howards of Virginia* (dir. Frank Lloyd, with Cary Grant), *Angels over Broadway* (dir. Ben Hecht and Lee Garmes, with Douglas Fairbanks, Jr.), *Arizona* (dir. Wesley Ruggles, with William Holden); 1941: *Texas* (dir. George Marshall, with William Holden, Glenn Ford, and Claire Trevor), *You Belong to Me* (dir. Wesley Ruggles, with Barbara Stanwyck and Henry Fonda), *The Men in Her Life* (dir. Gregory Ratoff, with Loretta Young).

Despite this sprinkling of prestige productions, the basic recipe remained much the same as before. There were lots of low-budget Westerns (a dozen or so in 1940) directed by Lambert Hillyer, a veteran of the Columbia lot, or Joseph H. Lewis and starring Bill Elliott or Charles Starrett. The studio made several series: a number of films based on Blondie, the cartoon character, the Lone Wolf series of thrillers, an Ellery Queen mystery series, and so on. There were light comedies from Alexander Hall, more light comedies and musicals from Walter Lang, and plenty of crime films (a few titles at random from 1938: *Women in Prison*, *When G-Men Step In*, *Penitentiary*, *Highway Patrol*, *Reformatory*, *Convicted*, *I Am the Law*, *Juvenile Court*, *Smashing the Spy Ring*).

What is one to conclude from what emerges of Columbia's production policy in this period? Aware that a viewing of all the films might prove one wrong, it could be said that there is no evidence of Columbia's deliberately following a line favorable to the

New Deal. Of course, it could be objected that a similar scanning of the titles of Warner Bros. films of the same time would fail to reveal what an actual viewing of the films shows: a detectable if not pronounced leaning toward Rooseveltian attitudes. But this much seems likely: the policy of bringing in outside stars and directors (and writers, too) for big budget productions would have worked against the continuity required for a deliberate political policy. At Warners a built-up nucleus of stars, writers, producers, and directors was capable of producing pictures that fused the thrills of crime with social comment, but at Columbia the occasional film (such as *Man's Castle*, directed by Frank Borzage in 1933) that took the Depression as its subject was a one-off, with the exception of Capra. And it does seem as though Capra *was* an exception. As far as one can tell, the directors who did not have his freedom at the studio did not follow him in the direction of social comment, and neither did directors brought in from outside with a similar amount of freedom. And Capra's films, after all, despite his standing within the studio, are only a tiny proportion of all the films Columbia made in the 1930s.

If one can say that the presence of Giannini on the trust controlling Columbia did not lead to films predominantly favorable to the New Deal, then can one not also throw doubt on the assumption that control of a studio by interests favorable to the Republican Party led to films (such as *Young Mr. Lincoln* and *King Kong*) designed to make propaganda for that party? No one would argue that there was a total lack of correlation between ownership and the content of films. No studio in the 1930s would have tolerated outright Communist movies or anything very close to that. (Nor for that matter would a Fascist film have stood any chance of being made.) Within these parameters, however, considerable diversity was possible, a diversity, moreover, that it is dangerous to reduce by the simple expedient of labeling all the films as bourgeois. The differences in political attitudes between, say, *The Good Earth* (MGM, 1937) and *The Grapes of Wrath* (20th Century-Fox, 1940)—two films with not totally dissimilar subjects—are not negligible and relate to real political and social events of the time. But they cannot be explained simply in terms of who owned the studios or in terms only of social attitudes at the time. Any explanation would require that many factors be taken into account, and not least of these would be the exact nature of the institutions that produced them.

The history of the American film industry, then, forms a kind of missing link in attempts, Marxist and otherwise, to make connections between films and society. As we have seen, many of the materials needed to forge that link are missing, which is why the title of this essay, "Notes on Columbia Pictures Corporation, 1926–1941," is intended to imply more than the customary academic modesty. The problems of producing such a history are both practical and the result of a massive ideological prejudice, and I am aware that the information I have produced on Columbia in the 1930s amounts to very little in the way of real knowledge. But this information has been the result of a few hours in the library, not of a large-scale research program. If one considers how much has been learned, for example, about British labor history in the nineteenth century, the possibilities for further research do not seem hopeless. As a subject labor history would appear equally as unpromising as the history of the film industry. Apart from newspapers there are few written sources, and the people involved are all dead. The history, therefore, has to a great extent to be reconstructed from the material objects that survive: buildings, institutional structures, the customs and practices of a people. But full-time academics and research students have been working in the field of British labor history for years. The study of the history of the American film industry has scarcely begun.

Afterword for This Volume

My article on Frank Capra and Columbia first appeared in 1975. What an age of innocence that now appears! In Britain, film studies had hardly intruded into the academy at all. There was scarcely a single full-time university teacher in the subject and no institution at which one could major in the history, theory, criticism, or practice of cinema. Admittedly, in America things were already more advanced and scholars more professional. Douglas Gomery, in an article published in a following issue of *Screen*, rightly admonished me for a cavalier disregard of accepted academic practice with regard to citations. But, even if some serious work had already been undertaken, one cannot fail to be struck by both the

sheer volume of scholarship that has poured out in the intervening period and the degree of methodological sophistication that
has been achieved. If my article proceeded most immediately out
of a protest at the poor quality of film history, that lament has in
large measure been answered.

So much so that I would be inclined to regard my own text as
itself no more than an historical relic, were it not that some of the
questions it asks about the particular nature of the regime at Columbia Pictures and the consequences for Frank Capra's creative
autonomy seem still not to have found definitive answers. The
terms of my inquiry centered around the extent to which the precise financial situation of the studio (i.e., from exactly which fraction of capital it derived its support) might have had an influence
on the studio's political ideology, or at least that part of it which
is located in Capra's films. My intention was to get beyond thinking in terms of the political monoliths of capitalist and socialist, or
even Democrat and Republican, and to look at the actual political
alliances of the time, between, for example, the Rooseveltian New
Dealers within the Democratic Party and elements of a populist,
or at least not antireformist, faction within business and banking.
If the Giannini brothers were populist bankers and pro-New Deal,
did this mean that the studio they backed would be more recep-
tive to scripts that espoused a New Deal philosophy?

One of the most notable advances of the past few years has
been the growth of our detailed knowledge of the inner workings
of the film industry, as a result of the opening up to film scholars
of the written records of individual filmmakers and production
companies. In place of the ghosted memoirs and inaccurate and
self-serving recollections of retired filmmakers, we have history
written from the documentary evidence recorded in studio memos,
scripts, accounts, and correspondence.

Unfortunately, although such studios as Warner Bros. and
United Artists have been extensively researched from primary
sources, we have not thus far been given the same insights into
Columbia. If there are papers relating to Columbia Pictures, they
do not seem to have been deposited in public libraries. Joseph
McBride's 1992 biography of Capra throws light on the questions
that remain, but we do not yet possess a history of the Giannini
brothers' activities in the film industry. We still, therefore, lack any

internal proof that would allow us to complete the circuit that runs so suggestively from the point of financial control to the ideology on the screen. The evidence that populist bankers led to populist movies remains circumstantial, if intriguing.

Looking back, I think the chief impetus behind what I wrote, besides a genuine interest in the particular circumstances that gave rise to a group of highly interesting films, was a desire to rescue the, as it seemed then, sickly infant of film history from the clutches of two equally malignant stepmothers. On the one side was auteurism, a convenient shorthand for a bundle of ideas drawn from traditional aesthetics. According to this view, the essential task of film history was to recount the cinematic achievement of great men, tracing the details of their artistic development, the formation of their personal style, and the evolution of their moral vision. Film history was the record of significant individual accomplishment; within this perspective the film industry received consideration only as an impediment over which the man of genius triumphed.

By the end of the 1960s, the radicalization of intellectual life that accompanied such major shifts in the political climate as the protests over the Vietnam War had extended to film studies. Beginning in France and soon spreading to Britain and America, there was a revolution against anything suspected of the taint of bourgeois idealism. The auteurist approach to film history, which located the point of origin of the work in the genius of the individual (the bourgeois category par excellence), fell squarely into that category. And so, instead of focusing on the filmmaker's aesthetic achievement, the historian and theorist (all historians had to become licensed theorists or fall into disrepute) turned toward the context in which the director worked. No longer was it talent that was seen as the spring which supplied the cinema's driving power; rather, it was the material conditions of production, and especially money.

Not for the first time in a revolution, some people got carried away with the excitement of it all and went too far. From arguing that due attention ought to be paid to the material conditions governing artistic production, since after all art was itself a form of material production, they progressed to the assertion that ownership of the means of production guaranteed that the ideology of films would be entirely consistent with the ideology of the ruling class. The meaning of the tune could be assumed once you knew who was paying the piper.

My intention in looking at the case of Capra and Columbia was simple enough: to hold on to the real advances that a materialist view of the cinema offered while rejecting the crudity that vulgar Marxism seemed to be trying to impose. In some ways the project as outlined now seems almost embarrassingly obvious in its appeal to moderation: retaining the power of economics and a materialist analysis of institutions to explain a social practice such as cinema, while resisting any attempt to collapse such a complex form of human activity back into its determinations. If the terms in which the question was posed, the desirability of uniting what conventional critical discourse separated out—cinema and the film industry, aesthetics and economics, Capra and Columbia—seem now a trifle utopian, at least in the manner in which they were expressed, nevertheless the project of film history is still substantially what it was: how to account for films as both the result of individual human actions and the product of impersonal forces.

It's an indication, perhaps, of how far we have come that so little of what I said in 1975 now seems exceptionable. In a sense we are all Marxists now, if only in the weak sense that, in contemporary film history, the mode of production is determining, though not all-determining. And the sheer variety of factors that need to be considered in producing a description of the mode of production goes far beyond any simple notion of "economics," so that determination itself becomes an elastic concept. Not that there no longer is determination, but no one factor can be said to prevail: in short, everything is overdetermined.

History always has the last laugh. There is a piercing irony in the coincidence of a Marxist model becoming the paradigm for film history during the very period that Marxism as a political force was in its death throes within its heartland, eastern Europe. How far film history will itself be determined by these historical forces we shall perhaps discover in the coming years.

BIBLIOGRAPHY

This bibliography provides a selected guide to writings concerning Frank Capra published since 1981, with an emphasis on Capra's career at Columbia Pictures; a comprehensive Capra bibliography through 1981 appears in Charles Wolfe, *Frank Capra: A Guide to References and Resources* (Boston: G.K. Hall, 1987). Included within this alphabetical listing is a selection of writings on Columbia Pictures, the Hollywood studio system, and film authorship.

Balio, Tino. "Columbia Pictures: The Making of a Motion Picture Major." In *Post-Theory: Reconstructing Film Studies*, ed. David Bordwell and Noel Carroll. Madison: Univ. of Wisconsin Press, 1996.

———. *Grand Design: Hollywood as a Modern Business Enterprise, 1930–1939*. History of the American Cinema, vol. 5. New York: Scribner's, 1993.

Basinger, Jeanine. "America's Love Affair with Frank Capra." *American Film* 7, no. 5 (1982): 46–51, 81.

———. "Collector's Choice: Meet Frank Capra." *American Film* 13, no. 3 (1987): 59–62.

Behlmer, Rudy. "A Dream and a Vision: *Lost Horizon*." In *America's Favorite Movies: Behind the Scenes*. New York: Ungar, 1982, 22–39.

Blake, Richard A. "The Screwball Comedy: *It Happened One Night*." In *Screening America: Reflections on Five Classic Films*. New York: Paulist Press, 1991, 103–27.

Bordwell, David, Janet Staiger, and Kristin Thompson. *The Classical Hollywood Cinema: Film Style and Mode of Production to 1960*. New York: Columbia Univ. Press, 1985.

Bowman, Barbara. *Master Space: Film Images of Capra, Lubitsch, Sternberg, and Wyler*. New York: Greenwood Press, 1992.

Carney, Raymond. *American Vision: The Films of Frank Capra*. Cambridge, England: Cambridge Univ. Press, 1986.

———. "Dreams, Deeds, Words, Gasps, and Glances—Frank Capra's *Mr. Deeds Goes to Town*." In *Notebooks in Cultural Analysis*, ed. Norman F. Cantor. Durham, N.C.: Duke Univ. Press, 1986, 3: 221–47.

Caughie, John, ed. *Theories of Authorship: A Reader*. London: Routledge & Kegan Paul, 1981.

Cieutat, Michel. *Frank Capra*. Paris: Rivages, 1988.

Crofts, Stephen. "Authorship and Hollywood." *Wide Angle* 5, no. 3 (1983): 17–22.

Dick, Bernard F., ed. *Columbia Pictures: Portrait of a Studio*. Lexington: Univ. of Kentucky Press, 1992.

———. *The Merchant Prince of Poverty Row: Harry Cohn of Columbia Pictures*. Lexington: Univ. of Kentucky Press, 1993.

Foucault, Michel. "What Is an Author?" In *The Foucault Reader*, ed. Paul Rabinow. New York: Pantheon, 1984.

Gabler, Neal. *An Empire of Their Own: How the Jews Invented Hollywood*. New York: Crown, 1988.

Gehring, Wes D. *Populism and the Capra Legacy*. Westport, Conn.: Greenwood Press, 1995.

Gomery, Douglas. *The Hollywood Studio System*. New York: St. Martin's, 1986.

Gottlieb, Sidney. "From Heroine to Brat: Frank Capra's Adaptation of *Night Bus* (*It Happened One Night*)." *Literature/Film Quarterly* 16, no. 2 (1988): 129–36.

Hillier, Jim, ed. *Cahiers du cinéma, the 1950s: Neo-realism, Hollywood, New Wave*. Cambridge: Harvard Univ. Press, 1985.

———. *Cahiers du cinéma, the 1960s: New Wave, New Cinema, Reevaluating Hollywood*. Cambridge: Harvard Univ. Press, 1986.

Kendall, Elizabeth. *The Runaway Bride: Hollywood Romantic Comedy of the 1930s*. New York: Knopf, 1990.

Levine, Lawrence W. "Hollywood's Washington: Film Images of National Politics during the Great Depression." In *Prospects: An Annual of American Cultural Studies*, vol. 10, ed. Jack Salzman. New York: Cambridge Univ. Press, 1985, 169–95.

Lourdeaux, Lee. *Italian and Irish Filmmakers in America: Ford, Capra, Coppola, and Scorsese*. Philadelphia: Temple Univ. Press, 1990.

Maland, Charles J. *Frank Capra*, rev. ed. New York: Twayne, 1995.

McBride, Joseph. *Frank Capra: The Catastrophe of Success*. New York: Simon & Schuster, 1992.

Mordden, Ethan. *The Hollywood Studios: House Style in the Golden Age of the Movies*. New York: Knopf, 1988.

Muscio, Giuliana. *Hollywood's New Deal*. Philadelphia: Temple Univ. Press, 1996.

Naremore, James. "Authorship and the Cultural Politics of Film Criticism." *Film Quarterly* 44, no. 1 (fall 1990): 14–22.

Neve, Brian. "Populism, Romanticism and Frank Capra." *Film and Politics in America: A Social Tradition*. London: Routledge, 1992, 28–55.

Perkins, V. F. "Film Authorship: The Premature Burial." *CineAction!* 21/22 (November 1990): 57–64.

Poague, Leland. *Another Frank Capra*. Cambridge, England: Cambridge Univ. Press, 1994.

Quart, Leonard. "A Populist in Hollywood: Frank Capra's Politics." *Socialist Review* 13, no. 2 (1983): 58–74.

Schatz, Thomas. *The Genius of the System: Hollywood Filmmaking in the Studio Era*. New York: Pantheon, 1988.

Staiger, Janet, ed. *The Studio System*. New Brunswick, N.J.: Rutgers Univ. Press, 1994.

Stricker, Frank. "Repressing the Working Class: Individualism and the Masses in Frank Capra's Films." *Labor History* 31, no. 4 (1990): 454–67.

Tomasulo, Frank P. "Colonel North Goes to Washington: Observations on the Intertextual Re-presentation of History." *Journal of Popular Film and Television* 17, no. 2 (1989): 82–88.

Truffaut, François. "A Certain Tendency of the French Cinema." In *Movies and Methods: An Anthology*, ed. Bill Nichols. Berkeley and Los Angeles: Univ. of California Press, 1976, 224–37.

Viviani, Christian. *Frank Capra*. Collection Special/Poche 2. Paris: Lherminier-Éditions des Quatre-vents, 1988.

Walker, Joseph B, and Juanita Walker. *The Light on Her Face*. Hollywood: ASC Press, 1984.

Weales, Gerald. *Canned Goods as Caviar: American Film Comedy of the 1930s*. Chicago: Univ. of Chicago Press, 1985.

Wood, Robin. "Authorship Revisited." *CineAction!* 21/22 (November 1990): 46–56.

Wolfe, Charles. "*Mr. Smith Goes to Washington:* Democratic Forums and Representational Forms," in Peter Lehman, ed., *Close Viewings: An Anthology of New Film Criticism*. Gainesville: University Press of Florida, 1990.

Woodward, Katherine Solomon. "The Comedy of Equality: Romantic Film Comedy in America, 1930–1950." Ph.D. diss., Univ. of Maryland, 1988.

Young, Kay. "'Inventing' Romantic Comedy." In *Look Who's Laughing: Gender and Comedy*, ed. Gail Finney. Langhorne, Pa.: Gordon & Breach, 1994, 257–74.

Zagarrio, Vito, ed. *Accadde una notte: Frank Capra (1928–1934) e la Columbia (1934–1945)*. Rome: Di Giacomo, 1988.

———. *Frank Capra*, 2d ed. Il Castoro Cinema 112. Rome: L'unita, Editrice il Castoro, 1995.

———. "Frank Capra *malgré lui*: A Filmmaker and the Contradictions of American Society, 1928–1934." Ph.D. diss., New York Univ., 1995.

FILMOGRAPHY

Complete filmographies covering Frank Capra's entire career are available in Charles Wolfe, *Frank Capra: A Guide to References and Resources* (Boston: G.K. Hall, 1987), and Patricia King Hanson, exec. ed., *Meet Frank Capra: A Catalog of His Work* (Palo Alto and Los Angeles: Stanford Theatre Foundation and National Center for Film and Video Preservation, 1990). The following filmography provides selective information concerning the twenty-five films that Frank Capra directed for Columbia Pictures from 1928 through 1939, in the order of the films' release dates. Abbreviations: Si: silent, Sd: sound, b&w: black and white, Prod: producer, Assoc: associate, Scr: screenplay, Dial: dialogue, Adpt: adaptation, Cont: continuity, Photog: photography, Art dir: art direction, Ed: editor, LP: leading players, min: minutes, VHS: available on video.

That Certain Thing, 1928. Si, b&w, 69 min. *Prod* Harry Cohn. *Story* Elmer Harris. *Titles* Al Boasberg. *Photog* Joseph Walker. *Art dir* Robert E. Lee. *Ed* Arthur Roberts. **LP:** Viola Dana (*Molly Kelly*), Aggie Herring (*Maggie Kelly*), Burr McIntosh (*A. B. Charles*), Ralph Graves (*A. B. Charles, Jr.*). VHS

So This Is Love, 1928. Si, b&w, 60 min. *Prod* Harry Cohn. *Story* Norman Springer. *Adpt* Elmer Harris. *Cont* Rex Taylor. *Photog* Ray June. *Art dir* Robert E. Lee. *Ed* Arthur Roberts. **LP:** Shirley Mason (*Hilda Jensen*), William Collier, Jr. (*Jerry McGuire*), Johnnie Walker (*"Spike" Mullins*).

The Matinee Idol, 1928. Si, b&w, 66 min. *Prod* Harry Cohn. *Story* Robert Lord and Ernest S. Pagano. *Adpt* Elmer Harris. *Cont* Peter Milne. *Photog* Phillip Tannura. *Art dir* Robert E. Lee. *Ed* Arthur Roberts. **LP:** Bessie Love (*Ginger Bolivar*), Johnnie Walker (*Don Wilson*).

The Way of the Strong, 1928. Si, b&w, 61 min. *Prod* Harry Cohn. *Scr* William Conselman. *Cont* Peter Milne. *Photog* Ben Reynolds. **LP:** Mitchell Lewis (*Handsome Williams*), Alice Day (*Nora*), Margaret Livingston (*Marie*), Theodore von Eltz (*Dan*), William Norton Bailey (*Tiger Louie*).

Say It with Sables, 1928. Si, b&w, 70 min. *Prod* Harry Cohn. *Story* Frank Capra and Peter Milne. *Cont* Dorothy Howell. *Photog* Joseph Walker. *Art dir* Harrison Wiley. *Ed* Arthur Roberts. **LP:** Francis X. Bushman (*John Caswell*), Helene Chadwick (*Helen Caswell*), Margaret Livingston (*Irene Gordon*).

Submarine, 1928. Si, b&w, 103 min. *Prod* Harry Cohn. *Story* Norman Springer. *Cont* Dorothy Howell. *Photog* Joseph Walker. *Art dir* Harrison Wiley. *Ed* Ben Pivar. **LP:** Jack Holt (*Jack Dorgan*), Dorothy Revier (*Bessie*), Ralph Graves (*Bob Mason*), Clarence Burton (*submarine commander*).

The Power of the Press, 1928. Si, b&w, 62 min. *Prod* Jack Cohn. *Story* Frederick A. Thompson. *Adpt and cont* Sonya Levien. *Photog* Chet Lyons and Ted Tetzlaff. *Art dir* Harrison Wiley. *Ed* Frank Atkinson. **LP:** Douglas Fairbanks, Jr. (*Clem Rogers*), Jobyna Ralston (*Jane Atwill*).

The Younger Generation, 1929. Si or part Sd, b&w, 75 or 95 min. *Prod* Jack Cohn. *Scr* Sonya Levien. *Dial* Howard J. Green. *Photog* Ted Tetzlaff. *Art dir* Harrison Wiley. *Ed* Arthur Roberts. **LP:** Jean Hersholt (*Julius Goldfish*), Lina Basquette (*Birdie Goldfish*), Ricardo Cortez (*Morris Goldfish*).

The Donovan Affair, 1929. Si or Sd, b&w, 83 min. *Prod* Harry Cohn. *Dial* Howard J. Green. *Cont* Dorothy Howell. *Photog* Ted Tetzlaff. *Art dir* Harrison Wiley. *Ed* Arthur Roberts. **LP:** Jack Holt (*Inspector Killian*), Dorothy Revier (*Jean Rankin*), William Collier, Jr. (*Cornish*), Agnes Ayres (*Lydia Rankin*).

Flight, 1929. Sd, b&w, 120 min. *Prod* Harry Cohn. *Story* Ralph Graves. *Dial* Frank R. Capra. *Photog* Joseph Walker and Joseph Novak. *Art dir* Harrison Wiley. *Ed* Gene Milford and Ben Pivar. **LP:** Jack Holt (*Panama Williams*), Lila Lee (*Eleanor*), Ralph Graves (*"Lefty" Phelps*).

Ladies of Leisure, 1930. Sd, b&w, 102 min. *Prod* Harry Cohn. *Dial and adpt* Jo Swerling. *Photog* Joseph Walker. *Art dir* Harrison Wiley. *Ed* Maurice Wright. **LP:** Barbara Stanwyck (*Kay Arnold*), Ralph Graves (*Jerry Strong*), Lowell Sherman (*Bill Standish*), Marie Prevost (*Dot Lamar*).

Rain or Shine, 1930. Sd, b&w, 90 min. *Prod* Harry Cohn. *Dial and cont* Jo Swerling and Dorothy Howell. *Photog* Joseph Walker. *Ed* Maurice Wright. **LP:** Joe Cook (*"Smiley" Johnson*), Louise Fazenda (*Frankie*), Joan Peers (*Mary Rainey*), William Collier, Jr. (*Bud Conway*).

Dirigible, 1931. Sd, b&w, 100 min. *Prod* Harry Cohn. *Story* Commander Frank Wilber Wead, U.S.N. *Adpt and dial* Jo Swerling. *Cont* Dorothy Howell. *Photog* Joseph Walker. *Ed* Maurice Wright. **LP:** Jack Holt (*Commander Jack Bradon*), Ralph Graves (*Lt. Frisky Pierce*), Fay Wray (*Helen Pierce*).

The Miracle Woman, 1931. Sd, b&w, 90 min. *Prod* Harry Cohn. *Scr and dial* Jo Swerling. *Cont* Dorothy Howell. *Photog* Joseph Walker. *Ed* Maurice Wright. **LP:** Barbara Stanwyck (*Florence Fallon*), David Manners (*John Carson*), Sam Hardy (*Hornsby*), Beryl Mercer (*Mrs. Higgins*).

Platinum Blonde, 1931. Sd, b&w, 90 min. *Prod* Harry Cohn. *Story* Harry E. Chandlee and Douglas W. Churchill. *Adpt* Jo Swerling. *Dial* Robert Riskin. *Cont* Dorothy Howell. *Photog* Joseph Walker. *Art dir* Stephen Goosson. *Ed* Gene Milford. **LP:** Loretta Young (*Gallagher*), Robert Williams (*Stew Smith*), Jean Harlow (*Ann Schuyler*). VHS

Forbidden, 1932. Sd, b&w, 83 min. *Prod* Harry Cohn. *Story* Frank Capra. *Adpt* Jo Swerling. *Photog* Joseph Walker. *Ed* Maurice Wright. **LP:** Barbara Stanwyck (*Lulu Smith*), Adolphe Menjou (*Bob Grover*), Ralph Bellamy (*Al Holland*), Dorothy Peterson (*Helen Grover*).

American Madness, 1932. Sd, b&w, 75 min. *Prod* Harry Cohn. *Story and dial* Robert Riskin. *Photog* Joseph Walker. *Art dir* Stephen Goosson. *Ed* Maurice Wright. **LP:** Walter Huston (*Thomas Dickson*), Pat O'Brien (*Matt Brown*), Kay Johnson (*Phyllis Dickson*), Constance Cummings (*Helen*), Gavin Gordon (*Cyril Cluett*).

The Bitter Tea of General Yen, 1933. Sd, b&w, 87 min. *Prod* Walter Wanger. *Scr* Edward Paramore. *Photog* Joseph Walker. *Ed* Edward Curtis. **LP**: Barbara Stanwyck (*Megan Davis*), Nils Asther (*General Yen*), Toshia Mori (*Mah-Li*), Walter Connolly (*Jones*), Gavin Gordon (*Dr. Robert Strike*).

Lady for a Day, 1933. Sd, b&w, 88 min. *Scr and dial* Robert Riskin. *Photog* Joseph Walker. *Art dir* Stephen Goosson. *Ed* Gene Havlick. **LP:** Warren William (*Dave the Dude*), May Robson (*Apple Annie*), Guy Kibbee (*Judge Blake*), Glenda Farrell (*Missouri Martin*), Ned Sparks (*Happy*), Walter Connolly (*Count Romero*). VHS

It Happened One Night, 1934. Sd, b&w, 105 min. *Scr* Robert Riskin. *Photog* Joseph Walker. *Art dir* Stephen Goosson. *Ed* Gene Havlick. **LP:** Clark Gable (*Peter Warne*), Claudette Colbert (*Ellie Andrews*), Walter

Connolly (*Alexander Andrews*), Roscoe Karns (*Oscar Shapeley*), Jameson Thomas (*King Westley*). VHS

Broadway Bill, 1934. Sd, b&w, 90 min. *Assoc prod* Samuel J. Briskin. *Scr* Robert Riskin. *Story* Mark Hellinger. *Ed* Gene Havlick. **LP:** Warner Baxter (*Dan Brooks*), Myrna Loy (*Alice Higgins*), Walter Connolly (*J. L. Higgins*), Helen Vinson (*Margaret Brooks*), Douglas Dumbrille (*Eddie Morgan*). VHS

Mr. Deeds Goes to Town, 1936. Sd, b&w, 115 min. *Prod* Frank Capra. *Scr* Robert Riskin. *Photog* Joseph Walker. *Art dir* Stephen Goosson. *Ed* Gene Havlick. **LP:** Gary Cooper (*Longfellow Deeds*), Jean Arthur (*Babe Bennett*), George Bancroft (*Macwade*), Lionel Stander (*Cornelius Cobb*), Douglas Dumbrille (*John Cedar*). VHS

Lost Horizon, 1937. Sd, b&w, 132 min. *Scr* Robert Riskin. *Photog* Joseph Walker. *Art dir* Stephen Goosson. *Ed* Gene Havlick and Gene Milford. **LP:** Ronald Colman (*Robert Conway*), Jane Wyatt (*Sondra*), Edward Everett Horton (*Alexander P. Lovett*), John Howard (*George Conway*), Thomas Mitchell (*Henry Barnard*), Margo (*Maria*), Isabel Jewell (*Gloria Stone*), H. B. Warner (*Chang*), Sam Jaffe (*High Lama*). VHS

You Can't Take It with You, 1938. Sd, b&w, 126 min. *Prod* Frank Capra. *Scr* Robert Riskin. *Photog* Joseph Walker. *Art dir* Stephen Goosson. *Ed* Gene Havlick. **LP:** Jean Arthur (*Alice Sycamore*), Lionel Barrymore (*Martin Vanderhof*), James Stewart (*Tony Kirby*), Edward Arnold (*Anthony P. Kirby*), Mischa Auer (*Boris Kolenkhov*), Ann Miller (*Essie Carmichael*), Spring Byington (*Penny Sycamore*). VHS

Mr. Smith Goes to Washington, 1939. Sd, b&w, 125 min. *Prod* Frank Capra. *Scr* Sidney Buchman. *Story* Lewis R. Foster. *Art dir* Lionel Banks. *Ed* Gene Havlick and Al Clark. **LP:** Jean Arthur (*Clarissa Saunders*), James Stewart (*Jefferson Smith*), Claude Rains (*Senator Joseph Paine*), Edward Arnold (*Jim Taylor*), Guy Kibbee (*Governor Hubert Hopper*), Thomas Mitchell (*Diz Moore*), Eugene Pallette (*Chick McGann*), Beulah Bondi (*Ma Smith*), H. B. Warner (*Senate majority leader*), Harry Carey (*president of the Senate*). VHS

ABOUT THE CONTRIBUTORS

EDWARD BUSCOMBE was until 1996 head of publishing at the British Film Institute. He is now a freelance writer and teacher. With Roberta Pearson he edited a collection of essays on the Western published by the British Film Institute in 1997.

CHARLES J. MALAND is Lindsay Young professor and chair of the Cinema Studies Program at the University of Tennessee, where he teaches courses in film studies and American culture. His books include *Frank Capra* (Twayne, rev. ed. 1995) and *Chaplin and American Culture: The Evolution of a Star Image* (Princeton Univ. Press, 1989), which won the 1990 Theater Arts Association Award for best book in film, television, or radio studies.

RICHARD MALTBY is head of screen studies at the Flinders University of South Australia and visiting professor of film studies at Sheffield Hallam University, Britain. He is author of *Hollywood Cinema: An Introduction* (Blackwell, 1995) and *Harmless Entertainment: Hollywood and the Ideology of Consensus* (Scarecrow, 1983). He is completing *Reforming the Movies,* a history of censorship, politics, and regulation in classical Hollywood.

GIULIANA MUSCIO is associate professor of cinema at the University of Padua, Italy. She is author of *Hollywood's New Deal* (Temple Univ. Press, 1996) and of works in Italian on screenwriting, the Hollywood blacklist, and the relation between Hollywood and Washington during the 1930s.

THOMAS SCHATZ is Philip G. Warner Regents Professor in the Department of Radio-Television-Film at the University of Texas at Austin. He is author of *Hollywood Genres* (Temple Univ. Press, 1981) and *The Genius of the System: Hollywood Filmmaking in the Studio Era* (Pantheon, 1988). He has completed *Boom and Bust: The American Cinema in the 1940s*, volume 6 of the ten-volume History of American Cinema (Scribner's, forthcoming).

ROBERT SKLAR is a professor of cinema in the Department of Cinema Studies, Tisch School of the Arts, New York University. His book *Film: An International History of the Medium* (Abrams, 1993) won a Kraszna-Krausz Foundation award. His other recent books are *City Boys: Cagney, Bogart, Garfield* (Princeton Univ. Press, 1992) and *Movie-Made America: A Cultural History of American Movies* (Vintage, rev. and updated, 1994).

BRIAN TAVES is a film historian at the Library of Congress. He is author of *Robert Florey: The French Expressionist* (Scarecrow, 1987), *The Romance of Adventure: The Genre of Historical Adventure Movies* (Univ. Press of Mississippi, 1993), and *The Jules Verne Encyclopedia* (Scarecrow, 1996).

CHARLES WOLFE is chair of the Department of Film Studies at the University of California, Santa Barbara. He is the author of *Frank Capra: A Guide to References and Resources* (G.K. Hall, 1987), editor of *Meet John Doe* (Rutgers Univ. Press, 1989), and co-editor (with Edward Branigan) of the American Film Institute Film Readers Series.

VITO ZAGARRIO teaches film history at the University of Florence and film analysis at the University of Rome III, Italy. He is author of studies in Italian on Francis Ford Coppola and Frank Capra and of *Non solo Hollywood: Percorsi e confronto del cinema centenario* (Bastogi, 1996), among other books. Also a filmmaker, he has directed two feature films, *La donna della luna* (1988) and *Bonus Malus* (1993), and a documentary on the film director John Waters, *Divine Waters* (1983).

Index

This index lists references to Frank Capra's films and to principal individuals, institutions, and subjects discussed in the essays. Because his name appears on nearly every page, Frank Capra is not included here.